So There We Were: River Running in the Hudson Gorge

jeff dickinson

Lauren: Enjoy with a cold one and nice of you to stay in at Alarm Clock

Jeff Dickinson

A river trip is more than a competition between man and water. It is a journey through time with the flowing water a link to the past and future. In a span of a few hours it is possible to learn not only to live with the river but, perhaps, to better see (a person's) role in the complicated interplay of nature now and through the ages.

Wayne Trimm, *The Conservationist*, May-June, 1976

ISBN: 1480083313
ISBN 13: 9781480083318

Dedication

This book is dedicated to all Hudson river runners past, present, and future. It has been an honor and privilege to be a part of this lineage.

I also dedicate the book to the memory of my parents, my mother who passed away in 2011 and is probably passing copies of it around up in heaven. From my father, who passed away in 2013, I seemed to have inherited my flare for storytelling. Now you all know where I get it from!

Acknowledgements

One never realizes what writing a book entails until one does it, particularly the help and support that is needed to complete it. I give thanks to those people that I have talked to over these last few years, whose stories are contained in this work. They provided a great deal of important primary source information that helped to complete the story this work tells.

I would also like to take this opportunity to thank and acknowledge those that are not mentioned in the book, who played important roles behind the scenes in the completion of this work.

To begin with, Jerry Pepper, of the Adirondack Museum, provided guidance while I rummaged the files and bookshelves in the Museum's Reference Library for pre-rafting information. Dr. Charles Yaple, chair of my graduate committee at SUNY Cortland, proof read parts of the text and gave very helpful suggestions and direction. Rob Rubendall, of the SUNY Cortland Outdoor Education Center in Raquette Lake, proof read the text, providing a reader's perspective. My younger brother Jon also proof read parts.

Eric Kaza of the Northville DEC office gave me access to several large files of letters, documents, and notes on the early years of commercial rafting. Thanks goes to Indian Lake Town Clerk Julie Clawson and her office at Indian Lake Town Hall for access to the minutes of past Indian Lake Town Board meetings, another important source for primary information. The librarians at the Lake Pleasant Library in Speculator helped me as I reviewed back issues of the Hamilton County News.

Kristeen Eldridge, at the Indian Lake Chamber of Commerce, gave me access to the forgotten attic files in the Chamber Information Building. The librarians at the Town of Long Lake were helpful in retrieving past articles of Newcomb river runners. Bill Zullo, Indian Lake Town Historian, let me look through material in the Indian Lake Museum. Historians at the Town of Newcomb gave me contact information for river runners still alive in the area.

A special note of thanks goes to Susan Uttendorfsky of Adirondack Editing who edited the entire manuscript with warmth, support, and professionalism.

Finally to my wife Nina who helped proof read, provided ideas, and who patiently has waited for the completion of this work.

Invitation

History is never complete as it continues on past the limits of any written work. The interpretation of history is never complete either, as new facts, information, and stories surface. As such I hope this work is not the end of telling the Hudson Gorge story, but just the beginning. I recognize that there are other stories that have not been told. If the reader has such stories to tell, I'd love to hear them as it will help to fill out and document what the Gorge and the Upper River have to say. Let me know as there is a lot of catching up to do with the Lower Hudson!

jtdickinson@yahoo.com

Table of Contents

Introduction: The Whys

One of the more famous and well-known river runners of the past probably would not be old enough to do a commercial raft trip today with most outfitters, especially those on the Hudson. Huckleberry Finn and his partner, Jim, rafted the Mississippi River in an effort to get away from the everyday life they knew: Huck escaping an abusive parent, and Jim seeking freedom as an individual. They became quite adept and comfortable with their wooden raft as they rode the current downstream. Granted, it wasn't a trip down a raging Class V run, but it was a raft trip none-the-less, similar to the rafts that first rode the flat parts of the Hudson.

After witnessing the brutality of feuding neighbors, including the killing of a boy his age who he had befriended, Huck ran, both figuratively and literally, for the river and his friend, Jim. Huck summed up both of their feelings about rafting when he exclaimed "...there warn't no home like a raft. Other places do seem so cramped up and smothery, but a raft don't. You feel mighty free and easy and comfortable on a raft." [1] Many of today's river runners, both guide and guest, can certainly relate to those words and feelings, that there warn't no home like a raft or a river!

So what is it that makes people want to do this? Of all the outdoor activities and jobs one can do, what is it that makes one want to follow Huck Finn and run rivers? While an entire section, or even a book, could be devoted to this subject, only a few paragraphs will do here before delving into the history of Hudson River running.

There are a lot of good reasons to run rivers. For loggers and fur traders, the reason was simple: a practical way to transport extracted resources out of the wild interior. Loggers floated logs down from camps deep in the woods to the mills farther downstream as a means to get the product to market; diesel trucks were not around then! Trappers and fur traders went up and down the rivers and waterways for beaver pelts for much the same reason. While some of these past river runners may have experienced a certain degree of adrenaline, for the most part, their motivation was economic. For many modern river runners, the motivation probably lies deeper.

Henry David Thoreau, who ran several New England rivers, wrote, "Who hears the rippling of rivers will not utterly despair of anything." [2] T.S. Elliot spoke of a river as "a strong brown god – sullen, untamed and intractable...watching and waiting...the river is within us." [3] Writer Eddy Harris, an African American who canoed the length of the Mississippi River from Lake Itasca to New Orleans, quoted Elliot as well, and commented on how growing up around the Mississippi, the river had gotten within him and "captured my imagination when I was young and has never let go." [4]

Loren Eiseley wrote, "If there is magic left upon this planet, then it is contained in moving water." [5] In the book *Time and the River Flowing: Grand Canyon*, Eiseley continued, saying that if a person could have one compressed moment to feel part of the eons of time, it would have "something to do, I am sure, with common water. Its substance reaches everywhere; it touches the past and prepares the future; it moves under the poles and wanders thinly in the heights of air." [6]

Doug Wheat wrote that to a river runner, moving water is a "living force to mount and ride," with all river runners looking for that tonic of a wild river as they learn to interact with what the river is, flowing and not forcing. [7] Journalist Dean Krakel II moved to Montana to do research on the Yellowstone River, figuring it to be sufficient to just travel the highways next to the river without actually going on the water. "But there came a time when the current's pull proved irresistible," for by only driving the roads next to the river, Krakel could never get completely close enough. The voice of the river, he said, "created an ache inside of me that only the going could satisfy." [8] In his anthology book Adirondack canoe patriarch

Paul Jamieson quoted Paul Brooks: "Each mile on a river will take you further from home than a hundred miles on a road. You will see more in an hour than a motorist will see in a week." [9]

Pat Dickerman spoke directly to rafters, saying that the lure of river running was the opportunity to have a wild ride through a rapid set against a beautiful landscape. [10] Similarly, Lloyd Armstead quoted Dave Brown of the group American Outdoors when Brown wrote about the "thrill and adventure" of river running amidst the scenery of free-flowing rivers. Raft trips enable river runners the opportunity to experience their wilderness heritage along with the sense of discovery felt by the first settlers. Rafters also find that river running "offers a perfect escape from the pressures and tensions of their daily lives," [11] similar to what Huck and Jim felt.

In his book, Jeff Wallack, a guide for the western outfitter O.A.R.S., wrote that commercial raft trips "make it possible for many folks to confront the only version of a wilderness frontier they're ever likely to encounter" and test themselves within this frontier. On a river trip, Wallack writes, a person can encounter life away from the familiar patterns of living to experience a trip across an unknown, unfamiliar, and potentially dangerous environment, where they depend on a guide to get them through the encounter. Here, raft guests not only encounter the physical frontier, but also the "inner frontier." [12] A river trip, then, allows a person "the rare opportunity to confront their true selves" where this inner frontier resides.[13]

For raft guide Julie West, there are special restorative qualities in a river. In Judith Harper's article in the *Adirondack Explorer*, West explained that while rafting on the Hudson was a small part of her income, it was a valued part of her life. "It's important for my sanity… There's something about rivers. Moving water is healing. What's kept me going over the years is my bond with the Hudson… I see it through the seasons, and…each day is a different experience…" [14]

Sue Goodspeed, writing in the *North Creek News Enterprise*, also gave some thought to the attraction of a river, telling the legend of a boy who grew up near a river and who continually returned to the same river throughout different stages of his life. Goodspeed wrote:

> On each trip back to the water the man would be
> amazed that his own reflection was captured in still-
> ness by perpetual motion.
>
> Looking down, the old man saw not the reflection of a
> weather beaten face aged by time but rather the face
> of his youth, a young Huckleberry Finn staring back.
> Then he was the face of a young man, and again an
> older man, then the face of his youth yet again.
>
> In the constancy of their motion, the waters reflected
> not just the evolution of his life, but captured also the
> timelessness of his youth. The boy (old man) wondered
> how many others returned to water to retrieve time. [15]

For me, running the Hudson becomes a one-on-one spiritual
encounter with the Creator, absent the distractions and comforts of
everyday life. As finite beings, we are forever attracted to the infinite, fascinated by that power beyond our control, or comprehension.
Theologian Paul Tillich referred to this attraction as the "passion for
the Infinite." [16] At the same time, though, we are repulsed and afraid
of it; a yin and yang tension, as Taoists would say.

This attraction to the infinite, and the tension it creates, can be
experienced on the river as one floats through calm water and becomes
awed by the scenery. The tension is then felt as one approaches a
rapid, allowing a great opportunity for engagement and response. On
the Hudson, nothing creates this opportunity like floating past Blue
Ledges, then trying to keep a raft pointed straight while going down
the Narrows in big water!

Yet the tension this encounter creates can revert to praise at the
bottom of the rapid as the river calms down and flattens out. As John
Muir had his encounters with resulting praise in Yosemite Valley, so
do I have them in the Hudson River Gorge. While there, I can be in
the presence of the Almighty's handiwork, the finite encountering the
infinite, and not fall to the *fear* of the encounter, but rather, *rejoice*
in it. While I feel the Infinite more personally when kayaking the

gorge, working as a raft guide offers me the chance to share this communion experience - the bread and wine, so to speak - with others.

Most of all, though, is the reason that Charles Farnum gave the two women he met when running the Hudson River from North River to Albany in 1880. When asked why he ran the rapids instead of going around them, Farnum said, "I liked the fun of running such water." [17] Like Farnum, I can have a great time on the river and share this good time and feeling with the community of my fellow guides and guests, and perhaps both will rejoice from the encounter. We can all feel much like Huck and Jim and exclaim "there warn't no home like a raft"!

Why this book on river runners in the Hudson Gorge?

It started with an innocent event several years ago at the Whitewater Challengers (WWC) North River base. *So there I was*, as any good guide story starts out, sitting around one of the prep tables in the WWC kitchen one summer afternoon after the end of a large river trip. Large numbers are fun, but for most Hudson guides, a lot of hard work goes into getting 100 plus people on and off the river. When the after-trip meal was done, the cleanup completed, and the guests had left, I was ready to relax.

Joining me was Marko Schmale, the WWC river manager, Mike Hawkins, a veteran guide from another company, and Jake Haker, one of the more seasoned WWC guides. The trip was done, the afternoon was long, raft guides relaxing after a long day; a situation *ripe* for telling guide stories. And told we did! Stories about the day's trip, about a particular guest who fell out and swam, heroic tales of their rescue, something about a particular guide or outfitter, current issues of procedure and conduct on the river, the cute blond in another raft, etc.

The more fascinating part came when the conversation turned to the early days of rafting on the Hudson and what it was like back then. Stories of chasing guides down the morning of a trip, dealing with aftermath of the night before, who had paired with whom, the challenges of using bucket boats, etc. I sat and listened intently, for it was fascinating to hear about what had gone on then and appreciate the efforts of those who had laid the groundwork for those of us who followed.

I have always felt fortunate and honored to know many of the guides and people that were spoken of, the "hall of famers", as I refer to them. I have also felt fortunate to know and work with the current generation of guides. By knowing and working with both, I feel as if I have a connection with both generations.

When the stories stopped, the cooler emptied, the evening fell, and all of us ready to head home, I felt a little awed. The day gave me more than I expected and I felt fortunate to have stayed that day to enjoy the company of these guides, for I had been communing with living pieces of Adirondack rafting history. Listening to these stories, I felt as though I was a part of the history of river running in the Hudson River Gorge, a history that now spans three centuries, beginning with the log drivers of 1849.

It then occurred to me that these stories deserved to be recognized, recorded, and honored; raft guides should take their rightful place in the river-running lineage of the Hudson River. I also thought that if these guys had so much to tell, other guides might, too. This history should be recorded and documented before we are all incapable of remembering it. So began the journey of finding and talking to these people by phone or in person, reaching out to more living pieces of Adirondack river-running history in Maine, Florida, Ontario, New York, Pennsylvania, California, and Washington, talking to the Hockmeyers, Haleys, Cromies, Schurmans, Clarkes, Kowalskis, Powleys, Staabs, Briggs, and others.

But history rarely happens in a vacuum. As I heard these stories, I came across stories from other river runners who ran the gorge in aluminum canoes and World War II surplus rafts before commercial rafting began. Men like Doug Garard of Newcomb, New York, who ran the gorge in the late 1960's with less-than-adequate clothing and equipment, concluding, after making the run, that he and his friends were all nuts to have done so! Ed Hixon, Clyde Smith, and others who made the run in aluminum canoes helped to establish the recreational value of the gorge. Fran Monthoney's friend, who ran the Narrows in one of the logging boats, and "Yankee John" Galusha, who told of the loggers who pushed the envelope and dared to run the rapids of the Hudson in wood boats in April with no neoprene, dry suits, helmets, or lifejackets!

As my research expanded to include other Upper Hudson runners and explorers of the area, something else became apparent. In his introduction to Charles Farnum's account of running the Hudson, Roland Van Zandt wrote that the Hudson River, as a "turbulent mountain stream leaves little for history to say," and compared to the lower Hudson, not much has happened on the upper Hudson. In terms of the chronicles of history, the Hudson River south of Glens Falls offers "an embarrassment of riches; north of it they are virtually nonexistent." [18]

Van Zandt then continued to say that what the upper Hudson lacked in history, it made up for in scenery. For some early writers, the upper Hudson River and the region around its shores had value because of this absence of historical importance. To them, the upper Hudson River belonged to "the splendors of the natural, rather than the human history." [19] While I can certainly agree the Upper Hudson region has an unparalleled scenic quality (I do admit a bias on this account!), I will disagree that, in terms of history, the Hudson River north of Glens Falls has little to say.

The Upper Hudson region has a natural and human history that is of interest and of significance to the region, the state, and the nation - *it has a lot to say*! Just ask the loggers who moved up the Hudson to provide a growing nation with the wood products it needed. How uninteresting was it to run these rivers in the spring, spending twelve to fourteen hours a day in freezing cold water, poking, prodding, and herding logs like cattle to make sure that the logs for these needed products made it to Glens Falls to be processed and shipped out for a growing nation? Or to float the wood products farther downstream on a large wood raft, like Huck and Jim? Or one could ask members of the Henderson mine group, who struggled to make a promising iron mine profitable for this same growing nation. How uninteresting was it to be part of the first group on the summit of the highest point of land in the state, or experience the excitement of determining the high source of water for this famous river? But there is more to say!

Imagine coming to an undeveloped region so close to a major urban area and experiencing the romantic feeling of being in the midst of a wild place, a less-hurried getaway that helped provide balance to the business of this growing nation and industrial culture. How important was it for early recreationists in the area to experience the wilds, as Farnum said, simply for the fun of it and perhaps achieve this balance?

How true was this for modern-day river runners, who began to ply their craft on the river just as the loggers were leaving? How important was it that these recreational river runners placed a *different* kind of value on the river than just as a mere dammed-up water tank for distant downstate urban sprawl? How significant is it to have a thriving industry today in an economically depressed region where the business of river running now spans four generations in one family? How uninteresting or unimportant is it to hear the stories of the creation of an industry that allows the continuation of this 150-year-old tradition of running the Hudson River Gorge, a tradition that continues to this day?

I believe that part of this unknown quality concerning the Upper Hudson region is historic, dating back to the 1600s when the Upper Hudson region was bypassed for more productive transport and migration routes; history seems to have continued the bypass. While humans were a part of the Hudson River landscape south of Glens Falls ever since the Lenappe moved in from the west, hearing the story of the lower river is only part of what the river has to say. Just as the lower section has both interesting history and marvelous scenery, *so too does the upper section!* It just hasn't been talked about that much. This work, then, is an attempt to start that conversation.

So there we were!

The Adirondacks in General

The Adirondack region, like the Upper Hudson, can be a mystery for people, even for those who live in New York. For many years, the area was unknown but to a few wanderers, trappers, and Native Americans. Later, it was bypassed in the western migrations of the 1800s and by the northern water route to Canada, remaining relatively unsettled until later that century. Even then, the Adirondack region was not well known, explored, or mapped. Lewis and Clark made it out to the west coast and back almost seventy years before the public knew about Lake Tear of the Clouds being the highest pond source of water for the well-known Hudson River. While this is not the place for an exhaustive work on the history of the region, a few factoids will help the Adirondacks become a little less of a mystery and a little more familiar, for it is here that the mighty Hudson has its birth and early life.

If one looks at a map of New York State, the Adirondack region fills up a great deal of the northern part of the map. The region essentially is bounded by the Black River to the west, Lake Champlain to the east, and the Mohawk Valley to the south, with the north-northwest slope dwindling down to the St. Lawrence River. One could fit several states within this range, and even a couple of national parks. Within the "Blue Line", as the official Adirondack boundary is known, are 3,000 lakes and ponds, 1,000 miles of rivers, and 30,000 miles of brooks and streams.[1]

The highest mountains in the Adirondacks are in the High Peaks area, just south of Lake Placid, with elevations over a mile high;

Mount Marcy leads the way at 5,344 feet. The 1980 Winter Olympic alpine ski events were held on the fifth highest mountain in New York, Whiteface Mountain. These "High Peaks," as they are known, tend to arch out from this mountainous region, creating a bowl-shaped range with cracks that radiate out in several directions. Through these cracks, or geological fault lines, flows the runoff water. One of these cracks becomes the Hudson River. In his book, Mike DiNunzio referred to the Adirondack range as a "mile high turtle shell". [2]

While the Adirondacks have mountains, they are also rich with water features such as ponds, lakes, and a variety of wetlands. DiNunzio called the water features of the region the "jewels of the forest," [3] many of which are not more than 10,000 years old, relics of a retreating glacier. The sizes range from small one or two acres (Lake Tear is only two acres), up to Raquette Lake, with over 100 miles of shoreline, or even Lake George, at over thirty-two miles long from the south end tourist trap of Lake George Village to the north end, near Ticonderoga. At 125 miles in length and a width ranging from one to twelve miles, Lake Champlain was referred to by Barnett as an "inland sea". [4]

The Adirondack region, then, in essence, is a "Whitman Sampler," with a multitude of land and water features that provide diverse opportunities for outdoor activities. There are longer rivers to raft, higher mountains to hike, longer canoe trips to take, higher rock faces to climb, and more open water to kayak, but rarely does one get the chance to do all of these in one area.

Mixed amongst this diverse outdoor landscape are several large villages and towns that help account for a year-round population of 130,000. [5] All or part of twelve counties are contained within the Adirondacks, with Hamilton and Essex being the two that are completely inside the Blue Line. Several state and local highways thread through the valleys, with an interstate freeway cutting through the east border. A claim to fame for Hamilton County is that it is the only county in New York State without a traffic light.

At six million acres, the Adirondacks are the largest state park in the nation, including Alaska. The largest national park is, of course, Wrangle-St. Elias in Alaska, at over 13 million acres. The

Adirondack Park itself is larger than Yellowstone, Glacier, and Grand Teton National Parks combined.

That very word, though, often leads to some misconceptions about what the Adirondacks are, for one may think of a park as an area completely open to public recreation where a person can roam free and uninhibited wherever they want. While this is true for the wildlife that calls the area home, it is only true to some degree for humans, as there is privately owned land within the Adirondacks. People live and work in the region. Thus, the Adirondacks do have some limitations on public use. As such, it is not a good idea to camp out in someone's backyard; the land owners may extend the full force of Adirondack hospitality in an unexpected way.

The state-owned land in the Adirondacks, and the Catskill range in the southeast part of New York, have the strongest land protection of any in the nation. There is federally owned and managed land across the nation, but that was set aside by the normal law-making process: Congress passes legislation, the president signs the bill into law. National parks are created this way, as are national wildlife refuges and national forests. Lawmakers giveth and they can taketh away, depending on the winds of political change and a particular constituent. State parks, in all the states, have a similar genesis and are vulnerable to the same Armageddon. Not so in the Adirondacks and Catskills.

Public lands in these two regions are protected by the New York State Constitution, Article XIV, known as the "Forever Wild" Amendment. It states that "The lands of the state, now owned or hereafter acquired, constituting the forest preserve as now fixed by law, shall be forever kept as wild forest lands".[6] What that means is that in order to develop state land in the Adirondacks or Catskills, sell it, or to cut, remove, or destroy the timber on it, there must be a constitutional amendment approved.

In New York, an amendment, unlike standard legislation, must pass two sessions of the state legislature with the final nod in that process being a vote of the people of the entire state. Article XIV was originally put into the New York State Constitution in 1894 in an effort to ensure a water supply for the state's water transport system, which was seen as being jeopardized by the logging of the region at that time. This public land is known as the "Forest Preserve".

The public land in the Adirondacks and Catskills is further classified as Wilderness, Wild Forest, Primitive, Canoe, Intensive Use, Historic, Administrative Areas, Travel Corridors, and Wild, Scenic, and Recreational Rivers. Each designation carries different management policies with an aim toward different types of usage. Land with a *Wilderness* designation has to have a certain amount of acreage and does not allow motorized usage, whereas *Wild Forest* can be a patchwork of land pieces which do allow motorized usage. *Primitive* is land managed much like wilderness but essentially can't meet all of the criteria for Wilderness. *Canoe* is a place where the waterways and the surrounding land allow for a wilderness-like experience. [7] River corridors are also classified *Wild, Scenic,* or *Recreational* depending on usage, as well as river and shore conditions. More on that in a later chapter.

The boundary of the Adirondacks is often referred to as the Blue Line, a term which goes back to the days when the Adirondack Park was first created in 1892.[8,9] After the state spent so much time and effort trying to get rid of the land it owned in the region, it decided it wanted it back to create the Adirondack Park. Phil Terrie wrote that the Forestry Commission, as part of the request for the creation of the Adirondack Park, requested the power to purchase private land to create "one grand, unbroken domain". [10] When the boundaries of this proposed domain were being drawn, the lines were marked in blue, with the idea to eventually acquire all the land within the blue line, excepting the land inside village and city limits. Although the Blue Line was re-drawn in 1929, the state has long abandoned the idea of acquiring all the land within it, even though some conspiracy theorists insist the opposite is true.

The name for the Adirondacks has an interesting, varied, and complicated background. To begin with, Professor Ebenezer Emmons, after he completed his survey of the High Peaks area in 1837, proposed to call the region "Adirondack". The word Adirondack is commonly thought to be an Iroquois slur name applied to their hated rivals, the Algonquins from Canada. The story goes that when the hunt did not go so well, the Algonquins often had to chew on bark to sustain themselves while in the Adirondack region. The Iroquois, who also hunted there, noted this and, to make fun of their hated enemies, referred to the Algonquins as *hadarondas,* or *barkeaters.*[11]

According to Terrie, though, the origin of the word Adirondack is not that simple.[12] Several Mohawk and Huron words are strikingly similar, such as *Aderondackx,* a Mohawk term for the French and English, *Attiwandaronk,* a Huron word for someone who speaks a different language, *Rondaxes,* a Mohawk word for the Hurons, and *Adyranthaka,* a Mohawk name for the French-allied Indians of Canada. It does seem, though, that the word Adirondack had its origin in the Mohawk language as a term applied to the Algonquins, and possibly other foreigners.

Steven Sulavik, in his book, *Adirondacks: Of Indian and Mountains,* wrote how the word Adirondack was derived from the Mohawk word *atiru`itaks,* literally meaning "tree eaters".[13] Because there was no written Mohawk language when the name was thought to have originated in the late 1500s, spellings of the word vary. The first recorded mention of the word was a 1627 Dutch reference to distant Indian tribes that the Dutch traded with. The earliest definitive record of the word Adirondack has the word spelled *Rontaks* and was used by a French Jesuit missionary in 1724. Later on, another Mohawk word, *ratirontaks,* meaning "they eat trees," became common.

While it is easy to think of the traditional application and reference of the word Adirondack being a Mohawk slur word given the Algonquins, ethnologist J.N. Hewitt suggested that the word was mistakenly applied.[14] Terrie writes how Hewitt further postulated the possibility of the word Adirondack coming from a reference to a St. Lawrence tribe known as *Arendahronon,* meaning "those who eat rocks." The Mohawk translation of the word was *Tatirontaks,* and since the Mohawks lacked a word for rock, they substituted one for tree and added the prefix *ad,* meaning "to eat".[15]

Sulavik noted that several tribes of similar heritage and language - such as the Hurons, Algonquins, and Montagnais - lived along the St. Lawrence River, and suggests that it was to them that the Iroquois applied this infamous name. The Montagnais tribe of the lower Ottawa River valley was the most likely tribe to be derided by the Mohawks as "tree eaters," as they lived a more nomadic way of life than the other two tribes. Sulavik also noted that in the book, *History of the Five Nations,* published in the 1800s, Cadwallader Colden equated the word Adirondack with the Algonquins and was probably the point of reference that Emmons used when he recommended the name Adirondack for the region.[16]

There is evidence to suggest that there were even older names applied to the region than the one Emmons proposed. Nathan Sylvester noted that the governor's territorial map of New York dated 1776 had the following inscription written across the Adirondack territory: "This vast tract of land which is the ancient Couchsachrage, one of the four beaver hunting countries of the six nations, is not yet surveyed." [17] As with Adirondack, the word *Couchsachrage* is of Iroquois origin.

The first known name applied to the Adirondack region appeared on a 1562 map, not long after Jacques Cartier's exploration of the St. Lawrence River region.[18] *Avacal*, a derivative of *Avacum* or *Havacum,* was quite possibly a Latin word applied to a hilly region of the southerly providence in Belgium. Since Dutch and Belgian map makers were influential at that time, it would not be unreasonable to assume the name was used to describe a similar region found in the New World.

Another early name for the region came from Father Simon LeMoine, who, in July of 1654, was on a trip to establish a mission amongst the Onondaga Iroquois of central New York. LeMoine paddled up the St. Lawrence for three days, stopping at a place called "Lake St. Francis" and, looking to the east, saw a "chain of high mountains" which he named "the Mountains of Saint Margaret" in honor of St. Margaret.[19]

William White also listed several other early names for the Adirondack region. The names include The Mountains of St. Marthe, Mohegan Mountains, Black Mountains, Clinton's Mountains - after DeWitt Clinton of Erie Canal fame - Macombs Mountains, and Corlears's Mountains, after a Schenectady man who tried to make peace between the French and Iroquois. Additionally, there was the Aganushioni Range, the Iroquois name for "long house," and Peru Mountains, a name some of the early French used.

In areas south of the Adirondacks, the region was often known as "The Great Northern Wilderness," which stayed for some time.[20] By contrast, E.R.Wallace reported that in areas north of the Adirondacks, residents along the St. Lawrence River referred to the Adirondacks as the "South Woods".[21] *Couchsachrage,* one of the early map names of the Adirondack region, was sometimes translated to mean "place of winter". The Dismal Wilderness, Beaver Hunting Grounds, the Place of Beaver Dams, Deer Hunting Country, and Irocoisia - which also referred to part of Vermont - also vied for the first name applied to the present Adirondack region.[22] Thus, the background of the region's name was not just a simple matter of Emmons suggesting the name for tree-eating Algonquins.

The geological history of the region is a little more clear, but no less complicated. According to Yngvar Isachsen, the Adirondacks are an old mountain range, with the exposed bedrock seen today being over 1.1 billion years old.[23] The bedrock is part of a larger rock base that protrudes south from Canada. Very few places in the United States have this extension. As such, the Adirondacks are not part of the Appalachian chain, as is sometimes believed.

Isachsen continued to describe how the Adirondacks are essentially an uplifted dome of metamorphic rock, 120 miles long and 80 miles wide, with cracks and fault lines that typically run north-northeast.[24] That is why one can see the various mountain ranges positioned along this northeast orientation, including the ones that form the High Peaks, Snowy Mountain, Thirteenth Lake, AuSable Lakes, Long Lake, and Indian Lake.[25] As early as 1837, state geologist Ebenezer Emmons described the Adirondacks as "one great uplift with gradual but unequal slopes on all sides". The first major uplift occurred 1.1 billion years ago, thrusting up layers of accumulated rock and soil to heights of 25-30,000 feet. This uplift was the result of the collision of two tectonic plates, or continents, and is refered to as the Grenville Orogeny. Thus, the Adirondacks are "a product of global plate tectonic processes".[26]

As a result of this process, some of the sediments and minerals leftover from the encroaching sea water were thrust down under great pressure where they were altered, changed, and intruded upon by igneous rock.[27] Over the course of millions of years, this mix underwent high temperatures and tremendous pressure, changing the mix to the metamorphic bedrock we see today. Quite often, one can see this mix in the rock formations of the Hudson River Gorge, such as in Cedar Ledges, where rock types mix, change, and are undercut.

As the exposed layers of rock and sediment from the uplift became weathered and eroded away, this sublayer of metamorphic rock began to rise to form the Grenville Providence. About 58 million years ago, a small protrusion of this rock, shaped like a dome, began an uplift, the result of a small hot spot under the rock.[28] This small protruding thumb of bedrock that crosses into New York from Canada along the Thousand Islands area is known as the Frontenac Arch.

The most recent geological force in the region were glaciers, advancing and retreating several times across this uplifted dome.[29] The last major advance took place 21,000 years ago, with the last remnants retreating 10-12,000 years ago. At its height, the glacier was some two miles high. Glaciers had a profound effect on the landscape, bulldozing soil, plucking and sculpting exposed rock, plugging rivers, and creating new water bodies. Thus, as the uplifts gave the Adirondacks its shape, the glaciers carved the details we see today.

As the glaciers retreated, they helped create the growing conditions that incoming plant species found by sculpting the exposed rock and till, depositing this material on the sides of mountains and in the bottoms of valleys.[30] Pioneering plants, such as lichens and mosses, then moved in, paving the way for the forest communities that followed. The environmental conditions left by the glaciers, such as elevation and types of soil, helped determine where these communities would develop.[31] From these varied conditions, several distinct types of forest communities have evolved.

Ed Ketchledge refered to these forest communities as "site types".[32] The most common of these types of forest is the northern hardwoods, which grow best at elevations below 2,500 feet. Sugar maple, yellow birch, and beech are the predominant types of trees in this grouping and all can grow in areas without direct sunlight (shade tolerent). The sugar maple is the dominant species of the three and can be used to help define the boundaries of this forest type. [33]

The Adirondacks also have one of the most southerly extensions of the boreal forest, with tree and plant types being similar to that found in the Canadian north woods.[34] The word "boreal" comes from the name of the Greek god Boreas, who took care of and was in charge of the North Wind.[35] Ketchledge calls this boreal forest type *Spruce/Fir,* as those tree species, along with some yellow birch, are the predominant tree types in this range. [36] Barbara McMartin listed some of the special animal species that live within this range, such as the rare spruce grouse, moose, boreal chickadee, Canada jay, and the arctic three-toed woodpecker.[37]

Ketchledge listed the other types of forest sites that exist in lower elevations as *Spruce-Swamp,* seen in wetland type areas; *Pine,* seen in areas slightly elevated from wetlands; and *Mixed Woods,* where both pine and hardwoods share a habitat. [38] Jane Keller refered to this forest collection as a "museum of eastern trees".[39] In a sense, the Adirondacks are a meeting ground for the northen hardwoods and the boreal forest - a melting pot of forest types.

A unique forest/plant habitat found in the Adirondacks are the small "islands" of plants similar to those found in the arctic tundra of Alaska and the high northern Canadian latitudes.[40, 41] These mosses, lichens, grasses, and shrubs are found on about eighty-five acres of land on eleven of the High Peaks, and represent some of the rarest forms of vegetation in the area.

Human activity in the area has been short compared the geological forces. Native Americans passed through the area, but only on a seasonal basis. There were never any permanent settlements, although there is some evidence to indicate a presence near the Upper Saranac Lake area and near North Elba.[42] That being said, there were several well- established travel routes through the area, but no indication of one going downriver through the Hudson River Gorge. The closet travel route to the gorge was the one mentioned by Aber & King in the *History of Hamilton County,* referred to as the Sacandaga Trail. [43] This old pathway went up the Sacandaga River Valley from the Johnstown-Gloversville area to the Indian Lake area, following the Hudson up from the Indian River to Newcomb and the Upper Works area.

The earliest Europeans to see and explore the Adirondack region were the French of the late 1500s to early 1600s. The most likely European of record to have first seen the Adirondacks was Jacques Cartier, but that, as White said, depends on what type of day October 2, 1536, was in the area along the St. Lawrence River. [44] That day, Cartier was led up to a hill that over looked the present Montreal area; if it was clear and sunny that day, he would have seen the Adirondacks in the distance some seventy miles away. Regardless of the weather, he was told by the natives of "an unexplored region of lakes, of mountains, and delightful plains" to the south.

Samuel de Champlain was the first European of record to have actually ventured into the region in July of 1609, several months before Henry Hudson made his way up what was to become known as the Hudson River. [45] Champlain came up by way of the Richelieu River from the St. Lawrence and into a large lake that was eventually named for him. From the lake, he would have easily seen the Adirondacks to the west. He was accompanied by a band of Huron warriors and sailed to the head of the lake, where they met a band of Iroquois, the hated enemies of the Hurons. Naturally, a battle started and, with an ensuing shot that would be heard for centuries thereafter, Champlain killed two Iroquois chiefs with his firearms and, according to Francis Parkman's recounting of the incident, wounded another. [46] Not realizing it at the time, Champlain set in motion a whole course of history with this one act, setting the table for the French and Indian War and the sides of loyalty that the various regional Indian tribes took thereafter.

The first European of record to enter into the Adirondack region by land was a Jesuit priest named Father Isaac Jogues. [47] The priest was first captured by the Iroquois in 1642, escaped, and went back to France, but returned to the Champlain-Lake George area in 1646 in an effort to make peace with his former captors. [48] During the time of his captivity, it is possible that he was the first European river runner of record in the Adirondacks, if he followed the Sacandaga Trail from the south up to Indian Lake and the Hudson River.

Adirondack land was never the most popular or productive land in colonial times. White[49] and Graham[50] detailed how the land in the region was sold to speculators or given away by the state for war debts. Those who actually came to the area could not make a living from the land, with the area gaining a reputation for not being worth much. Farmers found the land uncooperative, as it is challenging to plant crops amongst the rocks and poor soil typically found in the region. Much more attractive and productive land lay out west and, with the Erie Canal in operation, most settlers bypassed the region. The only thing that it seemed good for, as the 1800s came around, was for lumber and a small amount of mining. Later in the century, it became a place of vacation and getaway for well-off urbanites, a function that continues to the present day.

A Whitman Sampler of outdoor activity in the Adirondacks.
Top left: Canoeing on Lake Lila. **Top right**: High Peaks from Gothics. **Bottom left**: Nina Dickinson snowshoeing at Limekiln Lake Campground. **Bottom right**: Fishing boat at Wilcox Pond.
All photos: Jeff Dickinson

The Upper Hudson River Itself

In the 1891 edition of his guide book, *"Adirondacks Illustrated"*, noted photographer Seneca Ray Stoddard recognized the lack of public knowledge or awareness concerning the Upper Hudson region. Dunwell quoted Stoddard: "The section where the great Hudson River and its higher tributaries rise are less known to the public than almost any part."[1] Benson Lossing, in his early guidebook on the entire length of the Hudson River, did spend time in the Upper Works area. However, he then left the river for the lowlands, picking up the Hudson again near Thurman, circumventing an entire section of the river. Even today, of the many books on the history of the Hudson River, ample mention is made of the part from Albany to New York City, but little of the upper region and the gorge. Roland Van Zandt, while providing excerpts from Charles Farnum's trip on the rapids of the Hudson, stated that not much of note has taken place along this section. One wonders if there is even an awareness of the upper river. For those who do wonder about the Hudson above Albany and Glens Falls, this chapter will serve as an introduction to both the river and the region from which it flows.

There are longer, better-known rivers in the United States than the Hudson, such as the Missouri, the Mississippi, the Rio Grande, and the Colorado. The Hudson itself is only 269 miles long from its highest source of water, Lake Tear of the Clouds, down to Manhattan, which is short compared to the 2,350 miles of the Mississippi, or even the 1,700 miles of the Colorado.[2] Like many rivers, the Hudson starts out as a small stream less than thirty feet wide as it comes out of

Lake Henderson; less than a few feet wide as it comes out of Lake Tear. Like the Mississippi as it flows out of Lake Itasca, one can leap across the Hudson at this point in one bound; wade for those who are leaping challenged!

Less than thirty miles from its source, though, the Hudson widens and deepens, becoming a world-class whitewater run as it drops over 300 feet through the Hudson River Gorge. Most of the whitewater that can be run on the Hudson is contained in the first sixty-five to seventy miles, from above Newcomb to the junction with the Schroon River near Thurman. By the time it travels the first 165 miles to Albany, the river has dropped over 4,300 feet.[3] In the next 150 miles to Manhattan, the elevation drop is around one foot.

Many people who have heard or know of the Hudson River, though, picture it as the quiet, calm body of water that flows between Albany and the island of Manhattan. They picture the skyscrapers of New York City reflecting off the Hudson's waters as it moves on by. Looking upstream, they realize that it comes from somewhere, but are not really sure where. Others do expand their vision of the river a little, perhaps picturing it as the tidal water flow that makes its way down from Albany. Perhaps, like many people before the 1800s, what they picture of the river ends there. But the river continues past Albany and the Glens Falls area, having its origins and early life in the Adirondack region of New York, with the highest sources of its water coming off the southwest side of the highest peak in the state.

Early maps indicate a lack of knowledge of where exactly the river came from above Albany.[4] Champlain's map of 1632 showed the lower Hudson going north from New York Harbor, but dwindling out just north of present-day Albany.[5] Another map dated 1656 showed the Hudson continuing north past Albany, paralleling Lake Champlain. In this instance, the map maker may have had in mind the Schroon River, as it follows a similar direction.

Almost 100 years later, a map dated 1756, published in *Gentleman's Magazine,* showed the Hudson ending just north of the junction with the Sacandaga River. Another map dated 1757 from the *Universal Magazine* accurately showed the Hudson flowing past Glens Falls and branching off at the junction with the Sacandaga River, which, on the map, was called West Branch of the Hudson. From here, the Hudson, as shown on the map, continued to flow from the north and was called North Branch of the Hudson River. On this map the river ended in the Adirondack region, which was marked "parts but little known".

A map dated January 4, 1779, and reprinted in 1844, showed the Hudson going up somewhat accurately from the Glens Falls area to the North Creek area, past a "very remarkable mountain" (most likely Gore). The map continued to portray the path of the river fairly accurately up to the Boreas River, but from there accuracy drops off, with the Hudson River Gorge not being shown. It did show the junction with the Indian and Cedar Rivers, but then was shown heading north, curling around Newcomb, then heading west before going southwest toward Long Lake and the Blue Mountain Lake area. Here it was called West Branch of the Hudson River. Many of these maps can be found at the Adirondack Museum[6] in Blue Mountain Lake, New York.

A map dated 1838 did show the Adirondack High Peaks region with the Hudson River flowing out of it, but the gorge section was not accurately portrayed. It was only as recent as Verplanck Colvin's survey maps of 1873 that the path of the Upper Hudson River and the Hudson River Gorge was accurately shown.[7] So while much of the lower Hudson River had been explored, known, and was written about, much of the upper river, particularly the gorge, remained unknown for a long time.

The name for the Hudson itself, and its geological background, like the Adirondacks, is varied. As with many names for Adirondack features, there is an English name and a Native American name for the Hudson River. According to Nathan Sylvester, the Algonquin name for the river was *Cahotatea,* which meant "the river that comes from the mountains."[8] The Mohawk name *Skanentade,* which translated meant "the river beyond the open woods," with the Iroquois name translating to "the river beyond the openings." Henry Hudson translated the Algonquin name to "river of the mountains." Early Dutch settlers used the names of old Holland families "Nassau" and "Mauritius". [9, 10] Hudson did not apply his name to the river he explored, leaving it to the English after they gained control of New York from the Dutch.

Robert Boyle reported that the "Mahican" (Lenni Lenape) Indians that lived along the Hudson were fascinated at the back and forth movement of the Lower Hudson. [11] Having little elevation loss from Albany down to the Atlantic Ocean means the Hudson is influenced by the tides. As such, river water here moves both downstream and upstream. The tribe called the river *Muhheakunnuk*, which meant "great waters constantly in motion." Dunwell also confirmed this name and gave a few more details. The name, according to tribal historian Hendrick Aupaumut, *Muhheahkunnuk,* or *Mohicanituck,* is a word whose translation is "great waters or sea, which are constantly in motion, either flowing or ebbing."[12]

The present name of Hudson was applied by the English in honor of their countryman who had explored the river. The name Hudson, though, rivaled another European name for the river at that time, North River, which was given by early Dutch settlers in the region. The name referred to the geographical location of the river in relation to the Delaware River, which was known then as the South River. The name North River continued to hold sway in some trading and commerce circles of the day. Presently, there is a community along the upper Hudson River that bears the name North River. North River was also the name frequently applied to the Hudson between Newcomb and North Creek in the 1800s.

As to specific geological background, the general direction of the river was first determined by the geological uplifts in the region. [13] As the uplifts raised the underlying bedrock, cracks, or faults, in the rock allowed water to drain in between the cracks. Essentially, the Hudson flows through these exposed fault lines, which have bedrock of varying degrees of hardness. The draining water cuts easily through bedrock that is soft and is forced to change direction when running into harder rock, such as what happens in the gorge. As the river flows south from Lake Henderson and to the confluence with the Opalescent River, it cuts through soft, leftover glacial deposits. It then hits a layer of weak Greenville marble as it turns west toward

Lake Harris in Newcomb. [14] Here, the river runs across a smooth layer of folded rock to again flow south for twelve miles.

At the confluence with the Indian River, the Hudson again hits a zone of softer marble bedrock along a fault line as the river abruptly turns east. [15] Some of these marbles are severely undercut, as seen along Cedar Ledge Rapids on river right (right side as you go down the river).[16] For the next eight miles, the river cuts through alternating layers of soft Greenville marble and harder syenite as it courses through the fault line. After leaving the Gorge area near the confluence with the Boreas River, the Hudson runs into another hard layer of syenite at Dutton Mountain, forcing the river south, before being re-directed east, toward the uplifted ledge that creates the Greyhound Rapid.

The river follows this eastern course, past North Creek, where it continues to flatten out. Several of the major rapids in this section are caused by the water flowing over uplifted ledges, such as those at Greyhound and Diagonal (located downstream from Riparius). The river gradually turns south as it flows toward the confluence with the Schroon River, where it begins a long flat section until it pours over a steep ledge at Lake Luzurne, known as Rockwell Falls. Several miles south from here, the river once again turns east toward the Glens Falls-Hudson Falls area, where it makes its final turn south toward New York City.

The river itself has its origins in the High Peaks Wilderness Area and, as with other things in the Adirondacks, is open to interpretation; what is meant by the source of the river can be confusing and is not always clear. The waterway to which the name Hudson River is first given by the US Geological Survey is the stream that flows out of Henderson Lake. [17] The lake, according to Alfred Donaldson, was named after Dave Henderson, one of the principals in the McIntyre mining operation. [18] The name came about on the exploratory trip that Henderson and others took from Lake Placid, over Indian Pass, and down to the lake and the infant Hudson River. The group was exploring the claim of their Indian guide as to the amount of possible iron ore in the Hudson riverbed.

The first dam on the Hudson is about ten feet from the outlet of Henderson Lake. The first bridge over the Hudson, located less than 100 feet downstream from Henderson Lake, is a simple wooden foot bridge with a hiking trail crossing it, definitely more quaint, and not as much traffic (and no tolls) as the Brooklyn Bridge has. From here, the river is more of a backcountry stream as it cascades over and between rocks and ledges, dropping down to a flatwater area near the old iron ore furnace of the McIntyre mine operation. An early map of the Upper Works region identified this section of the Hudson between Henderson Lake and Lake Sanford as Adirondack River.[19]

Here the Hudson begins to course gently, taking on the character of a wild, wetland river before opening up to what is left of Lake Sanford. Carson cited the name of the lake as most likely coming from Major Reuben Sanford, who helped survey the Upper Works area for the McIntyre operation in 1837. [20] Here can be found the remnants of the second dam on the Hudson River, near what was known as the Lower Works.

Lake Sanford has changed since the days of the McIntyre mining operation, as later mining from NL Industries dumped the tailings from their titanium processing into Lake Sanford. The lake is more of a wide, flatwater stream for two and a half miles as it passes by the newer mining site. Stoddard, in his 1874 guidebook of the Adirondacks, described Lake Sanford as being "four miles long, the shores low and marshy, looking more like a broad river than a lake..." [21] Smith, in *The History of Essex County,* also noted the length of the lake to be four miles. [22] Joel Headley, in the 1800s, described it as a "beautiful sheet of water" with no marks of civilization apparent and islands that "smile on you from every point" with "countless peaks" rising in "grand composure" off the far shore; much different than today. [23]

By the late 1940s, when the NL Industries titanium mine operation was going on, Paul Schaefer commented on the condition of Lake Sanford being "no longer a gem of the north glistening in the sunlight but a black, murky sewer into which poured a never ending stream of refuse from the mine." [24] The lake has become a mere ghost of what Stoddard knew as a result of the open pit operation, yet, in some places, it has begun to heal. After leaving what is left of Lake Sanford, the river changes back to a winding, wetland watercourse before it joins with the Opalescent River, which contains water from the highest pond source of water for the Hudson.

This first Hudson water to flow down toward New York City comes from the southwest slope of the highest point of land in the state, Mount Marcy. The peak was named for William Learned Marcy, the New York state governor at the time of the Redfield-Emmons expedition of 1837, replacing the unpretentious name of "High Point of Essex" that William Redfield applied to it. Two months later, Charles F. Hoffman bestowed the name of "Tahawas" to it.

Water that comes off the east and northern slopes of Marcy finds its way to the Ausable River and eventually, to the St. Lawrence. The Hudson-bound water from the southwest slope eventually finds its way to Lake Tear of the Clouds and out Feldspar Brook, descending for one and a half miles down to the Opalescent River. Geologically speaking, Lake Tear is a glacial cirque, the result of smaller parts of a larger glacier thawing and freezing again, according to geologists Jaffe & Jaffe. [25]

It should be noted that Lake Tear, like the name for the Adirondacks and Hudson, also has had multiple names and was known for years before Verplanck Colvin came upon it. One of the earliest names was Lake Perkins. Stoddard referred to Lake Tear as Lake Perkins in his 1874 guidebook of the region and also referred to it as the true high pond source of the Hudson. "Old Mountain" Phelps also calls Lake Tear "little Lake Perkins" in his descriptive essay on the Adirondacks. [26] Sandra Weber told how adamantly Phelps insisted that the name remain Lake Perkins, despite what Colvin and the state legislature would have called it. [27]

As to whom the name Perkins refers to, Donaldson mentioned an amateur artist of that name who "strayed" into Keene Valley around 1852 and was "captivated by its charms." [28] Carson mentioned an amateur painter from Milwaukee, Wisconsin, named Frederick S. Perkins, who came to Keene Valley in 1852 - probably the same one that Donaldson referred to. [29] Carson further noted that "Old

Mountain" Phelps guided Perkins to the top of Mount Marcy in 1857, where the two were supposed to have named several of the previously unnamed High Peaks. Perhaps it was then they named the little pond they saw southwest of their view, now known as Lake Tear of the Clouds.

Bill Healy, in his book on Phelps, mentioned that another early name for Lake Tear was Summit Water. [30] Sylvester also noted this name in his book, *Historical Sketches of Northern New York and the Adirondack Wilderness*. [31] Both Donaldson [32] and Weber [33] note that "Summit Water" was the name Colvin applied in his description of its discovery before the New York State legislature adopted the romantic term Colvin used when describing the lake in his report to the state, "a veritable tear of the clouds". E.R. Wallace also referred to Lake Tear using these older names. [34]

Water from Lake Tear dribbles out the west end and becomes Feldspar Brook, flowing for one and a half miles down to the Opalescent River. Had the Emmons-Redfield party followed it instead of the Opalescent on their way to Mount Marcy in 1837, they would have been the ones to determine the correct direction of flow for Lake Tear instead of Colvin. The Opalescent then makes a continual drop for the next two miles, coming out just upstream of Flowed Lands. Peter Lorie followed this part of the Opalescent when he carried his canoe to start his decent of the Hudson to New York City in 1992. Both Opalescent and Feldspar are named from the minerals found in their beds. The Opalescent was also known as the East River, in reference to other branches of the Hudson, a name still found on some trail signs in the High Peaks area.

Flowed Lands is the name of a small, half-mile section of backed-up Opalescent water and is surrounded with mountain views. It was created during the McIntyre mine operation to re-divert water down Calamity Brook to use at the mine located at Upper Works. To accomplish this, a trench was dug from a low point of Flowed Lands in the southwest corner to Calamity Pond, then known as Duck Pond, and an impoundment built on the south outlet. The trench can still be seen today as hikers come upon Flowed Lands on the Upper Works Trail from Calamity Pond.

The Flowed Lands outlet is in the far southern corner, where the New York City-bound water flows over the breached dam and downstream a mile to Hanging Spear Falls. The falls are quite a sight, with water shooting forth from the top of a ledge, plummeting down into a pool of water before continuing on through a mini gorge. Past the falls, the Opalescent cascades and meanders down for some two to three miles before joining the outlet from Lake Henderson.

From the Hudson-Opalescent junction, the river meanders for five miles before the start of a steep one-and-a-half mile descent over Class II and III waters under the Upper Works Road bridge. The Hudson then flattens out for the next six miles to Newcomb, with several Class II drops interrupting Class I meanders. A small Class I riffle under the Route 28N bridge and the Lake Harris outlet in Newcomb ushers in an open wetland area through which the river meanders.

In less than one and a half miles, the river constricts into a narrow channel and begins a Class II drop called Long Falls. The river flattens out for a mile before dropping over Ord Falls, a heavy Class II run with a good size wave train, which can approach Class III at high water.[35, 36] The Ord Falls name goes back at least to E.R. Wallace, who mentioned it in his guide book of the Adirondacks. [37] The 1898 USGS topographic (topo) map, Newcomb quadrangle, also names this feature Ord Falls.[38] This was also the site of the Ord Falls Dam proposed by the Hudson River Regulating District in 1923.

For the next four to five miles, the Hudson widens and flattens, with calm water being punctuated here and there with short Class I and II runs. Near the Goodnow Flow Outlet, the Hudson begins a two-mile flatwater section known as the Blackwell Stillwater, the name given on the 1898 USGS topo map.[39] As of 2014, the buildings of the Polaris Club, an old log camp converted to a hunting camp, are located on river left (left side of the river as you go down).

An old splash dam, built by Hudson River "Maestro" Jack Donohue, and used during logging days, marks the end of the Stillwater. The dam is washed out and hardly noticeable, but the unnamed Class II-III run after it is very noticeable!

The river then continues to alternate between Class I flatwater and small Class II drops for two miles to the junction of the Hudson and Cedar Rivers. The junction is quite scenic, with steep ten to fifteen foot ledges ushering the Cedar into the Hudson. A beautiful campsite is located on river right just after the junction. Immediately after the junction, the Hudson makes a nice Class II to III wave train - referred to as Cedar Rapids on the Finch, Pruyn map [40]-then alternates between flatwater and Class II runs for the next two and a half miles to where the Indian River comes in on the right.

Just up from the confluence with the Indian River on river right is the former site of the Gooley Club, named after Mike and Olive Goulet, who ran a farm known as "Mouth of the Indian".[41] The name Goulet was later spelled and pronounced "Gooley". The couple originally came to the area to run the Essex Chain of Lakes camp owned by Harve Bonnie, working there from 1877-1893 before purchasing their own place, known as the "outer camp". The camp was located on a bank overlooking the Hudson just upstream from the confluence with the Indian River where the recent club house was. The couple catered to hunters, fishing people, and log drivers in season.

Mike Goulet came to be known not only for his guiding ability, but also for his ability to make snowshoes. Olive, like many other guide wives, did a good deal of the hard chores and day-to-day tasks of running a lodge and farm facility. During the spring season, she cooked for log drivers, feeding up to thirty at a time. Olive was also well read and known for her storytelling abilities, reciting "Tom Twist" and "The Cremation of Sam McGee". The Goulets eventually sold the camp to Finch, Pruyn, who leased the camp to a sportsman's club known as the Gooley Club.[42] The property passed hands again to the Nature Conservancy in 2007, and to New York State in 2013.

This next part of the Hudson, according to John Kauffmann, writing in the book *Adirondack Reader*, will "claim your entire consciousness" with the "wilderness spirit of the Adirondacks". [43] It certainly caught the attention of the log drivers! As one continues down from the Indian River confluence, one can feel this spirit, and perhaps a touch of anxiety, much the same way log drivers did, and rafters still do, in the awareness that the Hudson River Gorge lay ahead. On a

21

spring day, as Kauffmann alluded to, cool air sends a "tingle" along the spine. Summer raft season, though, can temper the coolness and the anxiety.

The Hudson River Gorge itself is a unique area in the Adirondacks. The large-volume river has cut through some of the softer, exposed rock to create a deep, steep-sided gorge. The main part of the gorge is six to seven miles long, with some side walls rising up to 900 feet in places, some almost directly from the river. The gorge is longer, wider, and deeper than other Adirondack river gorges such as High Falls on the AuSable, the AuSable Chasm, and the gorges on the West Sacandaga and on the Boreas.

Surrounding the gorge are thousands of acres of wild land, much of it protected from human intrusion. As of 2014, the state land immediately surrounding the gorge is classified as a Wilderness area, as New York State began to acquire some of the Finch, Pruyn land surrounding the river and gorge in 2012. The section of the river that flows through the gorge is also classified as Wild by the New York State Wild, Scenic, and Recreational Rivers Act. Two Wild Forest and one Wilderness areas complete the state land surrounding the gorge, which also contains several pond and peak hiking destinations as well.

The major attraction, of course, is the river as it flows, surges, and thunders through the gorge, dropping almost 300 feet of elevation between the Indian River and the Boreas River. Wilderness Tours raft guide Gaye Clarke referred to the run, including the Indian River, as a "16 mile long rapid". [44] At high water, the Hudson approaches Class IV-IV+, providing a wild, churning ride that can bounce rafters and rafts around like a pinball. Raft and kayak trips most often begin on the Indian River, downstream from the Lake Abanakee dam, and follow the Class II-III Indian River for three miles to the confluence with the Hudson.

The deepest part of the gorge begins at Blue Ledges, as the river constricts and starts to drop steeply and quickly. Kauffmann wrote that at high water levels, the river "roars and spumes through this canyon in drop after drop, tumultuous in giant waves and gushing chutes". [45] Summer runs tend to be less tumultuous, as the water level drops and one can take more time to admire the beauty of the gorge. Even with its chaotic water, the Hudson does have several quiet pools of calm water in the gorge that allow one to relax and partake of the wild beauty around. Raft people oftentimes take advantage of the pools for a swim. These can also be soothing tonics that relax both mind and body, providing a balance to the stimulation of the rapids.

When it comes to the names of river features in the gorge, though, like many other things in the Adirondacks, things become complicated. As photographer Jim Swedberg commented in reference to names in the gorge, "It's easier to herd cats than get outfitters to agree on anything".[46] Indeed, as Swedberg further pointed out, there are often multiple names for the same rapid, or feature, as we shall see. While there are some standard names, such as the towering 300-to-400-foot high uplifted wall of rock called Blue Ledges and the glacially carved dome called Kettle Mountain, what river feature is what often depends on whom one asks, which raft company they work for, or when in history they made the run.

Part of the problem with the names in this section of the river is that different sources have given different names to the same features at different times. The name given to a certain rapid by the USGS topographical map may differ from the name used by some old-time river runner or a current raft guide. It is not the goal of this work, though, to try to standardize these names or set the record straight, but just to present the multiple sources and reference names.

The topographical map archives of the US Geological Service provide a good starting point. The 1898 Newcomb quadrangle (quad), which contains the Hudson Gorge, lists several familiar names of river features while omitting others.[47] On the quad, the course of the river itself is accurately portrayed, unlike previous maps of the time period. Amongst the familiar names are Ord Falls, Blackwell Stillwater, both located between Newcomb and the Indian River. Downstream from the Indian River confluence Blue Ledges, Kettle Mountain, and Carter's Pond are named. No name is given for any of the waterfalls such as OK Slip, Virgin, or Mink, nor for any of the rapids in the gorge.

The 1901 update of the Newcomb quadrangle is similar to the 1898 map, as are several of the reprints of the 1901 map over the next fifty years. The 1954 update does expand to name OK Slip Pond, Harris Rift Mountain (but no Harris Rift), and Pine Mountain along the gorge. The 1988 reprint of the 1954 map showed no rapids named. [48]

By 1989 the USGS had switched to metric measurements on the topo maps, splitting the old Newcomb quadrangle that contained the Hudson Gorge and putting it in the Dutton Mountain quad. [49] This map does have rapids named, including Indian Head, Gooley Steps, Cedar Ledges, and Dunk Pond Flats, which was located between Cedar Ledges and Blue Ledges. Virgin Falls is named as the stream on river left just above the start of Blue Ledge Rapids that drains Huntley Pond, with no name for the falls on the stream that drains Mink Pond. Blue Ledge Rapids is named, as are Blue Ledge Narrows, Osprey Nest, Beaver Dams (below Osprey Nest), Kettle Mountain, Gunsight, Harris Rift, and Fox Den (the rapid located just above the railroad bridge). In 2010, the USGS again changed the map, splitting the gorge between the Bad Luck Mountain and Dutton Mountain maps.

Other sources, of course, such as the 1928 Finch, Pruyn map, forest ranger rescue maps, and various guidebooks, present a variety of names and origins, as shall be seen.

Downstream from the Indian River is a mile-long, Class II-III rapid commonly known as Cedar Ledges, named, one would suppose, for the steep ledges that drop down from the side into the river with white cedar trees growing out of the ledge cracks. Many present-day river runners refer to it by this name, as does Alec Proskine in his river guide.[50] This was to be the location of the proposed Gooley #1 Dam in 1923 and 1968.

The flatwater section, punctuated by four short Class II drops that follow Cedar Ledges, is referred to as "Deers Den" on a map compiled by Dick Carlson,[51] the same name as was on the Finch, Pruyn map of 1928. A map in Wilson's book also gave the "Deer Den" name to the section between Elephant Rock and Mink/Virgin Falls. [52] The Deer Den name was also applied by the log drivers to a section of the river below Blue Ledges that Hugh Fosburgh spoke of. [53] Proskine referred to this flat section preceding Cedar Ledges as Black Hole, a name that North River residents applied, during the log drive days, to the major Class III ledge drop after the D&H Railroad bridge, called Greyhound today by many. [54]

A large rock in the middle of this "Deer Den" section is listed on the Carlson map as both Fish Rock and Elephant Rock; Proskine used the latter name. Several raft guides now refer to the rock as Jump Rock, as people use it to jump into the river. The next two short Class II runs have no names except the "Deer Den" name Wilson applied to them.

On river left, a mile above the beginning of Blue Ledge Rapid, is a large, scenic waterfall that can be viewed from the river. The falls are fed by the Mink Pond Outlet and are called Mink Falls on a USGS-based map[55] and in Proskine's book. [56] Some river runners refer to it as Virgin Falls, but both the 1989 USGS topo, and Miller's USGS-based map, gives that name to a cascade that drains into the river just above the start of Blue Ledge Rapid on river left; it is fed by water from Huntley Pond.

Pete Burns of Beaver Brook Outfitters, grandson of the Hudson River "Maestro" Jack Donohue, attributed the origin of the present-day Virgin Falls story to the fertile mind of Wilderness Tours guide Gaye Clarke in the early days of commercial rafting. [57] On a trip that he was a part of, Pete remembered Gaye telling a "guide tale" on the spur of the moment to raft guests about the cleansing and restorative powers of the water at the falls; hence, the name Virgin Falls. Naturally, the tale has grown over the years to include Native Americans bringing the women they would marry up to the falls to restore their virginity by passing them under the springtime water of the falls. As there is no solid evidence that Native Americans came to the gorge for any reason, Pete's explanation is very plausible and is not denied by Gaye himself! [58]

The long, Class III-IV rapid just above the sheer wall of Blue Ledges is commonly referred to as Blue Ledge Rapid, and is almost a mile long. It is here that the river begins to constrict and drop more steeply. The Blue Ledge name applied to this rapid is found on the 1928 Finch, Pruyn replica map,[59] as well as a 1967 *New York Times* article by Robert Hall.[60] The name, of course, refers to the exposed wall of blue-colored rock rising directly out of the river and is one of the more spectacular sights in the gorge. At the end of Blue Ledge Rapid, on the far river left, is a hole (or hydrolic) at medium to low water known as Jiffy Pop, Guide Sucker, and Chuck's Hole (for Adirondack River Outfitters guide Chuck Butkas).

Downstream from Blue Ledges, the river continues to constrict, funneling the river water like a pinched garden hose through an opening in the rock bed. Most sources refer to this rapid as the Narrows, or, as one map calls it, Blue Ledge Narrows.[61] It is a short but rolling wave train and is a Class III-IV+ run depending on the river level; at high water, the Narrows is one of the most exciting rollercoaster rides one can ever imagine! A Vermont paddling club, in their 1980 journal, referred to this rapid as Staircase.[62] Dick Carlson cited the log drivers referring to the Narrows as Blue Ledge Carry, as drivers would not run this section in boats, usually carrying or lining the boats down instead.[63] Both the Carlson map[64] and Proskine[65] referred to the next rapid as Osprey Nest, a short Class III drop.

Carlson's map listed three different names for the next rapid, beginning with Carter's Landing (Carter's), which refers to the flat area on river right were Carter's Creek comes in from Carter's Pond.[66] Notes from Irwin Miller record Carter's Pond as having been called Nate's Pond at one time.[67] The flat landing on river right was the location of one of several log driving camps. Both the Carlson and the Miller maps also list the names Mile Long for the rapid, undoubtedly referring to the length of the rapid, and Split Rock, which refers to the large boulder on river left that seems to be split down the middle. At the end of Carter's, the open ledges of Kettle Mountain can be seen in the distance on river left as it rises above the gorge.

Between Carter's Rapid and OK Slip Rapid is a short Class III run known as Wrap Rapid. OK Slip is a common reference to the Class III run that begins after OK Slip Brook comes in on river right. OK Slip was the name listed on the Finch, Pruyn replica map and, according to Rick Fenton, the name comes from the logging days. [68] At several places in the gorge, loggers built slide-like flumes to send logs down to the river; when it was time to let another log down the flume, the call "OK, slip" was given, the gate at the crib dam on the pond was raised, and another log was sent down the flume to the river.

The name also refers to the falls three quarters of a mile up from the river, which is one of the highest waterfalls in New York State at over 200 feet tall. OK Slip Falls cannot be seen from the river, but can be seen from the ledges of Kettle Mountain on the other side of the river. To look at the falls from this point is reminiscent of the view of Yosemite Falls from Glacier Point in Yosemite National Park, as the water shoots out from a notch in the top of the cliff and falls some 200 feet to the rocky floor below. The water for the falls comes from OK Slip Pond, which was used during the logging days. There is also a marked public hiking trail that leads to the falls from Rt. 28.

The small rapid after OK Slip Rapid is noted on the Carlson Map[69] but with the words "No Name" in parentheses, indicating that it had no name, which is what some present-day river runners call the rapid because it has no name, which, of course, is a name, meaning that the rapid is mis-named; got it?

The steepest drop on the river comes next, a Class III-IV+ run known by several names: Givney's Rift, Soup Strainer, Big Nasty, and Kettle Mountain Rapids. The Kettle Mountain name refers to the mountain of the same name that towers over the rapid on river left. Soup Strainer refers to the rock in the middle of the rapid that can act like a strainer and create a pin situation if river runners are not careful to avoid it. Big Nasty is the name that the Buck[70] article and the Miller map[71] used. That name probably refers to the steepness of the drop and the risk factor involved in running it in open canoes. Big Nasty is also the name some river runners give to several large holes found in Carter's Rapid. Kettle Mountain Rapid is the name given the run on the Miller map, combining the No Name and Givney's rapids into one.[72]

Gunsight Rapids is the name given to a series of short Class III runs after Givney's. They are sometimes differentiated into Gunsight In and Gunsight Out, respectively. [73, 74]

Harris Rift[75] is a Class III-IV run that was one of the most feared rapids of the log drivers, perhaps because of the series of three holes on river right located about two thirds of the way down. Harris is also the name of a lake in Newcomb that feeds the Hudson and a mountain to the right of the rapid just before the railroad bridge. The Harris name can be traced back to the log driving days and possibly referred to a John Harris who was an important log boss in the early days on the river. [76] The name Harris also appeared on at least one logging contract as the last name of several of the workers. [77] Harris was the name referred to by the 1928 Finch, Pruyn replica map.

Fox Den and Bobcat are the next two features named on the Carlson Map downstream from Harris Rift. [78] Proskine referred to these rapids by the same names, but reverses their order.[79] One of the popular surf holes in Bobcat is referred to as Fluffy Box of Kittens by several of the current generation of guides.[80]

As the river water exits Harris Rift, the turbulence that the gorge creates subsides. Fox Den and Bobcat rapids are followed by a half-mile flatwater section that leads up to the D&H Railroad bridge, which marks the exit from the Hudson River Gorge. This part of the rail line was extended from North Creek all the way up to the Upper Works to mine titanium as part of the World War II effort. [81] Seeing a threat to the supply of foreign titanium from German submarines, the federal government looked to the Upper Works area, improving the road system and the transportation of the mineral out, 130 years too late for the Henderson mine! The building of the railroad required, though, a federal override of Article XIV of the NYS Constitution, much to the objections of the state.

The river flows under the D&H bridge toward the Dutton Mountain ridge and the junction with the Boreas River on the left. From here, the Hudson starts to widen noticeably as it makes a 90-degree turn south. One mile downstream from the Boreas, the river makes another sharp turn to the left and drops over a long ledge that sticks out almost the whole way across the river. It is a Class III run and today is commonly called Bus Stop or Greyhound, but was known as Black Hole by local residents during the log drive days; the Miller map lists both names.[82]

One source of the origins of the Greyhound name, among several, was reported in the *Adirondack Daily Enterprise.*[83] In an article on rafting, Hudson River Raft Company guide Chris Shaw of Keene said Greyhound was named because "the hydraulics could turn over a Greyhound bus". Several versions of this story abound, including one that says that the ledge is big enough to park a Greyhound bus under and another that says if rafters aren't paying attention, they could, just like at a bus stop, exit from the raft! After Greyhound, for the next two or three miles to North River, the Hudson continues to be wide, making several Class II attempts at rapids.

At the hamlet of North River, one starts to feel the change from the wild, sometimes tumultuous river of the last forty miles as more signs of civilization begin to appear. The Barton Mines plant appears on river right, as does Route 28 and the hamlet of North River.

The first two rapids seen along State Route 28 are referred to as Mouse Tail and Perry Eller. The Mouse Tail name is derived from the unique black coloration on the upstream side of the rock ledge that sticks out into the water on river left and was used as a river level gauge during the log drive days by the "Maestro," Jack Donohue. Jack's daughter, Milda, gives credit for the naming of Mouse Rock to her father.[83] An earlier name of the ledge was found on a Verplank Colvin photo taken in 1898, with the name of Morse Rock listed as being above a rapid called Sabael Rapid.[84]

Sabael Rapid was quite possibly a reference to the present-day Perry Eller Rapid. Perry Eller was a resident of North River who owned a cottage on the property now owned by Whitewater Challengers, who built their raft center around the cottage. Five miles farther downstream, the village of North Creek comes in on both sides and the D&H Railroad rejoins the river and is a constant companion for the next thirty-five miles to Hadley-Luzurne.

In his river guide, Proskine commented on the wild scenery of the section of the Hudson downstream from North Creek.[85] Indeed, if it were not for the D&H railbed on river right, this section might be classified as Wild instead of Scenic. A mile or so downstream of North Creek is a Class II-III ledge drop called Bird Pond Falls.

A mile above Riparius is the three-quarter-mile-long rapid Proskine called Spruce Rapid, the same rapid that Charles Farnum and his friend had a problem in when they ran the river in 1880; they referred to it as Spruce Mountain Rapid. [86] Two or three miles downstream from Riparius is a Class III run named Race Horse Rapid. Farnum called it "Horse Race," with the name probably having something to do with the motion of the current. The other major rapid is a Class III run referred to as Diagonal Ledge. There is also a very noticeable rock island on this section that is not officially named, but is referred to as Rock Island by present-day river runners.

Shortly before the Route 28 bridge at The Glen, the Friends Lake Road can be seen on river left. As The Glen is approached, Route 28 makes its presence known for the last time, crossing over the river just above a Class II-III run. Less than a mile below the bridge, the river makes a sharp, 90-degree turn to the left, dropping over a large ledge that produces a very dangerous hole on river right at high water. For the next seven miles, the river is a Class I-II run at low water, with the Schroon River coming in on the left as the Route 418 bridge is approached in Thurman. Here, the Hudson begins a large flatwater section for the next thirteen miles to the last rapid before the dams, backwater, and larger doses of civilization begin that most associate the Hudson with. Rockwell Falls is a Class IV-V drop just before the junction with the Sacandaga River comes in on the right. E.R. Wallace referred to this falls as "Rockwell or Jessup's Little Falls." [87]

From here down to the Glens Falls-Hudson Falls section, there are several backwater impoundments as the upper section completes the transition to become the lower section. For the rest of its journey to New York City, the Hudson essentially is the wide tidal river most people know - very different from its wild beginnings.

Hudson River high waters
Left: Lake Tear of the Clouds.
Right: The beginning of Feldspar Brook.
Jeff Dickinson photos

Hudson River firsts
Left: 1st dam on the Hudson River as it leaves Henderson Lake.
Right: 1st bridge over the Hudson River just below Henderson Lake.
Jeff Dickinson photos

The remains of Sanford Lake.
Jeff Dickinson photo

Raft at Blue Ledges.
Jeff Dickinson photo

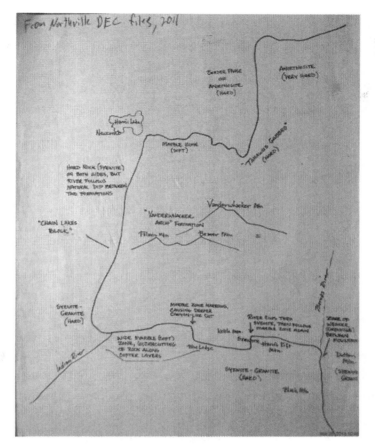

<u>Sketch map of Hudson River geology.</u>
Northville DEC Office

Early Hudson River Runners and Upper River Explorers

Writer and former National Park Service employee John Kauffmann wrote glowingly about the Upper Hudson River in Paul Jamieson's book, *The Adirondack Reader,* saying that "The Hudson is the shining, roaring gateway to the Adirondack wilderness".[1] Indeed, the river roars very loudly as it goes through the Hudson River Gorge, as log drivers attested to many years ago and rafters confirm today. Before logging, though, few actually went through the Hudson gateway, bypassing it on the way north by using the water route via Lake George and Lake Champlain. In the 1800s, settlers of the Mid-west and Plains states also bypassed it via the Mohawk River and Erie Canal. This chapter looks at some of those who did not bypass the gateway, opting instead to go through to explore the Upper Hudson region.

The first humans of record to see the Hudson River, of course, were the Native Americans who came to the Hudson River valley below Albany. Although the exact date of their arrival in New York is hard to know, archeological evidence indicates a presence of pre-historic humans in the area around 12,000 years ago; in New Jersey, evidence goes back 8,000 years. Lenni Lenape legends give a more exact date of 1300 AD when, according to the "Walam Olum, or Red Score," these people arrived on the Atlantic Shore from the north via the midwest looking for a "river that flowed two ways." [2] These Lenni Lenape people were often called the Delaware, spoke an Algonquin dialect, and inhabited most of New Jersey, the upper reaches of the Delaware River, and the lower western shore of the Hudson.

The first Europeans to see and know of the Hudson River sailed to the area by the mid to late 1500s.[3] Betty Buckell went back even farther, theorizing that a Viking, Thorfinn Karlsefni, a contemporary of Lief Ericson, saw the Hudson River as early as 1010, predating the Lenape.[4] Sailing along the coast of New England in a south-southwestern direction after passing Cape Cod, Karlsefni eventually came upon a fjord that he called Steamfjord. As the only other fjord would have been north, along the Maine coast, Buckell concluded the fjord Karlsefni saw was on the Hudson (probably the fjords above New York City). She further reasoned that if it was the Hudson, then Karlsefni may have been the first river runner on the Hudson, as it was a Viking custom to follow a fjord or river as far upstream as possible. If this is so, then Karlsefni would have made it all the way up to the Albany area, predating Henry Hudson by some 500 years.

The first European of record to see and describe the river was Giovanni de Verrazano, in 1524, while sailing for the French king. Verrazano described the New York landscape as "a pleasant situation among some steep hills, through which a very large river, deep at its mouth, forced its way to the sea".[5] The crew stopped in New York Harbor and, as they were not familiar with the river or its depths, sent out a small boat, passing Brooklyn and Staten Island while watching the natives work. They proceeded up-river to New York Bay before weather forced them to return to the ship. Arthur Adams, in *The Hudson Through the Years,* recorded the first European name given to the river, stating that de Verrazano called it the "Grand River" or "River of the Steep Hills".[6]

Adams also told of other explorers to the Hudson and some of the other early names applied to it.[7] A Portuguese man named Estevan Gomey came to the area the year after de Verrazano, 1525, sailing for the Spanish. This explained names such as Rio de Gomez, Rio de Guamas, and Rio San Antonio given to the Hudson. In 1569, the Hudson appeared as "Norumbega River" on some charts. Buckell also listed many early names for the Hudson, including sixteen Native American names and twenty-five European ones.[8] There also seems to have been some French and Dutch visitation between 1525 and 1609. Boyle noted the mouth of the river as it appeared on European maps dated 1556 and 1569.[9] Thus, the presence of the Hudson was known for some time before 1609.

The first known European of record to extensively run the Hudson River was the man for whom the river was eventually named. Henry Hudson was an English explorer who began a voyage to North America in April of 1609.[10] Hudson was working and sailing for the Dutch East India Company, looking for a short water route to Asia. Carl Carmer, in the book *The Hudson,* wrote that Hudson made it as far south as Virginia before working his way up the Atlantic coast, including a short stop at the mouth of the Delaware.[11] Hudson's ship was a small, shallow-bottomed, high-decked 80-ton yacht named the *Half Moon* and toward the beginning of September, Hudson found himself around the shallow, sandy coast of New Jersey.

On the morning of September 2nd, the crew woke to see "a great fire that seemed to hang in the sky, for no land showed beneath it". Later, the sun burned away the mists and they saw land "all like broken Ilands", sailing into a bay fed by a big, flowing stream. The light of the sunny afternoon mellowed and the evening calm came as they dropped anchor in the quiet harbor. When the stars began to show through the clear air, they saw to the north "high hills, bluer than the deepening blue of the sky." Crew member Robert Juet noted that "This was a very good land to fall with and a pleasant land to see". [12]

For the next several days, the crew studied and explored the river and the surrounding land as they followed the course of the river north, encountering both friendly and hostile natives. As Hudson and his crew drew closer to what is now the Albany area, the riverbed became increasingly shallow and hopes of finding a water route to Asia dwindled.[13] Hudson sent out a crew in a small boat to search farther up river, returning after reaching unnavigable water. It is commonly held that Hudson made it to where the Mohawk empties into the Hudson.[14] Hudson and his crew started the return trip downstream on September 23rd, after it was determined there was no further advance to be made, reaching the mouth of the Hudson River on October 4th.

A few years later, on another voyage to North America, Hudson discovered the bay in northern Canada that bears his name. Apparently, his crew did not think much of this feat, or of Hudson, for they mutinied, setting him and several others adrift in a small boat in the bay, never to be heard from again.

As to early explorers on the Upper Hudson and Adirondack region, there is scant information. William White told how there was not much permanent Native American presence in the area.[15] Keller wrote how the Algonquin and Iroquois did not appear in the region until around 2000 BC, with any trips being seasonal in nature.[16] Some evidence, though, is interpreted to mean that a settlement might have been made along what is now the carry between the Raquette River and Upper Saranac Lake, known today as the "Indian Carry".

The tribes had well-known and well-traveled routes through the Adirondacks.[17] The Lake Champlain-Lake George waterway of *Last of the Mohicans* fame was part of a major travel route that came up the Hudson River Valley to the Glens Falls area. Travelers then carried over to Lake George from the Hudson along present-day Route 9, bypassing the upper Hudson on the way to Lake Champlain and the St. Lawrence River. Both Dave Beetle[18] and White [19] reported on another overland water route up the Fulton Chain of Lakes near Old Forge, to the Raquette River system, over to the Saranac system at the Indian Carry, and down the Saranac to Lake Champlain. Another route turned east from Lake Placid and followed the Ausable River down to Lake Champlain.

There is also documentation on a route that led up the Sacandaga River valley from Johnstown to Speculator, up to Indian Lake, then to Newcomb, through Indian Pass and to Lake Placid, ending at Saranac Lake, most likely at the Indian Carry.[20] Aber and King refer to this route in *The History of Hamilton County,* calling it the Sacandaga Trail.[21] Father Joques was said to have traveled this route on a hunting and fishing trip in 1642 with his Iroquois captors.

The written record concerning the upper Hudson picked up as the eighteenth century approached. Carson wrote of how one of the earliest upper Hudson River runners, Sabael Benedict, made his way to Indian Lake in August 1762 from Lake Champlain to the High Peaks area. [22] From there, Benedict made his way to Indian Pass, continuing over to the Hudson side and down to Lake Henderson. Here Benidict paddled down through Lake Sanford, down the Hudson River, past Newcomb and the Harris Lake outlet. Benedict then followed the Hudson twelve miles downstream to the Indian River and up to Indian Lake to become the first person to settle there. An interesting side note is that Benedict was from the Penobscot tribe in Maine, predating future Hudson river runners from Maine by some 200 years.

There is evidence of a Mohawk presence in the High Peaks-Lake Placid area, as indicated by recovered arrowheads. [23] Weber wrote of a connecting route from Upper Works and Lake Henderson, up to Preston Ponds, and from there to the Raquette River system. Although tribes passed through the High Peaks–Upper Hudson area, there was not much of a reason for these travelers to climb peaks or run whitewater in the area. The first people to go near the mountains or climb the summits were surveyors such as Charles Brodhead, who was in the area in June 1797, coming within a few miles of Mount Marcy.

One of the first European groups to extensively explore and develop the Hudson headwaters region and also account for several names in the area was the mining operation led by Dave Henderson. Arthur Masten, in his book *Adirondac,* gave a history of the operation that centered in and developed the Upper Hudson area.[24]

The beginning of the operation actually started out with a failed mining operation in the Lake Placid area.[25] In 1811, Archibald McIntyre began the Elba Iron and Steel Manufacturing Company near the present-day Plains of Abraham. The operation was built along the Chubb River and brought a touch of prosperity to the area before going under in 1817. In 1826, some of McIntyre's relatives and associates, including Dave Henderson, came back to the area to start mining for silver. It was then that Henderson and the group met up with Sabael Benidict's son Elijah, the Native American who showed them a sample of iron ore and told them he knew where there was much more.[26]

The group started out for the Upper Works area from Lake Placid, following Benedict over Indian Pass. Sandra Weber also recorded one of the first African Americans in the High Peaks region, a manservant of the group simply referred to as "Enoch". [27] While the group was in Indian Pass, he was reported to have wondered what possessed a man to come out to a region such as this.

Henderson described going up Indian Pass and coming upon what was thought to be the Hudson River summit waters: "We at length gain'd the summit of the Notch, the very fountain head of the AuSable River, where we found another stream running south, which appears to be the principal source of the Hudson River". Camping that night on the Hudson side of the pass, Henderson told of "the infant murmurs of the giant River Hudson, the music which lull'd us to sleep".

The next day, the party made their way downstream, coming upon several deposits of iron ore. Three of the party continued on down to explore a large lake, naming it Lake Henderson, while the others stayed to search for more ore. [28] Jim Shaughnessy added to the narrative, saying how the group, upon arriving at the foot of the lake, viewed a small cascading stream that formed the outlet of the lake, the infant Hudson River. [29] It was the ledge of iron ore across the outlet helping to hold the water back that was of particular interest to the group.

The party continued downstream to Upper Works and, seeing enough ore to spark dreams of wealth, made plans that night around a campfire to develop a mine facility, forming the Adirondac Iron Works, which would later become the Adirondac Iron & Steel Company. The next day, the group hurried out of the area, traveling quickly and quietly to Albany to lay claim and buy the land.

Acquisition of the title to the land had to go through the state land office, which sent out a survey party to the area in 1827, headed by John Richards and Major Reuben Sanford. Sanford, a war hero in the Battle of Plattsburgh, was serving as a state senator and came from Wilmington, New York. They provided an early description of the area, referring to the Opalescent River as "the east branch of the North (Hudson) River" and reporting the difficulties they had in the survey process. [30] Despite these challenges, the Henderson group was issued a title for the land, which allowed development of the facility to begin.

Development began the next year, with a furnace built along the banks of the Hudson (which can still be seen today) to process the ore. Lee Manchester, in his anthology work *Tales From the Deserted Village,* noted that as part of the mine development, a dam was constructed on the river to provide slack water navigation between the Upper and Lower Works. [31] The operation grew to a small village, with plenty of boat and float trips on the infant Hudson River for both recreation (probably fishing by the mine crews) and commerce. [32] Arthur Masten even wrote about Dave Henderson taking a raft trip across Lake Henderson on his way to Indian Pass. [33]

Judge McMartin wrote in July of 1830 of meeting a couple of men who were exploring the area after coming up from Montgomery County by way of the Sacandaga Valley similar to the route Sabael Benedict followed. They reported taking a canoe down the Jessup and Indian Rivers to where the Indian junctions with the Hudson, carrying a short distance over land to a lake, and up to Newcomb and the Upper Works.

By August of 1830, Iddo Osgood, who came to survey a road in, wrote about a boat trip that he took on the Upper Hudson. Arriving at a bridge below Lake Sanford the party split up, with some going by foot to the Upper Works, and some by water. The water party set about to build a raft to transport themselves upriver, and when this failed, a canoe was made the next day from a large pine tree. Osgood and his friends toiled all day, making their way upstream to within three quarters of a mile of the head of Lake Sanford to meet up with the rest of the party.[34]

As part of the initial development of the Upper Works, Carson noted that Henderson brought in a group of associates, including a friend, David Colden, as well as the distinguished scientist, William Redfield, to make a survey of the property.[35] Carson noted that one of the major contributions of these expeditions was adding to the knowledge of the area, providing some of the first sound information on the peaks and headwaters in the upper Hudson River area.

Upon their arrival, the group made their way to the Opalescent River, referred to then as the East Branch of the Hudson River. [36] The initial going was difficult, and by noon they made it to the junction with the Opalescent, finding the decent of the Hudson at that point to be "very gradual". Redfield noted that the group continued to make slow progress up the Opalescent, having to wade at times. The group set up camp about 4 p.m. on the banks of the river, building a shelter with poles and a fire pit in front.

The next day, the group continued upriver, passing Hanging Spear Falls and, in the late afternoon, coming upon "a beautiful lake situated between two high mountains," [37] naming it Lake Colden after David Colden. The next day, Redfield, Henderson, and one other person continued up the Opalescent from Lake Colden for about two miles. Here, Redfield notes: "From this point I mounted a hill about 150 feet on the south bank and saw a third high peak," that was "surmounted by a beautiful dome of rock," that third high peak being Mount Marcy. The party made their way back down to Upper Works the next day, but Redfield returned the next year with another survey party to make the first recorded ascent of the peak that Redfield called "The High Peak" or "The High Peak of Essex," bestowing the first European name to Marcy.

From the beginning, the mine project had continuous problems making a profit, most notably being the transportation of the product out of the remote region. [38] The initial plan was to build an access road toward Lake Champlain to transport the processed ore out, where it would be transported by boat through the Champlain Canal to the Lower Hudson. Such a route proved to be insufficient and costly, as McIntyre noted as early as 1833. [39]

E.R. Wallace described the problem, too, that the "expense attending the transportation of the iron nearly 50 miles over corduroy [wood log based, JTD] roads to Lake Champlain rendered the business unprofitable". [40] If a railroad was considered at that time, there still was the problem of the terrain surrounding the Upper Works area, which presented an "awesome barrier". [41] Henderson, in a letter to McIntyre, noted the profitability problem, despairing that if these issues could not be rectified, the operation should be considered a loss. Thus, while the mine had plenty of ore to process and enough wood to fire the furnace, the transportation issue continued to be a problem, and the initial prosperity the Henderson–McIntyre mine had was short-lived.

The project was dealt a severe blow with the untimely death of Henderson at Calamity Pond in 1845. Seven years later, in 1852, the Sackets Harbor & Saratoga Railroad proposed a line from Saratoga up through North Creek to the Upper Works area, and from there continuing west to Watertown and Lake Ontario.[42] The initial plan was to take the line along the Hudson from North Creek, crossing the Hudson where the present-day railroad bridge is, upstream from the Boreas River, then following the Boreas up to Upper Works. The prospect of such a transport system gave hope to the failing mine operation, already on life support since the death of Henderson. The hope was short-lived, though, as the line never materialized and the life support plug to the mining operation was pulled.

Over the next forty to fifty years, there were other proposals to build the railroad line to the Upper Works, with the land and the idea changing hands several times. Thomas Clark Durant, whose son, William, developed Great Camp architecture in the Raquette Lake region, did build a line up to North Creek, but had no obligation to go farther. The land and the idea were bought by the D&H Railroad in 1889, with no further attempts at extending the line until World War II. [43]

One of the other problems that the Henderson mining operation faced was an impurity in the ore now known as titanium.[44] By World War II, the very mineral that had proved a nuisance to the Henderson mining efforts became important in industrial processing and, with the outbreak of the war, there was concern that foreign supplies of titanium would be jeopardized. Seeing the potential in the iron ore of the Upper Works area, National Lead (NL) bought the mine in 1941. When war broke out and the federal government began looking at domestic sources, the Upper Works facility became an attractive option. NL began to mine titanium, initially shipping the mineral out to North Creek by truck, and from there by rail, beginning in July of 1942.

It became clear, though, that this system was inadequate to meet the full potential of the mine. Work on extending the rail system from North Creek began in 1942 when the Defense Plant Corporation, a federal agency, secured a right of way through state land, overriding the protection of Article XIV of the New York State Constitution. Under contract with the federal government and NL, the D&H Railroad laid down the track from North Creek to Upper Works that Dave Henderson had so desperately needed 100 years before.

The track took two years to complete the thirty-three miles from North Creek to Upper Works, which included building a bridge across the Hudson upstream of the Boreas River confluence. The first load moved out on the new line on June 19, 1944, and was not well publicized due to security concerns. The mine continued on for some years after the war, with an entire village being built to work the mine. The facility eventually ceased production, with the last load of titanium leaving the mine at 7 a.m. on November 16, 1989. [45] The track was abandoned and presently serves as a multi-use recreational trail. As of 2013, it was being considered for use as a tourist ride.

The same year that Redfield was in the Lake Colden area, 1836, Ebenezer Emmons and James Hall climbed Whiteface Mountain to measure and study the mountains, noting what seemed to be a higher peak to the south.[46] Snow prevented them from continuing and, like Redfield, they postponed further exploration to the next year, including a summit climb of the higher peak. The report that Emmons filed with the state legislature became the first published reference to Mount Marcy.

Donaldson outlined the traditional view of the first ascent of Mount Marcy on August 5, 1837, with the group being led by Professor Ebenezer Emmons.[47] Donaldson lists the party as consisting of Emmons, his son Ebenezer Jr., Edward Hall, William Redfield, Asa Torrey, Professor Story, Professor John Miller, Achibald McIntyre, Dave Henderson, Charles Ingham, and guides John Cheney and Harvey Holt. Carson told how the party ascended to Lake Colden, with the chief objective to explore the high sources of the Hudson River and the surrounding peaks.[48] The party camped that night on Lake Colden in the spot that Redfield camped at the previous year.

The next morning, Friday, August 4th, the party made their way up the Opalescent River, camping that night in a small gorge in the upper reaches of the Opalescent between Mount Marcy and Mount Colden. Redfield noted that they passed a small feeder stream to the right of the Opalescent as they made their way up, commenting that it might provide a shorter way to Marcy, but he did not pursue it. Had he done so, he would have discovered that the stream, now known as Feldspar Brook, was the outlet of Lake Tear of the Clouds and the high pond source of the Hudson River. Redfield referred to the camp spot on the Opalescent as "Holt's Camp," with the name most likely coming from their guide.[49]

The next day, Saturday, August 5th, the party made their way up the northwest side of Marcy, following the last trickles of the Opalescent to a high meadow that drained both to the Hudson and St. Lawrence. The group continued to follow the northern flank of Marcy, arriving on the summit sometime in the late morning to early afternoon. Redfield, though, recorded two different times for the group reaching the summit - 10 a.m. and 12 noon. While there, the group gave several names to the surrounding peaks.[50]

Current research has raised several questions concerning who exactly stood on the summit of Mount Marcy that August day, who was the leader, and what time the group made it to the summit. Phil Terrie, in his introduction to Carson's book, detailed how recently discovered documents showed that Miller, Strong, and McIntyre were not part of the party that made it to the summit that day.[51] John Miller's diary indicated that he awoke sick the morning of August 3 and said that his condition would prevent him from accompanying the party when they left from Upper Works that day for Lake Colden.

The same diary also noted in the next day's entry, August 4th, that McIntyre, Strong, and two others arrived at Upper Works that evening. This, of course, meant they could not have been with the climbing party at Holt's campsite on the Opalescent that night, nor been with them the next day when they summited Marcy. If they had, it meant that they would have had to go from Upper Works to the summit in a half day; a tall feat, even today!

A letter written by James Hall on the summit, dated August 5, 1837, substantiated this, as Hall listed Professor Emmons, Dr. Torry, Ingham, Henderson, Redfield, and Hall as being on the summit, ommiting McIntyre, Strong, and Miller. A letter by McIntyre himself, addressed from Upper Works, was dated August 7 - the same day the climbing party was at Avalanche Lake. Hall's letter also indicated the party reached the summit at 2 p.m. and that the name of Marcy was bestowed upon the peak that day. Weber named the group as Emmons, Redfield, assistant state geologist James Hall, artist Ingham, state botanist John Torry, Dave Henderson, Cheney, Holt, and three other guides, as well as the younger Emmons.[52]

As to the time the group made the summit, Weber noted that Redfield indicated the group stayed on the summit for five hours. When considering this, she felt that it accounts for the discrepancies between Redfield's notes and Hall's letter if the group arrived on the summit at 10 a.m. and left at 3 p.m. Both Redfield and Hall gave similar accounts, with Redfield noting that the air on top of Marcy "was found to be cold and bracing and the aspect of the morning was splendid and delightful." [53]

Redfield also noted the temperature that morning was 33 degrees, with the group making it to the meadow at the head of the stream, now known as the Plateau, at 8:40 a.m. From there, they spent the next few hours making their way through stunted pine on their way to the top. With the group poised where they were at 8:40, a late morning summiting was entirely within a reasonable timeframe. Weber put the departure from the summit at 3:30, with the group making it back to the camp within an hour after leaving the summit, altering the route from the morning ascent. The next day, they made their way to Lake Colden, spending the next few days climbing Algonquin Peak and parts of Mount Colden, exploring Avalanche Lake and Indian Pass before returning to Upper Works on August 9[th.]

George Marshall, brother of Bob Marshall, writing in Carson's book, reiterated the suggestion that Redfield did not receive due credit for his work in the High Peaks area and for his leadership in the 1837 party.[54] He felt that given Redfield's work the year before, and with his credentials as a scientist, he would have been at least a co-leader with Emmons. McMartin, in her guidebook on the area, agreed, noting that according to Redfield's son, Redfield thought of himself as the "real leader" of the 1836 and 1837 trips.[55] The son further felt that, perhaps, the name of the peak should more rightly be Redfield, after the man who first saw it, helped lead the group who first climbed it, and who took the first measurements of its height.

James Hall provides the first published description of the view from Mt. Marcy:

> From this mountain we have one of the grandest views imaginable on the south, east, west and to a considerable distance on the north we have mountains extending before us; sometimes for a little distance they appear to form ranges, and again and for the most part, they are irregularly disposed, and present all the appearance of the ocean in a violent storm. Some of these mountains are clothed in evergreens to their summits, others are laid bare by slides leaving a crest of naked rock. Innumerable little lakes and streams are seen in all directions - Lake Champlain is visible on the east, and beyond that the Green Mountains, and beyond the low parts of this chain, we see the White Mountains, extending along the horizon like a dark cloud. [56]

Within months of the Redfield-Emmons party, Charles Hoffman came to the Upper Works and High Peaks area. Hoffman was a New York City writer who had traveled up the Mississippi River valley, sending back written accounts of his adventures for publication. Upon arrival back in New York City in the 1830s, Hoffman became editor of the *American Monthly* and continued to satisfy his romantic longing for exploring and writing about wild places with trips to the Adirondacks,[57] despite having only one leg.

In 1838, Hoffman published an account of his trip to Indian Pass and Mount Marcy, only months after the Redfield-Emmons first ascent of the peak.[58] In traveling to the Upper Works area, Hoffman wanted to "behold the real head of the river," referring to the Hudson. When he and his guide arrived, they paddled out onto Lake Sanford, where Hoffman could see "no sign of a house or clearing, nor any mark of the handiwork of man was to be seen anywhere". Hoffman continued describing a calm, silent setting full of solitude, punctuated by the reverberating sound of a loon, which was the only thing that seemed to move across the still landscape.

Several days later, after reaching Indian Pass and an abortive attempt at the Marcy summit, Hoffman commented on the wild character of the peak, which showed few signs of human presence. The wild inhabitants of these mountains "are almost the only living things that have their habitations in these high solitudes: and save when their occasional cry breaks the stillness, the solemn woods are on a calm day as silent as the grave".[59]

In his account of the trip, Hoffman refers to Mount Marcy as *Tahawus*, a name commonly thought to be a Mohawk or Algonquin name referring to the mountain and meaning "cloud splitter".[60] The name, though, seems to have its origin in the Seneca Nation of the Finger Lakes region of New York and means much the same thing. Hoffman was familiar with the Seneca Nation and would have known of the word Tahawus and its meaning. Hoffman's reference to the word Tahawus is the first of record to use that name. As such, there is more of a consensus today that Hoffman was the one who bestowed the romantic name of Tahawus to Mount Marcy, not the Mohawks or Algonquins.

Joel T. Headley, who, like William H.H. Murry was a pastor turned writer, published one of the first books on travel in the Adirondack region in 1849. *The Adirondack, or Life In the Woods* took the form an anthology of personal letters written to a friend from various locations Headley traveled to in the region. Headley's book was typical of the romantic literature of the region and nation, espousing the wonders of the wilderness. Headley's journeys took place over the course of several years and included a trip to the Upper Works and High Peaks areas. Part of the trip was a paddle on Lake Sanford, proceeding up the Hudson to the location of the McIntyre mine operation.

Headley commented on the remoteness of the location, calling the mine "the loneliest place a hammer ever struck".[61]

An interesting note in his writing was his disdain for the Adirondacks highest point being referred to as Mount Marcy. In a letter in his book dated 1846, Headley was preparing for an ascent of the mountain with his companions and describing his plans for the High Peaks area. The group was to make their way through the wilderness, then to "ascend Mount Marcy, as it is foolishly called, - properly Mount Tahawus, - and go through the famous Indian Pass".[62] Throughout the rest of the book, Headley continued to use the name Tahawus with reference to Mount Marcy.

It is also interesting to compare Headley's High Peak experience to that of today. On page 52, he describes that he would be carrying a "green blanket tied by a rope to my shoulders, a strong hunting knife and a large stick" to serve as a hiking stick. Dinner one night was done on a "blazing fire," with each person having "a piece of fat pork on a long stick" cooked over the fire. Without the benefit of marked and cleared trails, the group waded through spruce trees "with their dry limbs like thorns a yard long, stuck out on every side," to duck and dodge. Sinking in moss and utilizing some of the dead trees, the group continued "for two miles panting and straining up the steep acclivity, flogged and torn at every step." As the group ascended, the fir trees grew thicker and more dwarfish "till they became mere shrubs, and literally matted together," which made seeing ahead difficult. Present-day hikers, of course, have marked and cleared trails, backpacks with stoves, and aids for going over wet areas on the trail.[63]

Alfred Street was another early Adirondack explorer who took several trips to the Adirondacks in the mid-1800s.[64] Street, who was trained as a lawyer, moved to Albany in 1839, where he found work as a librarian and became director of the New York State Library in 1842. Street wrote accounts of his Adirondack journeys, always with a romantic bent to his prose. One of his notable books was *The Indian Pass: Source of the Hudson,* which described his trip to the High Peaks and Upper Works areas. The purpose of this trip, as Street wrote, was "To see the forest - the real, primeval, mysterious forest, where axe never rung save the hunter's, or roof never rose but the shanty of brush and saplings; the great stretching wilderness; to be buried alive in its fastness, and feel its influence in my inner most soul - this was the impulse of my nature, the warm desire of my heart." A romantic for sure!

At the time of Street's book in 1869, it was thought that the source of the Hudson lay in the springs of Indian Pass, as well as the collected waters of Lake Colden and Avalanche Lake. As he made his way through Indian Pass, Street described the trickle he believed to be the Hudson source: "Down, deep down trickled a blind rill, mining like a mole through a narrow tunnel of the broken, jagged rocks, and I knew that it was the infant Hudson whose birthplace oozed from the gashed heart of the monster..." [65]

While going through Indian Pass, Street began to have foot problems, forcing a layover of several days at Upper Works. It is here that he paddled onto Lake Henderson, Lake Sanford, and the upper Hudson River. Street described the experience from Lake Sanford:

> We found a leaky scow half-way up the sandy bank, with a pair of oars, and embarked. We passed a small island midway the channel, and presently opened upon the lake. It's waters appeared equally divided by a large island, reflecting the soft white clouds and "The (autumn) heaven's delicious blue".

> We rowed some distance down the lake and turned. The east sky-line was broken up by the ragged tops of enormous mountains, among which old Tahawas, the Dial, and Dix's Peak were the most conspicuous. We blended our voices for a response from Echo Mountain, swelling boldly from the lake. The echo bounded out like the blast of a thousand trumpets. Again, again, and again the wizard voice repeated our shout,- each time softer, sweeter, fainter, sweeter, fainter, far away, away, as if magic music was melting o'er the water "The horns from Elf-land faintly blowing" now the

shadow, now the flitting transparency of sound, until it died away into stillness, wafting our greath away with it.

Regaining the outlet. I glanced up, and lo! the Indian Pass in its splendid half-circle, seemingly as near as at Lake Henderson, and, like Mount Morris at Big Tupper's Lake, omnipresent except at the village. The hated sounds of man probably induced the old monster to shroud himself from gaze there in sublime disgust. Opposite also appeared the wooded capes of Mount McIntyre. Mooring our bark once more upon the bank, we returned to the village. [66]

As they made their way up to Mount Marcy, Street and his friends stayed at a camp on Lake Colden. Here, Street's guides built a log raft to float across Colden:

In a short time rose a hubbbub from the point, and the raft appeared, propelled by the planted poles of the guides, and ruffing up the rich enamel of the water. For a rod, the thing floated well enough, but in a few minutes, it struck and clung upon a small island of grass, and the guides waded ashore. This little incident over, the scene resumed its holy peace." Later the crew floated across Lake Colden in the stillness of the night. [67]

An early explorer to the region who actually ran a rapid on the upper Hudson was Benson Lossing, who wrote the book *The Hudson: From Wilderness to the Sea,* which described his journey, with a few exceptions, along the course of the entire length of the river. One of those exceptions, of course, was the river section between Newcomb and Warrensburg. At the time of its original publication in 1866, Lossing indicated that after its discovery, little was known about the Hudson River above Albany amongst the European settlers except for a few trappers, hunters, and some settlers. Exploration and knowledge of the Hudson's headwaters only occurred during Lossing's time, in part due to the attempts of Henderson, Redfield, Emmons, and romantics like Headley and Street. In an effort to gain "a personal knowledge of the beauty and wild grandeur" of the headwaters region and be able to inform others, Lossing made a trip up to the area in the summer of 1859. [68]

To get to the Upper Works region, Lossing traveled up from Albany to Lake Champlain and Port Kent. From here, the party followed the Ausable up to Keesville and over to the Saranac system via Lake Placid, ending up at Saranac Lake. The party then went through the Saranac Chain, carrying over to the Raquette system at Indian Carry and then up the Raquette River to Long Lake, where they stayed near Plumly Point. From there they did a carry over to Fountain Lake (now Round Pond) via the ditch that had been started as part of a plan to connect the St. Lawrence and Hudson River systems. The project was never completed, except a partial canal that was reached by the party after an arduous carry through a wetland on the north-northeast slope of Kempshall Mountain.[69]

Picking up the channel into Fountain Lake (Round Pond), they made their way down the lake carrying over to Catlin Lake, following it down to Fishing Brook, pausing long enough to visit the site of the sawmill a short distance upstream on Fishing Brook. The brook brought them to Rich Lake past where the Newcomb Visitors Center is located today, and down to Harris Lake and the settlement of Pendleton (Newcomb). Here the party stayed for a couple of days before heading to Upper Works and the High Peaks via the Hudson River.[70]

While at Newcomb, Lossing and others took a boat and headed down the Harris Lake outlet to the confluence with the young Hudson River. Heading downstream from there, Lossing noted running a rapid located just before a calm section on the river. The rapid he mentioned is most likely the small Class I rapid located under the present-day Route 28N bridge. The party made their way to a "rocky bluff," most likely the rock ledges just before Long Pond Rapids, about a mile downstream where the group could look back and see several of the High Peaks.[71]

Back at Newcomb, the party made their way to Upper Works, passing by Lake Sanford, which Lossing described as "a beautiful body of water nine miles long, with several islands". After exploring the region for several days, Lossing made his way down from Upper Works to Schroon Lake and the Schroon River, traveling by carriage to Warrensburg, where he picked up the Hudson again. Conspicuously absent in his descriptive prose was a trip by river from Newcomb, through the Hudson River Gorge, past North River and North Creek, and then down to Warrensburg.[72]

Before leaving the area, Lossing, with prose reminicent of John Muir's high praise of the Sierras, wrote glowingly of the High Peaks and Hudson headwaters region:

> No wild country in the world can offer more solid attractions to those who desire to spend a few weeks of leisure away from the haunts of men. Pure air and water, and game in abundance, may there be found, while in all that region not a venomous reptile or poisonous plant may be seen, and the beasts of prey are too few and shy to cause the least alarm to the most timid. The climate is delightful, and there are fertil valleys among those rugged hills that will yet smile in beauty under the cultivator's hand. It has been called by the uninformed the "Siberia of New York"; it may more properly be called the "Switzerland of the United States". [73]

Lossing did offer advice on what to wear for the trip and might well be considered some of the first recommendations for Hudson River running:

> A man needs only a stout flannel hunting shir(t), coarse and trustworthy trousers, woollen stockings, large heavy boots well saturated with a combination

of beeswax and tallow, a soft felt hat or cap, and strong buckskin gloves. A woman needs a stout flannel dress, over shortened crinoline, of short dimensions, with loops an buttons to adjust its length; a hood and cape of the same materials, made so as to envelop the head and bust, and leave the arms free, woollen stockings, stout calfskin boots that cover the legs to the knee, well saturated with beeswax and tallow, and an india-rubber satchel for necessary toilet materials. [74]

As to who was the first woman to climb Mount Marcy, Carson noted that Lossing's wife accompanied the group to the summit.[75] The guide on the trip, John Cheney, noted that she was the third woman to have done the climb. The first two, Miss Mary Cook and Miss Fannie Newton, climbed on a separate occasion guided by several Keene Valley guides, including "Old Mountain" Phelps. The climb was difficult, especially for Cook, who was of a large size and refused the aid of rope.

There are questions, though, as to who exactly was the first woman to make it to the top of Marcy.[76] Carson discounted the September 1859 article of T. Addison Richards in *Harper's Monthly* of Richard's climb of Marcy and the women who were reported to have accompanied him. The group was staying in the Upper Works area, where the ladies took fishing trips on Lake Sanford, making them some of the first women of record to have been on the upper Hudson River. The group started out for Marcy, with both the men and the women finding the way more physically challenging than they anticipated, but all made it to the summit. Richards later admitted to exaggerating in the account and it is on this point that Carson questioned the reliability of the account. Weber argued that the accompanying drawings show four women actively involved in climbing, with one of the drawings being dated 1853. With women being that prominent and given the date on the picture, Weber felt that these women were the first females on Marcy.

Further, while Weber did note Mary Cook and Fannie Newton climbing Marcy in 1858 and Mrs. Lossing the following year, she questioned the statement attributed to John Cheney concerning the first women on top of Marcy.[77] Lossing's field notes indicated no meeting with John Cheney and, as such, no opportunity to make the statement to Lossing. As with many descriptive and romantic writers of the era, adventures were often enhanced to make them more appealing. Also, the *Essex County Republican* reported Cook to be the first woman up Marcy, then retracted the statement, later saying Cook was the second. Thus, there is no certainty about who the first woman was, and there may never be certainty.

That being said, the fact these women even made it up Marcy was very commendable, considering the time and culture they lived in. Weber noted the challenges women faced climbing mountains during the 1800s.[78] Clothing options were few and the cumbersome fashion of the day included corsets, girdles, petticoats, and heavy, full-length skirts. Just as important, though, were the sociological aspects, as women at that time were considered to be too frail and weak to engage in mountain climbing and should show no athletic vigor or adventuresome spirit. These early women explorers deserve high praise and acclaim for doing what the men of the time did, but with a few more physical and sociological obstacles.

One of the more extensive explorations of the High Peaks area - in fact, of the whole Adirondack region - was done by Verplack Colvin, who led the detailed state survey of the region beginning in 1872.[79] Colvin was commissioned by the New York State government to explore, survey, mark boundaries, and map the area. For the next several years, he crisscrossed the region, taking readings and making observations. He produced several reports to the legislature on his work, some of which were in diary form and make for great reading.

Colvin was also the first to determine that Lake Tear of the Clouds was actually the high pond source of water for the Hudson and not Lake Colden and the Indian Pass area, as had been previously thought. For a long time, Lake Tear had been known - Emmons and Redfield must have seen it in 1837 - but local guides always thought it flowed into the Ausable River and into the St. Lawrence. No one had actually checked it out, though.

Colvin's account of that day is full of the exciting sense of discovery and wonder of an important find. The survey team descended from Mount Marcy on a cold, drizzly September day in 1872, following a ridge to Gray Peak to make some observations and take some readings. The dense growth ripped their cloths and one guide was shivering from the cold. The team continued down the south slope of Gray. The following account is from Paul Jamieson's *The Adirondack Reader*:

> At length we emerge on the edge of a little cliff at the foot of which runs a stream amid black mossy rocks, the bottom of the valley. Descending, we hasten to drink of the gurgling water. But scarcely have we sipped when we start back and gaze at each other with astonishment... This stream tells a strange story, and surely it flows westward to the Hudson... We can see the shoulders of a pass opening westward. Surely this must be one of the many branches of the upper Opalescent, the Hudson's highest springs. But it is the water of this stream that excites our wonder. The water is warm or tepid and has not the usual icy temperature of the mountain brooks. It must come from a pond or lake, and this lake cannot flow to the Ausable and the St. Lawrence, but to the Hudson...
>
> But the guide looks doubtful — "Perhaps this does not come from the little lake" he says "but from some marsh, or perhaps there are two ponds" - for all the guides avowed that the little lake from the top of Marcy "must go to the Ausable," though they never took the trouble to explore that valley, visit the lake, and be sure. Yet there might be a marsh; there might be another pond hidden from the view of Marcy, and interested, and excited, by the hope of discovery, we commenced to ascend the stream, hurrying along on the slippery boulders, leaping from rock to rock and at

times diverging from the stream's bed into the woods...
Suddenly, before us, through the trees gleamed a sheet
of water, and we shouted our "hurrah": for there were
Marcy's slopes beyond, while the water of the lake
was studded with those rocks which we had looked at
with our telescopes from Marcy. It was the lake, and
it flowed, not to the Ausable and the St. Lawrence, but
to the Hudson, the loftiest lake spring of our haughty
river!

But how wild and desolate this spot! It is possible
that not even an Indian ever stood upon these shores.
There is no mark of ax, no barked tree, nor blackened
remnants of a fire; not a severed twig nor a human
footprint; and we follow the usual rule in this region
and cut a broad blaze upon a tree and make it the reg-
ister and proof of our visit. I saw it there but a few
months since, already looking dark and gum-covered
with the exudation of the tree. And now, skirting the
shores, we seek the inlet and find that the numerous
subterranean streams from different directions feed
its waters. The meadow at the eastern, upper end is
full of wide-winding openings, in which deep streams
are gliding, and it is remarkable that, while the water
of the lake is warm, the water of these subterranean
streams is delicious, icy cold. The spring rills which
feed these streams come from far up on the sides of the
surrounding mountains, the water dripping from the
crest of Marcy. First seen as we then saw it, dark and
dripping with the moisture of the heavens, it seemed,
in its minuteness and prettiness, a veritable Tear-of-
the Clouds, the summit water as I have named it. [80]

Weber noted the day of September 16, 1872, as being the date
Colvin was on top of Marcy, with the weather being stormy. [81] When
the crew left the summit, most of them went down to Lake Colden,

while Colvin and guide Bill Nye set out to measure Grey and Skylite and "to visit a little lake" located between the mountains. Colvin reported reaching Lake Tear at 4 p.m., with boots filled with water and ripped and torn clothing. After exploring the lake, the cold and wet pair abandoned the climb of Skylite and made their way down to Lake Colden to join the rest of the crew.

In 1880, Charles Farnham and a friend came to the Upper Hudson River seeking whitewater, with Farnum paddling a decked fourteen-foot Shadow canoe and his friend chosing a Nautilus to paddle. [82] In September of that year, the two shipped the canoes to Boonville and went up the Moose River to Old Forge, paddling the boats from there up the Fulton Chain and across to Raquette Lake. From Raquette, they paddled up to Blue Mountain Lake, transporting the boats from there to North River. Both boats where decked and had covers over the cockpit, making them the first whitewater canoers/kayakers of record on the Hudson.

Farnum first published his account in *Scribner's Monthly* in April of 1881, and it was later reprinted in Roland Van Zandt's book, *Chronicles of the Hudson.* To start with, Farnum made sure his readers understood the part of the Hudson he planned to run "would not be from the old river where it sinks into the sea, but from its roaring, turbulent youths [sic] among the mountains". Although Farnham felt that "to shoot a rapid is to live a new life", he and his friend did not intend to go through the Hudson River Gorge, for he knew that the gorge was "so furious in a freshet that only the most reckless lumberman venture on its rapids." [83]

Farnum gave some vivid descriptions of running whitewater in a solitary boat, where the boater's own skill is a huge factor in the completion of the run in an upright position. Farnum and his partner started where the river was more easily accessed in North River, leaving amidst a mix of curious and skeptical locals. As they floated along, he noted the wild, remote nature of the scene with the "two little crafts, comely and fragile, already seem castaways in that wilderness."

At the head of Spruce Mountain Rapids, the pair of boaters focused their attention, as it was considered "the most dangerous place on the river." Here he became more detailed in his account, making for great adventure reading similar to John Wesley Powell's accounts on the Colorado. Farnum appreciated the dangers of running rapids, saying how a boat could capsize or get smashed on a rock and that the boater "might get your limbs broken by catching between the bowlders, you might be caught on a rock and held under by the pressure of the current, or you might be knocked senseless by hitting your head on the rocks." [84]

The pair began their descent of the rapid and, after a quick stroke to avoid a rock, Farnum realized that he was sitting "so low in the water that I cannot see far ahead, to choose a route." This was not a problem until he came to a part where he saw a combination of rocks and breaking waves ahead, strung across most of the channel: "There is no passage there; I must cross to the right bank. Safety depends on keeping the boat headed downstream; for, if she lies across the current while drifting, a rock may catch the keel and capsize her instantaneously." The boat made it across just in time for him to see that he needed to go back across the current to avoid some rocks: "I turn her bow somewhat across the current and make a bold rush downstream. But the channel ahead is only four or five feet wide; if I steer badly there will be a wrecked canoe in about ten seconds."

Farnum realized that the low water was making route planning challenging and that he must keep careful track of his strokes and "pray that the water may be deep enough to float her keel above rocks." Seeing the boat broadside in the current, Farnum thought the situation was "almost hopeless but I lay all my strength on a back stroke on the right, and then a forward stroke on the left makes her just clear her bow" and he made it to the head of the channel. [85]

"It would be a good plan to rest now and get breath again. But here is where the rapids begin in earnest" remarked Farnum, with things seeming to swirl around him as he tried to focus on the run. In a moment reminiscent of John Muir on Mount Ritter, when Muir felt he would fall and then relied on instinct to guide him, Farnum was only able to give a brief glance at the run "but that glance is my utmost effort to see and comprehend the situation. Then my mind seems supernaturally keen in deciding, and every nerve is flooded with electric power" and Farnum set out on the run:

> The canoe starts here and there as if mad. There is not an instant's pause. We turn suddenly right, then left; just miss a rock here, gain a channel there just wide enough to pass the boat like an arrow through a hole; she strikes her keel, but goes on; or she scrapes one side of her bottom on a rock, and rolls partly over as a startling abomination. We come to a line of rocks and swells too suddenly for escape; a rock just covered with water right ahead is the lowest leap; we put on all speed and steer straight for its rounded crown. She rides up it on her keel; I keep my balance and sympathetically tremble for the boat while her momentum carries her over...[86]

As he made it to the end of the run, Farnum exuded with the passion of the run, saying, "I can scarcely breathe, my blood boils with excitement." [86]

After eddying out on the shore, Farnum awaited his partner as he prepared camp for the night, and when the partner arrived, it was clear that he did not have a clean run; the boat had struck a rock and capsized, with the paddle continuing on downriver without him. The situation prompted the man to inform Farnum that he would not go on, catching the train and making his way back to New York City.

But Farnum continued on and completed the run to Albany, stopping along the way to camp and often speaking to curious and hospitable locals. After passing The Glen section, Farnum sensed pride in his achievements and desired to tell someone of his experience. At Hadley Falls (Rockwell), as he was contemplating the run, Farnum was approached by two women who asked why he did not carry around such places, to which he replied, "I liked the fun of running such water," [87] a sentiment that carried over 100 years later into the modern generation of river runners on the Hudson River.

Lake Colden from Beaver Point looking north.
Jeff Dickinson photo

View of Boreas Ponds from Mt. Marcy.
Jeff Dickinson photo

McIntyre mine blast furnace remains.
Jeff Dickinson photo

Loggers and Log Drives

One cannot delve into the history of river running on the upper Hudson River and Hudson River Gorge without going into the history of logging and log drives. So much of the early history of the rivers commercially rafted in the Adirondacks - such as the Moose, the Sacandaga, and the Hudson - is tied up in logging. Loggers were some of the first to venture down these rivers, the first generations of river runners to run the very rapids that are run today, although not necessarily done for the fun of it. Logging and log driving were very dangerous occupations, with injuries and fatalities a common occurrence. These men, though, were some of the first to gain intimate knowledge of the rivers and the rapids and to be able to fill in some of the blanks on the map. They were one of the main reasons for exploration, the mapping, and the running of these little-used and unknown areas in the Adirondacks.

Wood products became an important resource for the nation and New York State at the time of the early 1800s.[1] Economic growth after the Civil War created this demand for forest products and the Adirondacks proved to be a ready source.[2] Wood was used not only for homes and other buildings, but for furniture, ships, the budding railroad industry for the steam engines, and for fuel in homes and factories. In the salt factories in Syracuse, New York, for instance, roughly 200,000 cords of wood per year were needed to process salt. With one acre of forest averaging 60 cords, it took about 3,000 acres annually to keep up production. Charcoal from burnt wood was used to make soap and other products. Hemlock bark was used in tanning hides. Thus, wood was a vital resource for the growing state and nation. It was also the only thing that could be done with the land of the Adirondacks, as farming was poor and mining became challenging due to transportation costs.

Logging in the Adirondacks started early, beginning on the outer edges of counties such as Warren, Essex, Hamilton, and Herkimer.[3] Loggers were attracted to the large white pines and tanners to the hemlocks, but were then driven inland by the availability of spruce.[4] Logging began as local operations, with sawmills built to provide the immediate communities with lumber products. As the demand for wood products grew, larger operations went farther into the Adirondack region, reaching the central part by 1846.

Floy Hyde noted in the book, *A Century Wild,* that the first logging operations of commercial importance began on the Hudson at Glens Falls and on the Saranac River near present-day Plattsburgh.[5] Work moved up the Hudson, as Wessels noted that the Jessup brothers acquired land on the upper Hudson River ten miles upstream from Glens Falls (probably at Lake Luzurne) to set up a sawmill and a grist mill.[6] Hyde continued by saying that Ticonderoga became a leading Adirondack community, but waned as available timber became scarce and logging moved up the Hudson, Saranac, and Raquette rivers.[7] For the town of Minerva, logging proved to be the main industry, with logging of hemlock and spruce beginning there in earnest between 1840 and 1845.[8]

In notes provided by Irwin Miller of North River, loggers were selective in trees they cut.[9] The prized trees were the white pines, followed by the spruce, as these soft woods floated downriver easily to be processed into lumber. McMartin also cited the restrained nature of the loggers, countering the idea that loggers clearcut large tracts of forest.[10] The method of "sweeping" all available timber in the shortest period of time was seen as not conducive to long-term prosperity.[11]

Aber & King noted the tool of choice for cutting was an axe, with one man being able to cut up to seventy logs per day.[12] When the crosscut saw appeared on the scene in 1891, it allowed up to 160 logs per day to be cut between the two men who operated the saw. The saw also allowed for cutting to be done closer to the ground than with an axe. Merrill noted that the standard length for a cut log in the Adirondacks was thirteen feet, often with several extra inches left to allow for banging on rocks and the acquisition of pebbles while being driven on the river.[13] At the mill, the ends were cut off.

Merrill noted the fluctuation of the lumber industry.[14] Between 1831 and 1849, some 230 different log marks were registered at the Queensbury town office as logging on the Hudson became large scale. This expansion continued through the 1840s and on into the 1850s. Between 1852 and 1859, annual log counts reached 300,000. Pre-Civil War counts rose to 400,000 logs, with post-war counts rising to peak at one million in 1872. By the 1880s, production peaked on the Hudson watershed, as noted by the Forestry Commission report of 1885.

As lumber production declined, opportunities for wood pulp rose, providing a use for smaller timber not suited for lumber. Pulp wood came into being in 1867 when it was first produced in Massachusetts and proved to be another use for cut timber.[15] As opposed to wood for lumber, pulp wood could be made from several different tree species and of varying sizes. Thus, trees passed over for lumber could now be cut for pulp. Pulp wood logs were cut shorter than saw logs, with the length being around four feet from end to end. Even though pulp wood resuscitated the industry, the record days of log drives and lumbering on the Hudson were done, with only four mills remaining in operation through the early 1900s. The last log drive on the Hudson in 1950 for pulp wood saw only 28,838 cords come through.

Professor A.B. Recknagel of Cornell University, writing for *Forests of New York* in 1923, commented on how, at times, there seemed to be a romantic myth surrounding the life and work of a logger. The life of a logger was far from romantic, as Recknagel said: "He does his work as a matter of course, whether it be felling the trees, drawing the logs to the 'landing' or driving them down the turbulent streams of early spring. The lumber-jack of Northern New York is a man of hardihood and self-reliance. He lives under crude conditions which to most city dwellers would be actual hardships. He is often endangering his life by the exigencies of his work. The rivers of the Adirondacks could tell many an heroic tale - not all of the distant past." [16]

The actual process of logging began when a landowner or logger decided to commence an operation on a tract of land. He then let out a contract stipulating the amount of logs to be cut and the type of tree.[17] Different trees had different seasons that were better suited for them to be cut. Hemlock, whose bark was used in hide tanning, could only be cut and the bark removed between May and August, as the sap in the tree ran at that time, making it easier to remove the bark. Thus, some loggers began work as early as the start of summer. The process of contract forming was called "letting a log job," and the person with whom the principal made this contract with was called a "jobber".

With finances in place from the principal, the jobber commenced the operation with the construction of a log camp and a road into the camp. Most logging operations, excluding hemlock, started in the fall, with the main activity centering on the preparation of the area for logging.[18] This meant building or repairing the road into the area and the construction of the camp. This road, called a "tote" road, served as the means for transporting men and materials in and out of the camp.[19]

Bunkhouses were often built of logs and constructed close to the job site. At one end of the house was the kitchen, with the dinning room occupying the rest of the downstairs. The bunkroom upstairs often held up to 100 men. Another smaller barn was used to house the horses and the hay and oats to feed them. A blacksmith shop was also built to service the horses and repair tools. In larger camps, a separate office was built for the boss and other administrators.[20]

Aber & King noted that many of the logging crews were comprised of locals, but a significant number came from Canada.[21] Others were recruited from city taverns with promises of fortune and adventure. Fox noted that most Adirondack lumber camps had a French Canadian as a cook.[22] Women, for the most part, were not part of the camp, although in later years, some served as cooks.

Road building occupied a good deal of the late summer and early fall time for the logging crews, building or improving the main road into the camp and laying out the skid roads to transport cut trees to the staging area. In these summer and fall days, trouble spots on the Hudson River Gorge that produced jams for the log drivers in the spring were blasted with dynamite.[23]

The actual cutting began in the fall, with the hauling of the cut logs to the staging point on a river shore or lakefront taking place during the winter, using the snow and ice to haul heavy logs.[24] The fastest choppers felled the trees, some with almost pinpoint accuracy. Miller noted that the best choppers could fell up to sixty trees a day (Aber & King noted about 70 trees a day).[25]

One method that helped the logger's accuracy is one still commonly practiced today. Loggers cut a notch on one side of the tree, the side they wanted the tree to fall to.[26] Next, they completed the cut on the opposite side of this notch, with the weight of the tree pulling it in the direction of the notch and helping to keep the saw from pinching. When crosscut saws were introduced, notching continued, with the axe making the notch and the saw making the cut. On larger diameter trees, wedges were placed in the cut to keep the tree tilted properly.

After the tree fell, other men went in and lopped off the branches, followed by the men who cut the trunk to the desired length. These logs were then skidded (dragged) and piled up in tiers to await the winter snows, then hauled to the closest waterfront for transport in the spring. The logs were also marked and measured by a "scaler", who oftentimes had an assistant.[27]

Joel T. Headley, in his book *The Adirondack, or Life in the Woods*, gave an account of an interesting logging technique that he observed in one camp called "tree driving". While watching loggers in the Indian Lake area, Headley noted that they cut several trees, but not all the way through:

> Those choppers worked both down and up the hill, cutting each tree half in two, until they got twenty or more thus partially severed. They did not cut at random, but chose each tree with reference to another. At length a sufficient number being prepared, they felled one that was certain to strike a second that was half-severed, and this a third, and so on, till fifteen

or twenty came at once with that tremendous crash to the ground. Here is labor-saving without machinery. [28]

Hauling of logs to the waterfront began with the first deep snow of the winter, after the network of logging roads to the waterfront had been built in the fall.[29] These roads were scraped clean so as to be as smooth as possible, with few bumps to jar the sleighs filled with logs. At night, the roads were sprinkled with water drawn from a large tank so the water froze and coated the road with a layer of ice for the sleigh to glide over. On steep sections, brush, straw, and sawdust were spread in the road to help check the speed of the sleigh so it didn't get out of hand. Cables attached to the horse teams at one end and a pully on top of the hill were also used in an effort to control the downhill speed. The actual dragging and hauling of cut trees was done by teams of horses or oxen.[30]

With the delivery of the stipulated number of logs to the water-front, the job was done and the boss, or "jobber," settled up with the principal or contractor. The men were paid off and dismissed, with wages in northern New York running about $.90 a day, or about $28 per month including room and board. The men left for home, or the nearest tavern, until called on again, usually for the spring log drives.[31]

An article in the March 1896 issue of *Godey's Magazine* by Lee Vance, quoted in Merrill's book, gave a complete and thorough account of the lumber operation. Excerpted below is a synopsis of life in a log camp around 1896:

> About 4am, when the morning stars are still twin-kling, the cook rises and begins to get ready the break-fast. About half an hour later the men are routed out of bed, and by 5 o'clock they are sitting around the table, and eating by the light of lanterns hung overhead; for in winter it is dark till 6 or 7 o'clock... Breakfast over, the men are ready for their work in the woods. It is now dim daylight, and outside it is "a nipping and an eager air." The men are divided into gangs of tens

or twenties; one gang does the chopping, another the "skidding" and hauling of logs.

And so, from early morning till late at night the gangs of choppers and loggers are hard at work in the woods. Their day's labor is a long one, usually fourteen hours out of twenty-four. When pushed the men will work by the light of their lanterns far into the night. No wonder, then, that they return to camp tired, but with muscles warmed by work, and with severely sharpened appetites. They all do full justice to the evening meal, the bill of fare being much the same as at breakfast. Supper over, the men light their pipes and become more or less sociable in their way.

Indeed, the social side of a logging camp is seen best in the evening, when the rugged woodmen unbend, when their hard features relax and break into broad smiles. At one time the lumbermen gather around the table to take a hand in a game of cards, the favorite games being euchre, cinch, or pedro. There are always a number of lookers-on, who pass comments on the game or who inform the principals how they should play.

At another time the men "swap stories" of daring adventures and of "hair-breadth 'scapes," which are the more interesting, because many of the thrilling narratives are literally true. No man who has worked at logging any length of time is without some story which has an element of danger or the dramatic in it.[32]

When timber was cut in the forest, there still remained the problem of how to get it out to the mills and the market. McIntyre and Henderson's mining operation at Upper Works suffered from this problem, and it eventually proved to be its downfall. Loggers faced the same problem, but were able to manage it by locating near running water.[33] Tree-cutting and mill operations were located - not by chance - on or near rivers, with the water providing the means, one way or the other, to transport the logs and timber.

Rivers were utilized in several different ways, one of which was rafting. According to Merrill, rafting of timber and sawn logs as a means of transportation was quite common on northeast waterways, as lumber from sawmills was assembled into rafts, which were then floated downstream.[34] One of the first references to rafting on the Hudson system was the passage of an 1806 law calling for the marking of logs to protect them from theft. The law was to protect "those engaged in the rafting business" from the theft of logs.[35]

Fox, in his book *History of the Lumber Industry in the State of New York,* described the design of these rafts.[36] Typically they were wood platforms built upon floating wood and consisting of boards layered upon each other, with the boards at right angles to successive layers. Depending upon how many layers there were, a raft could contain up to 180,000 feet of board. At the corners, small saplings were used to strap and secure several rafts together, with the total size being up to 40 feet wide and 160 feet long. Most of the mass of the raft was submerged, with only six to eight inches above the water line.

Fox continued describing how oars were located in the front and back and were hard to use, requiring two or three men to handle them.[37] The blade of the oar was raised out of the water when not in use, and when dipped back into the water, the oar handles rose high over the men's heads. The oars helped provide both motion and steering, with the exact position of the oars being determined by the position of the raft on the river in relation to obstacles and current. Use of the oars was directed by a pilot, with a full raft crew consisting of between twelve to eighteen men. A shanty or cabin was built on top to house the crew. Under ordinary circumstances, rafts could make about forty or fifty miles a day. At night, the pilot found a calm eddy to pull the raft into and cabled it to shore. In an effort to appease the crew, the pilot tried to pull into a place close to a town or tavern. Imagine that - river runners seeking out local establishments after a day of rafting!

One of the earliest accounts of rafting on the Hudson was by a woman named Anne Grant in 1768. She described how, in the early spring when water levels were highest, communities gathered to construct rafts with the timber that had been cleared in the surrounding area. These rafts then floated downriver to Albany, where they were disassembled and the lumber shipped to New York City. Further progress downriver by rafts was impractical due to wind and tides. The crew used long poles to steer away from shallow spots and islands. At times, several people would ride; sometimes even families came along. "There is something serenely majestic," Mrs. Grant wrote, "in the easy progress of those large bodies on the full stream of this copious river," referring to the Hudson.[38]

Fox noted that rafting took place on several New York State rivers, including the Hudson.[39] In Harold Thompson's book, *New York State Folktales, Legends, and Ballads,* there is a section that details this early rafting. While the following description took place on the Delaware River, it provides an excellent shot of what a raft trip was like at that time:

> Food for the rafters themselves was carried along in big grub-boxes, but that supply might be supplemented by other rations when the raft was tied up at night. Steersmen considered night-running as dangerous; there were sharp turns in the river, swift currents, and great apron-dams to be run. The evenings might be spent at inns along the way, or the rafters might roll up in their blankets and sleep on the raft preparatory to an early start. A "night-cap" was obtainable right on a raft, from a large jug which was placed in the exact center of the structure, at the foot of a "shirt-pole".
>
> During the day, the steersman, who was always the boss of the raft and often its owner, stood in the rear, usually operating a big oar. On the small "colt" rafts there was one large oar in the front, worked by as many as three men, for it was very heavy and hard to push.

The big rafts had two oars on the front, and either two or (rarely) three aft. The forty-foot oars were set on sixteen-inch blocks and *pushed*, not pulled, breast high with the strength of the mightiest shoulders York State has known. At the top of his clarion lungs the steersman would cry: "Now, boys, pick it up lively. Give her three clips Jersey... Now two clips Pennsylvany... Holt!" As you went downstream Pennsylvania was on the right and New Jersey on the left.

It was an exciting life, full of danger to men and property. [40]

Donaldson recorded another early reference to rafts on the upper Hudson River.[41] In 1770, brothers Edward and Ebenezer Jessup bought land on the upper Hudson, about ten miles upstream from Glens Falls, near the Sacandaga and Schroon Rivers, and located a sawmill there. From this point they rafted their logs down these rivers to Glens Falls. If this account is accurate, this was one of the first recorded instances of rafts running on the Hudson and its tributaries, 200 years before the start of commercial rafting in the gorge. The last wooden rafts to ply the waters of the state were around 1880.

As logging operations outgrew their locations near flatwater and moved upriver, the need to figure out alternative ways of getting logs to mills from the deeper parts of the forest became apparent.[42] In 1813, a method was devised to bring logs to the river's side and float them downstream, as opposed to lashing them together in a raft, and the first ever river drive was completed on the Schroon River in Warren County.[43] The Fox brothers, Norman and Alanson, used this method to float logs from their Brant Lake tract down the Schroon to the Hudson, ending up at Glens Falls.

This method proved to be a savior of the logging industry in Glens Falls, for by the mid-1800s, the lumber industry had picked over the nearby forests and began to look upriver.[44] New York State helped this transport system by declaring that certain rivers were to be "public highways," allowing legal passage for logs and river drivers through private land. As log drives became familiar, sluice or crib dams began to be utilized on smaller tributaries and lake outlets, allowing loggers to move farther into the interior of the woods.

The first log drives in the Hudson River Gorge commenced in 1849, growing from 26 million board feet being transported on the Hudson River system in 1851 up to 213 million board feet in 1872.[45] A map entitled "Hudson River Log Driving System", based on a Finch, Pryne map, shows a large and long river system with over thirty sluice dams on the tributaries.[46] While other rivers were used, the Hudson became the major transportation watershed of the state, with its importance demonstrated with the proposed building of two feeder canals to redirect water and logs from the Raquette River system to the Hudson.[47] These canals would have been built between Blue Mountain Lake and Lake Durant and Long Lake and Rock Pond but neither was completed.

In an article in *Adirondac,* Francis Seaman gave some more details of the Long Lake plan, proposed by G.W. Benedict from the State Geological Survey.[48] A dam was to be built at the outlet of Long Lake, which would raise the level of the lake, forcing water down through the canal between Long Lake and Rock Pond and into the Hudson River system for use on the log drives.

Verplanck Colvin's Second Survey Report [49] contains a map that showed the Blue Mountain canal was to be dug near the southeast corner of the lake near where the present-day town beach is located, with the dam on the channel to Eagle Lake. Raquette River loggers, of course, objected to both plans and, although work had begun on the Long Lake canal, they were able to stop the plan. Parts of the Long Lake canal can still be seen today in the area of Hendrick Spring, west of Catlin Lake.[50]

When the spring thaw began, the river boss took a special group of brave men into the places were the cut logs had been stored and kept to begin the river drive.[51] This aspect of the logging operation was one of the most dangerous, with hardly a season going by without a death or serious injury. These men were of unique character - rugged, working from dawn to dusk, flirting daily with disaster and wet most of the time as they pushed logs, broke jams, rowed river boats, and generally watched out for each other.[52]

Fox continued by describing the men as needing unique physical abilities, since they had to be able to leap from log to log while balancing a pike pole in their hand.[53] This pole became a paddle if the logs broke loose and the driver had to ride out the rapid on a log. Barbara Bird also glowingly described the character of the river driver that, despite the clothing they wore, the men were very graceful "like that of a bird in flight, and his quickness, precise judgment and superb poise mean life and death," deciding with split-second accuracy the buoyancy of the logs.[54]

One early reference to the life of a log driver that also makes a reference to rafting rapids on the Hudson River, comes from a piece in Harold Thompson's book. The ballad is remembered by John Nichols, who retold it to give an idea of what lumbering was like in the 1870s with the ballad entitled *Shanty Boy*:

Transported I am from a handsome maid
　　To the banks of the Hudson stream,
Where the wolves and the owls and the panther's ugly growls
　　It disturbs our nightless (nightly) dreams.

Then springtime comes in, double hardship then begins,
　　With its waters so piercing and cold;
Dripping wet were our cloths, and our limbs were almost froze
　　And our hand-spikes we scarcely can hold.

Over rocks, shores, and dams, gives employment to all hands,
　　Our well-bounded raft for to steer;
Those rapids we do run, fierce – to us but merely fun,
　　To avoid all slavish fears. [55]

During the winter months, logs were cut and hauled to the waterfront, where they were stacked in piles which, in the Hudson region, were called "rolling bank".[56] With the coming of spring and the higher water levels, the blocks holding these rolling banks were removed, allowing the logs to roll into the stream, lake, or river. Logs piled on a lakefront were floated to the moving water of the outlet, either individually, or tied together as a raft on large lakes. Often these logs were moved at night to avoid daytime winds.

On smaller tributaries, sluice dams were built that backed up water, like at Lake Durant in Blue Mountain Lake, so water could be released at the proper moment to provide a temporary flood that allowed logs to float down to the main river.[57] These dams, also called splash, crib, or flooding dams, had gates that were opened in the spring to create the artificial surge.[58]

Harold Hochschild described the use of a boom to control the movement of logs on the river or lake, similar to the purpose of herding and fencing in the livestock industry.[59] The "Big Boom" was used just upriver from the mills at Glens Falls to corral logs floated from upstream. On the operation on Lake Durant, a smaller boom was constructed of logs linked by rope or chains and strung across the outlet near the dam to prevent the accumulated logs in the backed-up water from crushing the dam. A rear boom was also used to prevent the logs from being blown back across the lake.

On the day the logs were to be started downriver, the sluicegate of the dam was opened enough to allow water to start filtering downriver.[60] The water ran for a half hour before the logs were let loose in order to help cover rocks downriver, which helped reduce the number of jams. Similarly, Hudson raft trips today utilize a dam release on the Indian River, with rafts waiting for the release to filter downriver so as not to get stuck on rocks. It took from two to four weeks to empty all the logs out of the lake, depending on how many were cut and what the weather was like, as wind could easily push logs away from the dam. The dam was open from dawn to dusk, allowing the lake to refill overnight.

With the advent of pulp wood, wooden slides were constructed on tributaries to transport logs to the main river.[61] These slides were of varying length, with one on the Ausable River being seven miles long. The four foot length for pulp wood made the transportation and hauling much easier, including shooting down the wood slides. These logs were floated upon a shallow stream of water that ran along the bottom of the slide.

Men were stationed along the main part of the river to keep the drive rolling.[62] It was their job to keep the logs from becoming stuck in eddies, caught on islands, and, in an extreme case, to break up any jams. Still others followed along after the drive to ensure that as many of the logs as possible made it to the mills. There was also a cook who followed along with the drivers to prepare meals for them. On the Rock River drives, one of the jobs was that of a log rider, where a skilled driver rode on a floating log downriver in order to free up logs on the shore.[63] A log rider had to be highly skilled and possess a good sense of balance. Less skilled riders rode a "cooter" behind the more skilled rider, which was a raft of two logs bound together.

Log drivers worked long and varied days.[64] The work usually began at 6 a.m., with lunch from 11 a.m.-12 p.m. and the day ending at 6 p.m. Sometimes the men started at 3:30 a.m. with breakfast at 4 a.m., lunch at 9 a.m., dinner at 1 p.m., and supper at 6 p.m. or later. The work went on seven days a week, with no Sunday rest, as the river never recognized the Sabbath. The men were wet to the bone from the icy river water and open to the wind blowing through their wool clothes. Hochschild commented on the prolonged effect this had on the men: "By the time they were 30-35 many were crippled with muscular rheumatism". [65]

On the Moose River, some log drivers had to walk a mile or so from the camp to the river, work ten to twelve hours, then walk back to camp. On the Hudson River, log drivers stayed at various spots along the river. McMartin listed several locations, one at the mouth of Carter's Brook at the start of Carter's Rapid, one at OK Slip Brook, and one at the top of Harris, all three located on flat shoreline on river right.[66]

Dick Nason, historian for Finch, Pryne Paper in Glens Falls, confirmed this, adding camps on the south shore (river right) at the confluence of the Indian River and one where Carter's Brook comes into the Hudson (river right at Carter's) that remained until 1924.[67] The 1898 USGS topographical map, Newcomb quadrangle, also shows a camp at the confluence of the Indian and Hudson rivers, as well as a trail that leads from the camp to east of Blue Ledges and out to the highway. [68]

Notes from Rick Fenton also referenced Girard Arsenault, who worked as a cook on the drives of the mid-1900s.[69] Arsenault said that camps in the gorge were supplied by horse, with locations at the Boreas River confluence and one between Carter's Brook and OK Slip Brook. A note also referred to the camp the top of Harris where Barker Brook comes in.

The 1898 Newcomb USGS map notes several trails to locations on the Hudson.[70] As was noted above, a trail accesses both the camp at Carter's Landing and the Indian-Hudson confluence, presumably for the camps located there. Another trail follows the Hudson from North River upstream to the confluence with the Boreas River, ending at the Hudson and not crossing it. A third trail is noted that goes south from Newcomb, following the Hudson on the west shore, or river right, and ending a mile or two above where present day Goodnow Flow enters, probably to supply the log drive camps located there.

Notes provided by Miller described the camp at Carter's Landing as being a forty- foot long lean-to that slept from twelve to twenty men, often under one huge blanket.[71] The front of the lean-to had four fires burning in order to facilitate the continual chore of drying the wool clothing. The men amused themselves at night by playing poker, with pots of $2 to $3 considered large. Bob Savarie, whose father Henry was a log camp foreman for Finch, Pryne during the pulp wood drives, recalled how some of the drivers camped out in tents along the river, sleeping on straw.[72] Some of them did not even remove their wet clothing, drying them by standing next to one of the fires.

Both Miller and Savarie noted that fires were also used for cooking, with bean-hole beans being a common dish. Savarie notes a menu of steak, mashed potatoes, bean-hole beans, and "plenty of hardboiled eggs". [73] Miller described the cooking of the bean-hole beans, where the uncooked beans were put into a large iron pot and set in a hole three feet in diameter with a fire built over the pot.[74] The beans were started about 6 p.m. in the evening and were ready by 5 a.m. the next day.

Lunches, because they had to be carried to the men working away from the camp, were often cold mashed potatoes, hardboiled eggs, and cold meat. Coffee was made from river water boiled in buckets.[75] By comparison, in the early years of commercial rafting, when several outfitters cooked lunch on the river, steak and some form of potatoes was standard fare, along with coffee. Presently, lunch ranges from simple peanut butter or deli sandwiches to hot soup and fruit with tea or lemonade to drink, depending on the outfitter.

Donohue & Conroy also reported a camp spot along the Hudson River in the settlement of North River called Henry Bennet Flats.[76] Here, locals joined the drivers for a meal of "bean pole beans, steak, pickled eggs, fried potatoes, biscuits, store cookies, apple pies - all washed down with large tin cups of tea and coffee". Savarie also noted this in his article.[77]

John Galusha, also known as "Yankee John", was a log driver from Minerva working the Hudson in the 1870s when the thirteen-foot saw logs ruled the river. His recollections of log drives were documented in an article by Pete Fosburgh in *The Conservationist* dated April-May 1947.[78] A log driver's day started at 3 a.m. and Galusha remembered "standing around in the cold April rain on Blackwell's Stillwater waiting for it to get light enough to start work". So imagine river runners of today standing around on an early April morning with snow on the ground wearing nothing but wool clothing and leather boots. Compare that with the heated changing rooms, polypropylne, neoprene, and drysuits of today!

Galusha went on to describe the day:

> It was an easy day going down Blackwell's because the Hudson there was slow and deep, and each man used to pick a good log and ride it for two or three miles, smoking his pipe. Sometimes he would "run the wood" from log to log, just to pass the time of day with another driver across the river.
>
> But when the drive passed the Cedar and came to the mouth of the Indian there was a dull roar coming up from below, and that meant tough times ahead. This was the "jam stretch". A log would hang up on a rock,

others would tie into it, and finally the whole channel would be blocked by a network of wood, with more
coming down all the time. [79]

Anxiety levels still tend to surge when rafts enter the Hudson
from the Indian River on days when the water level is high, as
here, the river drops quickly through narrow stretches with steep-
sided ledges, boulder-strewn currents, hydraulics, and eddies of the
Hudson River Gorge. Log jams in this section had the potential for
death or serious injury due to these river characteristics. Whitewater
has a tendency to focus the attention of river runners both past and
present!

Galusha continued:

> If the river was good and it stayed good, you could put
> a log in at Newcomb and it would show up at the Big
> Boom in a matter of only two days.
>
> But with 13-foot logs, there was always trouble some-
> where. The Boreas was bad all the way down. The
> Hudson was bad at Ord Falls, below Newcomb, bad
> again just above the mouth of the Indian, and very
> bad on the big bend below Blue Ledge [probably refer-
> ring to the Narrows, JTD], near the Dear Den. Even if
> the drive got through those spots, it could always hang
> up on the Moulton Bars at Warrensburg. The worst,
> though, was always that stretch past the Deer Den. [80]

When an actual jam occurred, the river boss asked for volunteers
to go out and release the jam. As with river runners of the present, motives of pride and notoriety amongst peers prompted quick
responses from the crew; testosterone drove river runners back then
as well! Fox described how the volunteer, to the sound of applause,
took axe or handspike (peavey pole) as they would:

...leap over the treacherous logs and place themselves at the head of the jam. Behind them are thousands of logs, filling the angry stream from bank to bank, piled thickly to the bottom, some of them tossing, tumbling and leaping in the air as the dammed up torrent forces them about in wild confusion. Beneath them is the swaying, rocking, unstable mass, in which is seen the log that forms the key to the position. The crew of drivers gather on the banks below the jam, where they watch with intense eagerness and anxiety the man who volunteers to cut or loosen this log. They note every stroke of the axe wielded by the hero as, coolly and undaunted, he proceeds with his work. The critical moment is close at hand. There is some more prying with the handspike, a few more blows with the axe, and the huge threatening mass begins to move. Above the sound of the foaming waters a loud shout of warning comes from the men below, and then, leaping from log to log as the jam breaks, the brave fellow reaches the shore in safety amid the applauding cheers of his comrades... [81]

Headley gave a personal account of the breaking of a jam. He was on a journey in the Indian Lake area and stopped at the edge of a swollen river to observe log drivers in action. After watching them for some time, Headley was "struck with the coolness with which one would stand half under a huge embankment of logs, and hew away to loosen the whole, while another with a handspike kept them back". After watching the drivers for some time on a jam, Headley commented that it was "really an exciting scene" to observe, prompting him to try his hand at it, laying his coat down and grabbing a handspike. Using the spike, Headley tried to move a log, "tugging and lifting away" until the log gave way and made its way downriver with a sudden shout from Headley.

Headley observed this trait again when describing the work of a driver who, after a log jam had commenced, began to make his way across the logs in the water. The driver

> ...slowly and carefully steps from one to another, feeling with his feet and "handspike" to see where the "drag" is. When he finds it, he loosens, perhaps with a blow, the whole rolling, tumbling mass, and away it moves. Now look out, bold driver, thy footing is not of the most certain kind, and a wild and angry stream is beneath thee. Yet see how calmly he views the chaos. The least hurry or alarm and he is lost - but no, he moves without agitation - now balancing himself a moment, as the log he steps upon shoots downward, then quickly passing to another as that rolls under him, he is gradually working his way towards shore. [82]

Headley concluded by saying that the driver did not always make it ashore and ended up having to seat "himself astraddle of one, and darts like a fierce rider down the current".[83]

If the jam could not be reached from shore, a crew was assembled to boat out to the jam.[84] Here, one person, usually one of the expert boatmen, rowed out to the jam with one or two other men riding along. If the jam could not be freed from the boat, the crew had to get on the logs while the person rowing the boat held steady in the water, providing a place for the men on the logs to jump to when the jam got loose. The person in the boat had to row quickly so as not to be swept downstream by the logs or the water. The men were well paid for this hazardous work up-to $5 to $7 a day. In extreme situations, when a jam could not be moved by boat or pole, dynamite was used, [85] but, according to Galusha, this was a rare case.[86]

Galusha recalled the usage of "jam boats" on the Hudson, giving account of some of the first known river runners through the gorge:

> These were the old Adirondack *bateaux*, 14 feet long, pointed at both ends, and manned by an oarsman, a

bowsman, and a sternsman. Except in quiet water they were always rowed against the current and pointed directly upstream, because if they ever hit a rock while crabbed across the current they were almost certain to capsize. They followed every drive, even on the Boreas. There was a standing order that they were to be "roped" or "paintered down" through rough water, but there were plenty of good oarsmen who ran the Hudson all the way from Newcomb to North Creek, and more who tried. [87]

Although the bosses did not encourage it, [88] these were the first instances of boats running the rapids of the Hudson River Gorge.

Bob Savarie described a slightly different type of boat used later on during his father's days as a log driver on the Hudson.[89] "The river boats were large, sturdy crafts made from 1" thick ash lumber," Savarie said, and were pointed only in the bow with the stern flat and not pointed at both ends. As with Galusha, Savarie stated that three men crewed the boat, with the oarsman being the one who rowed.

By reading the water, he was able to navigate the rapids and put the boat in the proximity of the jam. In rapid water, the boat went downstream stern first. This reduced the push from the current and helped slow the boat. The bow man and the stern man handled pike poles to help stop the boat, and also were used to clear jams and move the logs around the rocks.

A type of boat similar to what Savarie described is on display at the Adirondack Museum.

Bird described the usage of boats to break a jam on the Moose River. Each boat had a crew of three men - one in the bow with a pike pole (peavey or handspike), one in the middle to row, and the third in the stern with a pike pole. The crew "moved swiftly out into the boiling stream. Rowing like mad, they swung over to the island." "Island" was what the jam of logs was referred to, with an island in midstream being called a "center" and one along the shore being a "wing".

Bird continues: "The bow man immediately caught hold of a solid log with his pike pole. As the boat swung downstream, the other two made fast with the peaveys. Bow man hopped out and held the boat while the other two disembarked, the rower first putting on his extra jacket". The rower had to hold the boat, waiting for the other two to break the jam and often got cold. When the logs gave way the other two men "leaped lightly from tumbling logs into the boat. There was hard work at the narrow oars until the boat was brought safely to the next center, or to shore, as the case might be." [90]

Hochschild stressed the importance of the skill of the man rowing the boat:

> The safety of the boat's crew depended mainly on the oarsman. Waiting at the edge of the jam for his mates, he had to exert himself to prevent the boat from being drawn under the jam and lost. Rowing away, he had to avoid becoming entangled with the loosening logs after the jam had begun to break. A failure of the oarsman's strength or skill was almost certain to bring death to the men by crushing or drowning. [91]

The skill of river runners today also is a critical element in the avoidance of disaster for them and their crews.

If the crew did not make it to the boat or shore, they had to deal with tons of cold springtime water and logs raging around them, nearly always causing serious injury or death. One account of a young fourteen-year-old William Brown, who survived a jam on the Cedar River, is taken from daughter Gertrude Brown's writing in the book *The Browns* and is quoted below. Here young Bill was enthralled with the work of log driving and, despite his father's orders, got involved with a log jam:

> In the excitement I ran out on the jam. There was a breathless silence for a second instead of the grinding

roar; an ominous foreboding of danger in the creaking and groaning of the mass from the pressure above. I knew this place, the great rock in the center of the river slanting upstream, the deep hole under it worn by many years of rushing water...

I saw a big log, its end protruding above the rock. I speared it with my pike pole. I pulled, pushed and pried with all my might. I thought it moved, then I thought I was moving. I heard a shout of warning. The whole mass was moving.

The men ran for the shore. My pike pole was caught fast in the log. Suddenly it shot out as if shot from a cannon, taking me with it. For a minute I was flying though the air, then I saw the whirling, thundering mass below me. I thought my end had come and closed my eyes. Then a calm came over me, I felt cool and steady. Opening my eyes I saw a big log in front of me. I struck it square on my feet, rode it for a few feet. My spikes held though it bucked and rolled and shot forward. I jumped to another log. Ahead of me was a bend in the river, my log was driving toward the shore. I knew there was another fall beyond the bend and that if I did not get ashore before reaching it I never would. I jumped from log to log toward the shore.

I saw a big flat rock. I jumped for it, slipped across it and into the water on the other side. I gained my feet and as my head came above the rock I was seized with horror.

I was ahead of the main mass and it was coming straight at me with a grinding roar that was deafening. It was on me. There was no time. I dropped under the rock. It slanted above me. The noise grew louder, swelled to an indescribable tumult, the water swept over me. I clung to a projecting root and braced my feet against a rock. The water sucked and dragged at me. For a second at a time my face would be above water and I gasped for breath only to be covered again. My rock moved and I was afraid that it would give way. Finally after what seemed like hours the noise grew less and died down to its usual roar. The water and logs were no longer going over my rock.

I succeeded in reaching the shore. I could hear the men shouting below me and soon came upon them. I heard a man say "here is the lad, I thought he was a goner'. Father said "I told you not to leave the shore, I should spank you," but there were tears in his eyes... I was now a full fledged river driver. Father sent me home for dry clothes. [92]

Bird also gave a good account of a log driver who was able to ride a jam out on a log. The jam let loose

...with a heave too sudden for the driver, working on the lower end, to reach the boat. There he was, riding a log into the rapids below. Gone was his pike pole. Tons of logs rushed past him, hitting the rocks with angry rumbling, pitching high in the air and falling with a great crash and splash. No man could stay upright long in such turmoil. Nor did he. Slipping down astraddle the log, he rode it like a cowboy on a bronco. The logs were hurled upon a promontory downstream. All eyes were upon one log ridden by the intrepid Hank. He landed. We saw heels kicked high in the air. Then he stood upright and signaled all was well. [93]

One of the more important jobs for river driving was that of the foreman, or agent, who oversaw the entire operation. When it came to conducting river drives in the 1900s on the Hudson, Jack Donohue was *the* man! He started to work for Jones Ordway up near Blue Mountain Lake when he was sixteen years old.[94] By the time he was twenty, in 1885, he was working for Finch, Pruyn and eventually ran the log drives for all eleven companies on the Hudson River for over fifty years. As part of his job, Jack had the authority to buy land and cruise the logging sites, marking the timber to be cut. But it was the log drives for which he gained his notoriety.

Jack resided in a riverfront house in North River, where he could be involved with the logging operations. Jack's house was one of few that had a phone, which helped him keep in touch with the men at the holding dams upstream. As springtime came and the time for the log drives approached, one of his daughters, Helen Donohue, recounted how Jack kept track of the weather and the wind direction. "He knew," said Helen in the book *River of Mountains: A Canoe Journey Down the Hudson River,* "the effect the wind would have in thawing the ice in the dams that held the water and the logs. He'd just pack up and head for Newcomb or wherever the holding booms were. In a matter of hours the first logs would be on their way..." [95] Daughter Milda Burns remembered riding with her father up to Newcomb in Jack's car. [96] Son Ray Donohue worked a few drives before working with his father on land. [97]

The water level of the river was also an important tool Jack used to determine the start of the log drives, as having sufficient water levels helped ensure an adequate amount of water to float the logs downriver. Jack used the large rock ledge on the other side of the river near his home as a river gauge.[98] Black intrusions in the rock created a mouse-like shape with a "tail" that curved down to the flowing water. Jack not only tested the water with his foot, but also watched the water level rise. When it reached the mouse's tail, he knew that the level was rising fast enough to start the drives. In present terms, daughter Milda said that the level of the river to start a drive would be about seven feet according to the North Creek USGS gauge.[99] Many river runners today continue to use the Mouse Tail rock in the Mouse Tail Rapid to determine the river level and understand what river conditions might be encountered.

An important part of the log drives was utilizing the releases from the crib dams to augment the regular flow of water. In a carefully orchestrated operation, Jack, "The Maestro", would instruct the crib dam operators to release water in stages to ensure there would be enough water to float logs to the Hudson River fairly easily. [100] It is interesting to note that Jack's river legacy continues today, as the third and fourth generation of Donohue-Burns, his grandson and great-granddaughters, run the river as raft guides and raft company owners.

Thus was the periless work of the first generations of river runners in the Hudson River Gorge and upper Hudson River. These river runners faced many of the same conditions that modern river runners do: cold water, cold air, recirculating holes, entrapments, rocks, pins, etc. They did it, too, without much of the safety equipment or management tools now in place. Lifejackets, helmets, wetsuits, and drysuits were not part of the wardrobe of these early river runners; wool clothing and leather boots were. Most of them, too, did not run the river for recreation, as it was one of the few reliable jobs available in the area. There were no backboards strategically placed along the river and no waiting ambulances in North River in case of trouble. Yet these runners cleared the way for the proceeding generations of river runners on the Hudson who would run the river for both fun and profit.

Logs ready to drive on Boreas Pond.
Milda Burns photo

Pulp logs on the way to Glens Falls from Boreas Pond.
Milda Burns photo

Jam boat on the Boreas River.
Milda Burns photo

Last log drive on the Hudson just below Perry Eller, 1950.
Milda Burns photo

The "Maestro", Jack Donohue, at his home in North River, NY.
Milda Burns photo

Recreational River Runners

Log drives on the Hudson ended in 1950. The upper Hudson River and the gorge, though, did not suffer from a void of activity or lack of interest in its resources during the thirty-year period after the end of the log drives and before the beginning of commercial rafting. The Hudson River saw numerous kayakers, canoers, and a few rafters during this period, as part of the national growth in outdoor recreation. During this time, the Hudson became known in river-running circles for its value as an outdoor recreation spot. It also caught the eyes of the New York State Water Resource Commission and the Army Corps of Engineers, who were not interested in the recreational potential of the river and the gorge but in their resources for quenching the thirst of New York City. This section, then, will look at the period of time on the Hudson River Gorge between 1950, when the log drives ended, and the 1980s, when a new generation of river runners took to the river.

When compiling a history of river running on the upper Hudson River, it is important not only to document what happened, but also why it happened, and note the context in which it happened. History rarely happens in a vacuum; there is almost always a precipitating event or events that set the stage, lay the groundwork, and lead toward the next event. So it was with the log drivers of the 1800s on the Hudson River. They did not wake up one morning and decide it was a good day to go riding logs down the treacherous Hudson River Gorge; they were responding to events and demands outside that realm. A growing nation increased its demand for lumber and logs;

these loggers fulfilled that demand. And so it was with recreational river runners on the upper Hudson River and the Hudson River Gorge, who took to the water in the context of a larger national trend that saw growth in outdoor recreation in general, and whitewater sports specifically.

Outdoor recreation saw a large period of growth starting in the 1950s and continuing through the 1960s and 1970s. Jensen [1] noted trends in visitor use to federally and state managed outdoor areas. In 1945, the Corps of Engineers, US Forest Service, and National Park Service recorded between 10 and 20 million visits to their land areas. Twenty years later, in 1965, the combined numbers for all these agencies had risen to between 120 and 170 million visits. Similar trends were seen in state park areas, with numbers going from 42 million visits in 1945 up to 345 million visits in 1965.

Jensen also noted an increase during the 1960s of several outdoor activities, including walking, camping, swimming, scenic drives, and boating. In 1960, Americans engaged in outdoor recreation on 4.28 billion occasions; by 1965, the numbers increased to 6.48 billion. McCall and McCall also noted a similar statistic, with 90% of the population participating in some form of outdoor recreation in 1960.[2] Membership in outdoor clubs and environmental organizations increased during this period as well.[3]

Similar trends in river running were found for the same post World War II time period. Roderick Nash [4] cited an increase in river trips down the Colorado River through the Grand Canyon National Park. During the 1950s, the number of people running the river ranged from 7 in 1950 to 135 in 1957, ending with 120 in 1959. Beginning in 1960, numbers started at 205 and reached 6,019 by 1969. By the 1970s, these numbers continued to grow, with Armstead [5] noting the steady increase in outfitters offering trips and Jenkinson [6] writing on the "phenomenal" growth in river runners.

Eastern rivers saw this increase as well, with Dickerman mentioning one Pennsylvania outfitter who started out with 5 rafts and 500 people in 1978 and rose to 350 rafts and 25,000 people five years later[7]. Rivers in West Virginia showed growth from a few avid paddlers and their friends down the New River in 1968 to over 200,000 in 1994.[8] The American Whitewater Affiliation (AWA) began publishing its journal in the late 1950s increasing the scope ever since.

This growth in outdoor recreation also created a need to secure both land and access to the land for this outdoor recreation to take place on, as well as management policies for the variety of users and interests. One such effort by Congress established the Outdoor Recreation Resource Review Commission in 1958, which made a study of the nation's growing demand for outdoor recreation and provided recommendations.[9] Several important actions were taken as a result, such as creating cooperative efforts with states in planning and acquiring land, including the expansion of the National Park System. Passage of the Wilderness Preservation Act in 1964 and the Eastern Wilderness Act in 1975 also established areas for outdoor recreation.

Of special importance to river runners was the passage of the Wild and Scenic Rivers Act of 1968 that protected certain sections of particular rivers in a "free and unimpaired flow" and preserved their "scenic, recreational, geological, fish and wildlife, historic, and cultural values".[10] The Act was originally intended to curb the advancement of dam proposals and protect rivers from shoreline development. It was passed within days of the defeat of the plan to construct a dam on the Colorado River within Grand Canyon National Park. The dam proposal was part of a larger effort to address water shortages in the southwestern United States by directing water from the impoundments to the more arid regions. A loophole in the legislation that established Grand Canyon National Park allowed the proposal to move forward, but the Wild Rivers Act plugged that hole and specifically mandated that rivers, or sections of rivers, were to be protected.[11]

So what does all of this have to do with running the Hudson River? It provides the context around which strikingly similar events were played out in the Upper Hudson River region and the gorge.

As with the nation, outdoor recreation in New York grew in the period following World War II. Canham wrote that New York felt the full impact of the boom in outdoor recreation, which was reflected in the increase in campground usage.[12] Paul Schaefer reported that total numbers of users at public campgrounds and day-use areas rose from 780,072 in 1950 to 1,065,455 in 1960, and up to 1.4 million in 1970, before leveling off just over one million in 1980.[13] Ski areas saw numbers go up from 59,040 in 1950 to 153,000 in 1960, and up to 556,457 in 1970. Use of undeveloped backcountry lands rose as well, going from 32,760 individuals in 1950 to 44,736 in 1960, up to 206,406 in 1970, dropping slightly in 1980.

As early as 1959, New York State responded when Governor Nelson Rockefeller directed the State Conservation Commission to inventory state outdoor recreation facilities and report back. As a result of this, money was allocated for the acquisition of land and the improvement of existing facilities.[14] Management policies of these lands, too, would have to accommodate the sometimes competing interests of these outdoor recreational users.

One of the more interesting and eye-opening land management ideas of that time came in 1967 when Laurance Rockefeller, brother of Governor Rockefeller, proposed the creation of an Adirondack National Park.[15] The proposal would have created a 1.7 million acre national park, to be administered by the federal government, from land in the central and north central areas, including the High Peaks region. Most of the major towns and villages within this area would have remained in local hands, with the rest of the public and private land deeded to the federal government.

The aim of the proposal was to secure valuable recreational land and limit development, but it had little support and a host of opposition.[16] Groups previously opposing each other on Adirondack issues came together to rally against the National Park idea. While the proposal was abandoned, the land management issues it raised by these competing interests remained.[17] Porter & Whaley referred to the National Park proposal as the "catalyst" that brought a realization of the need to address these issues in the Adirondacks.[18]

As a result of this realization, Governor Rockefeller, like any good politician, appointed a commission to study these land use issues in the Adirondacks and make recommendations for policy.[19] The Temporary Study Commission on the Future of the Adirondacks was created and put forth several proposals. The most well-known, far- reaching, and controversial was to create the Adirondack Park Agency (APA), giving it power to regulate land use in the Adirondacks.

The APA also implemented several different classifications for state-owned Adirondack land, with the primary ones being *Wilderness* and *Wild Forest* along with *Primitive, Canoe,* and *Intensive Use.* [20] Thus, recreational land would be protected for various recreational uses, with the APA classifications providing general management directions for the individual units of land. These legislative efforts helped ensure the recreational potential of areas like the Hudson River Gorge as log drives ended and a new generation of river runners took to the Hudson.

It should be noted that the state land around the Hudson River Gorge was initially classified as *Primitive,* meaning that the land is managed much like a wilderness area, with no motors allowed and little human impact.[21] This has changed as in 2012, New York State made a deal to acquire the land in and around the gorge that used to be owned by Finch, Pruyn. With the addition of surrounding land the gorge was re-classified *Wilderness* in 2014.

Recreational river running of the upper Hudson River and Hudson River Gorge, though, can be documented back to the 1800s, with one of the well-known river runners being Charles Farnum and his pioneering whitewater kayak/canoe trip in 1880. Ernest Ingersoll, in his *Guide to the Hudson River,* not only mentioned Farnum's trip, but also listed that part of the Hudson - from North River downstream - as a canoeable waterway.[22] He recommended putting in below Eldridge's in North River, where "even the hardiest canoeists dare put their boats," indicating that recreational runs through the gorge were still not a common occurrence. E.R. Wallace described this section of the Hudson River in North River as "a shallow but turbulent stream".[23]

Local residents - like the staff of the Henderson Mine and visitors such as Benson Lossing and Alfred Street - utilized the infant Hudson and its connecting streams and lakes for fishing or relaxing. William Redfield boated on Lake Sanford as he made his way to Upper Works in 1837.[24]

Mills told of a canoe trip in the Upper Works area in an article called "Tupper to Tahawas, 1908".[25] The trip went from Tupper Lake over to Long Lake, carrying over to Catlin Lake and down to Harris Lake and the Hudson. The plan was to follow the Hudson upriver from there to Upper Works and hike the trail from there to Mount Marcy, but some challenging rapids made them camp near Lower Works and hike the rest of the way. The writer described one flatwater area as a "desolate spot, full of dead stumps, floating logs, and half submerged snags".

A narrative written by George and Robert Shaw [26] of Long Lake began with an Indian named Tahawus who had been driven from his tribe. On page two, the narrative described how, during his journey to escape, Tahawus "built himself a camp on a small stream between two lakes, now known as Lake Sanford and Lake Henderson;" that stream, of course, being the Hudson River. The narrative was vague on how long Tahawus stayed there, but did say that he reached Albany the next season. A note on page fifteen indicated the date this account was to have taken place before 1826. The rest of the narrative centered on how Tahawus guided McIntyre and Henderson around the area after having met the two in Albany.

E. R. Wallace described boating in the Newcomb area in his book, *Descriptive Guide to the Adirondacks.* For the Rich Lake to Lake Harris section, he mentioned rapids at the head of Lake Harris and at the outlet, with boats passing between the lakes via three short carries. He also described a thirteen-mile water route from Newcomb to Long Lake that passed through Catlin Lake, up to Round Pond, and a one and a half mile carry to Long Lake. Wallace wrote that the last carry could be shortened by going up Spring Brook as far as possible to the outlet of Hendrick Spring, named for Henry Hudson. Wallace described the spring as "a fit retreat for the fairies." Wallace also referred to this lake and connecting stream system as the "Western Branch of the Hudson River". [27]

Lawrence Grinnel's book, *Canoeable Waterways of New York State*, provided documentation of several Hudson River trips in the 1950s, including a description of the River as a potential canoe run.[28] Grinnel, a professor at Cornell University as well as a member of the Executive Committee of the newly formed American Whitewater Affiliation, started out with an interesting description of how to prepare for a canoe trip.

On page twenty, Grinnel listed the following as necessary equipment: a dry change of clothing in a waterproof pack tied to the canoe, PFD or lifejacket, two rubber kneeling pads, first aid kit, sunglasses and sunscreen, knife, compass, matches, maps, and emergency food rations. Each boat should be equipped with the following: 15 or 17 ft. aluminum canoe, canoe repair kit, bow and stern lines each being 25 ft. in length, paddles, including a spare, a sponge, camping equipment if doing an overnight, with group leaders having 50 ft. of rope in both the lead and sweep canoes. Clothing for cold weather should be made of wool. Quite a bit different from the log drivers' list of necessities - wool clothing, leather boots, peavey poles, and a log!

Grinnel went on to describe several sections of the Hudson River based on trips he completed. On September 1, 1951, Grinnel ran the Thurman to Lake Luzerne section, presumably taking out before Rockwell Falls. Four years later, he took three days, May 28-30, 1955, to complete the North River to Thurman section. Grinnel described the section from Newcomb to North River as "much of this wilderness route is reported to be very steep and hazardous for canoes; some parts are reported as risky for foldboats." [29]

Grinnel also mentioned that the gorge was run by W.F. Burmeister, but gave no date or any other details except that downstream from Blue Ledges were the bigger, more challenging rapids with the highest potential for severe consequences in case of a problem. Mention was also made of a canoe trip done in late August of 1955 by C.L. King, L.F. Davis, P.T. Olton Jr., and E.L. Thorp in two seventeen-foot canoes. The group started out at the Indian River confluence, making their way downstream seven miles to a trail that led out to State Route 28 [possibly OK Slip or the log drive camp access trail at Carter's Landing, either of which would be quite a carry, JTD]. The water was low, but higher than average for August, but even so, the group carried around the bigger rapids.

Grinnel recommended the North Creek to The Glen section be respected and be done with at least three boats in the trip.[30] He also recommended that the run be done by experienced boaters with back-paddle and draw stroke skills and that boaters be ready to help each other. Grinnel also mentioned two canoe trips done on the Riparius to The Glen section, the first one taking place in November of 1954 with two seventeen-foot and one fifteen-foot aluminum canoes. The group started out from Riparius, with one of the seventeen-foot boats being pinned against a rock in Race Horse. The group left the canoe, returning for it a week later. The other trip took place in April of 1955, with a canoe flipping at The Glen.

Grinnel also documented one of the first people of record to run the gorge in a canoe for recreation.[31] George A. Robe of Montclair, New Jersey, in early August of 1948, did the gorge run as part of an exploratory trip of the Upper Works area. Robe started Monday, August 2, at Lake Sanford and ended up in North River several days later, using a fifteen-foot Old Town cedar canoe weighing about sixty pounds. On the first day, Robe made his way to the Opalescent River, polling his way up as far as possible and staying overnight on the Opalescent, as the Redfield expedition had done years before.

On day two, Robe made his way back downstream to the Upper Works bridge via pole, paddle, and carry, leaving the canoe at the bridge and hitching a ride back up to get his car. Day three saw him making his way down to Newcomb in order to leave the next day for the gorge. As he made his way down toward the Indian River on day four, Robe mentioned passing an abandoned lumber camp, probably the Polaris Club just down from where the Goodnow Flow comes in, reporting that here the "going was fairly easy".[31]

On Saturday, about two hours after starting, Robe flipped his canoe, after swamping it - probably in Cedar Ledges or Blue Ledges - losing some gear and having to stop and repair the canoe. Robe noted starting down the steeper section of the gorge with even bigger rapids, where attempting to run them would be "suicidal". To get around these drops, Robe had to "line her down foot by foot, clambering along the shore from boulder to boulder" with a fifty-foot length of rope being "indispensable". Saturday was a long day, with no lunch or supper, skipping Sunday breakfast as well as he continued to make his way down the gorge.

Robe talked about some of the difficulties of running this section of the river, saying how he had to rope the canoe around a ten-foot high boulder at the edge of a rapid, and one section of the gorge being steep enough to make it hard to climb out of or around. Midday on Sunday found Robe on a "slanting shelf of rock" - possibly at the top of Harris on river left or at Greyhound - that he got out on, camping the night there, and finishing the trip to North River the next day. [32]

The *American Whitewater Journal* recorded the account of a trip down the upper Hudson River written in poetic form. The date of the poem was 1952 and the trip was led by a New York piano maker named Ted Steinway and included two couples by the name of Ledoux and Duel, with the account written by A.B. Duel Jr. [33] According to the poem, the five people on the trip were looking for an experience different and apart from what they knew in their everyday lives. The trip was a two-day float trip on the upper Hudson, planned by one of the members, Ted Steinway, who insisted on the Hudson, "with its churning, boiling waters / Dashing wildly down the mountains". The group met at a North Creek motel on the weekend of June 7, with the weather threatening rain. The group, though, was excited, with their spirits high.

The group packed the next morning and headed to the put-in, which wasn't noted but was most likely Newcomb, with the down-river destination listed as "Gooley," which probably meant the Gooley Club at the confluence of the Indian and Hudson Rivers. The faces of the group still showed eagerness of the night before, but this was quickly tempered by the low water they encountered, as the river had "shrunk down to a puttering brook". [34] The Steinway boat, though, having minimal gear, easily drifted over the rocks. Others in the group with heavier boats had to get out and drag them through the rapids, which caused minor damage to both boats and spirits. The group camped on the river, possibly at the Cedar River confluence, although, again, it was not noted exactly in the poem. The steak dinner that evening was well attended by the local black fly population. The take out the next day was noted as "Gooley," again, probably referring to the Gooley Club.

In her book on Adirondack boating, Hallie Bond noted what might have been the first trips of record on the upper Hudson to use inflatable rafts, recording the adventures of the Northwoods Club in the early 1950s. [35] The club provided raft trips for their members starting in Newcomb and ending in North River. Pat Cunningham, who was involved with these raft trips, noted participants included members of the Foseburg family.[36] He said that the trips took place in 1955-56 and were done primarily as fishing trips. Wilson noted in her history booklet on the Northwoods Club that by 1949, the club had leased land from Finch, Pruyn on the Hudson near Blackwell Stillwater, giving them direct access to the river. [37] Thus, it was possible and much easier for the club to do float trips downriver from there.

Bond also noted the premier of an event that became an important part of the local North River–North Creek river culture. [38] In May of 1957, the first Hudson River Whitewater Derby was held in North River along the section of river that ran next to State Route 28. The event contained a downriver slalom race and became a premier event for the growing whitewater boating population, with one of the more notable participants being Senator Robert Kennedy in 1967. The event continues today, but not on the grand scale of the past. One of the important roles that the Derby played was in making the Hudson known as a whitewater run, music to the ears of budding eastern commercial raft outfitters in the 1970s.

North River resident Larry Wilke remembered taking a canoe trip through the gorge in 1959, "probably on July 4th, " with a yellow Old Town canoe and a Kennebec canoe. [39] Inspired by the Hudson River Whitewater Derby, the group began the trip at the confluence of the Indian and Hudson Rivers. Larry and his partner wrecked their canoe, camping overnight at Blue Ledges. While there, he recalled seeing a group going past the campsite on a fishing trip in a "small orange raft". This also became the standard itinerary for the next twenty-five years or so for running the gorge, with trips starting in Newcomb, overnight at Blue Ledges, and most trips ending the next day in North River.

During his college years in the early 1960s, Ed Hixon, along with John Rugge, Clyde Smith, and Chuck Jennings, canoed through the

Hudson River Gorge in open boats on many occasions. [40] Both Hixon and Smith continued to run the gorge into the 1970s, with Smith writing on these trips in a series of articles in *Adirondack Life* (1970-71) and publishing a book. Dr. Hixon recalled that the runs the group did were typically in spring or fall, with one trip having a water level so high they had to line the boats on the larger drops through the alder trees on shore.

In an article dated 1961, Randolph reported that the Connecticut chapter of the Appalachian Mountain Club was running the Hudson River Gorge with its members, then considering the run "the most difficult Class IV river which we run." [41]

One of the more successful raft trips of that time on the Hudson, and one with a great deal of notoriety, was the May 6, 1967, trip made by Senator Robert Kennedy and Secretary of the Interior Stewart Udall. Both men were involved on the national level with the passage of legislation such as the Wild and Scenic Rivers Act, which helped protect rivers like the Hudson from dam construction and other development, keeping them in a free-flowing state. Prime listed one of the important goals of the trip was to "dramatize river sports, water pollution control, and the pending Wild Rivers bill." [42] As part of this event, Kennedy and Udall ran the Hudson Gorge, with Kennedy participating in the Whitewater Derby the following day.

The group size for the raft trip totaled about sixty people and included family members from both the Udalls and the Kennedys, with a wide range of age and occupation. [43] Several rafting and kayaking professionals from the Kayak Canoe Club of New York (KCCNY), along with some local and out-of-state boaters, were part of the group, helping manage the safety aspects. [44] These experienced river runners did the trip through the gorge the day before in order to assess the suitability for the well-known boaters and their families. Journalists and photographers rounded out the trip and documented the occasion, all under the watchful eyes of Secret Service agents.

According to a *New York Times* article by James Clarity, the group consisted of Senator Kennedy; his wife Ethel; seven of their children, including Robert Jr.; Secretary Udall and his wife; James Whitaker;

and Caroline Kennedy, daughter of President John Kennedy. The flotilla of water craft included fifteen rafts, ten canoes, and six kayaks. [45] Prime also added that several uninvited media people followed the group in a helicopter.[46] Both Prime and Clarity noted the skepticism with which the trip was met, with Prime writing that, even then, many considered the Hudson River Gorge unrunnable.[47] Clarity mentioned that several local residents thought running the rapids of the gorge was "madness". [48]

In his remembrance of Kennedy a year later in the spring 1968 *American Whitewater Journal* trip leader Robert Harrigan talked about the self confidence the Senator showed before the trip. Kennedy talked to Harrigan about the Hudson, asking "what the river was like". [49] Harrigan responded, "I told him how the waters rushed through the Gorge – the banks lined with natural hemlock and white cedar. He never asked if he was equal to the task. He knew he was". The two also talked of the natural beauty of the gorge.

While some of the group stayed at Garnet Hill Lodge in North River, the trip participants met the night before at the Gooley Club at the confluence of the Indian and Hudson Rivers, where the trip would start. Clarity reported the day of the trip was "splendidly sunny," with water temperatures near 40 degrees. [50] Binger provided a brief log of the trip in *The American Whitewater,* the magazine of the AWA. [51] The water level was low, and by 10:30 a.m., rafts were being inflated, and by 10:45, the trip was underway. Kennedy was in a kayak and wore a wetsuit and a white helmet with orange PFD. By 11:30, the group was heading down Blue Ledges, where Senator Kennedy fell out of his boat, swimming the last steep section. Clarity reported that throw lines were unsuccessful at reaching Kennedy, who swam ashore in the calm pool at the bottom of the rapid, emptying his boat of water and continuing on. [52]

Lunch stop was at OK Slip at 1 p.m., where Binger reported that Garnet Hill owners had lunch delivered. [53] Kennedy, still damp and cold from his swim, shivered until he sipped on some hot chocolate. [54] Kennedy fell out twice more after the trip resumed, once probably at Givneys given his skill level, the location after lunch, and the steepness of the drop. Binger reported that the third swim was in Harris, where Kennedy's kayak was pinned to a rock by a raft during the rescue, but "nothing serious".[55] The rest of the trip was made without major incident, with the take out in North River and cocktails later that evening at Garnet Hill.

The attention that the trip drew to rivers and river running seemed to help, as Hawksley reported on final Congressional approval of the Wild and Scenic Rivers Act in September, 1967, with President Johnson signing the bill in October, 1967.[56] An interesting side note is that in the original proposal of the act, the Hudson River Gorge was included, but was omitted in the final version.

Local people ran the river during this period as well. Tom Butler of North Creek, better known as "Buckshot," told of how he and his friends rafted the Hudson in the North Creek area in the late 1940s.[57] This group of river runners collected logs that didn't make it down on the log drives, laid them next to each other, nailed them together with wood and nails, and floated down the river. "Buckshot" described it best in an article called "Confessions of a River Rat", printed in the *North Creek News-Enterprise* 1997 supplement on the Hudson River Whitewater Derby:

> Somewhere around 1949 or 1950, we gathered logs that the river drivers were herding down to Glens Falls, and kind of hid them in discreet places to be fashioned into rafts after the drivers had gone through. One of the local fellows, Pat Cole, (who is more like Huck Finn than Huck Finn), and myself set out down the river from the area just below the River Bridge, where some of the older guys had rat holed a raft already lashed together. It was the kind of day that only happens in dreams. The sun was high, birds were going it, all was right on heaven and earth and it was a Saturday with no school to torture us. We escaped with the "borrowed" raft without getting caught and as soon as we rounded the first bend, we settled back and lit up our corn cobs for a pleasant excursion to Riparius, some seven miles away.

Our ecstasy was short-lived however, as soon as we entered the Bird Pond Falls area, and discovered that we were amateurs. It only took a couple minutes for us to get dumped overboard a few times, whereupon Pat lost his glasses, I lost my jackknife, and we were fortunate not to lose our time left on earth a bit early. In only a few minutes, we were straddling a single log, the raft being somewhere below the Falls. Completely humbled and the long walk home gave us time to research and plan for future trips with a more stable vessel. We swaggered into town and of course, had to "let-on" to our buddies, that we had a marvelous time on our first raft expedition. It didn't take long for some of the older guys to get wind of our story and not much more time for them to figure that it was us who hijacked their raft. It got a bit warm for us for a while, but Pat and I had plenty of practice lying our way out of tough situations so we escaped again.

Buckshot goes on to say that there were other trips over the years on inner tubes and "assembled rafts of all sorts".

Doug Garand of Newcomb and some of his friends rafted the Newcomb to North River trip in the late 1960s, but did it a little earlier in the spring when the water was the highest. [58] Others in Garand's group included the Pratts and the Kellys from Minerva, Brian Sullivan from Olmsteadville, and Dan Carr of Newcomb. The group used military surplus rafts from the Town of Newcomb, which were twenty-eight feet long with D-rings on the side and part of the bottom removed to allow the water to escape, making it the first self-bailing raft through the gorge. It was more than twenty years before this technology found its way back to the river again, when self-bailing rafts became standard for commercial raft trips. The group also used PFDs, but not much else that offered protection and comfort from the cold water. The group left Newcomb in the morning and arrived in North River by the afternoon. Rafting the Hudson River Gorge in the high, early spring water without the wetsuits and other equipment for comfort and safety was, as Garand fondly recalls, "nuts".

Garand and his friends were not the only Newcomb residents to raft the gorge at that time. Breck Trautwein and several other workers from the Tahawas mine facility made the run from Newcomb to North River in early May of 1970 or 1971. [59] The group used a 943 vintage bridge pontoon boat from the Army they called *George* that featured a tiller on the back. The account of the trip appeared in the company magazine *Cloudsplitter* and listed the other intrepid explorers as Dan Carr, Jess Villar, Gordon Medena, Gary Carter, Bill Devine, and "Squeak" Porter. The group made it a two-day trip, staying overnight at Blue Ledges.

Like Garand's group several years before, the group met with skepticism about the trip down "the world's only horizontal waterfall," with "standing waves as big as a house," and that "a couple of people drown every year doing that." [60] Despite such encouragement, the group made ready for their trip.

Friday, May 7th, dawned "warm and clear," as Trautwein wrote, with the group loading the raft with gear, including beer, and lashing the gear to the raft. A picture on page ten of the group revealed plaid shirts and jeans for attire, no helmets, and old-style, collar-type PFDs with a can of beer on the raft in the lower left corner. Outfitted as such, the group made their way downriver and, after making Long Pond Falls and Ord Falls, relaxed on the flatwater of Blackwell Stillwater, feeling that if they could handle these rapids, "we could handle anything." Trautwein commented, though, as they got past the Stillwater and made their way to the Indian River, "the idyl was soon over." [61]

Dropping over the Class III run after Blackwell, the raft hit a log, snapping the steering oar into three pieces. After making the necessary repairs, the group approached the Indian River, fully aware that the worst stretch of rapids lay ahead. After hitting a rapid and being thrown about in the raft, Trautwein wrote that Porter had "found religion, 'cause he was kneeling there, hanging on." Arriving at Blue Ledges, the group was able to "catch our breaths, to stand on something dry and solid", making camp, cooking steaks, and washing it down with beer, hoping that the worst rapids had passed.[62]

By morning, though, the warm weather the day before had melted more snow, raising the level of the river as well as the anxiety level of the crew. Traveling about one and a half miles down from Blue Ledges - meaning that they had at least traveled through the Narrows and Osprey Nest - the crew decided that they had enough. Making their way to shore, they decided two of them would stay with the raft while the rest made their way downriver to the railroad bridge - a tall feat, considering the terrain! The group did make it out after regrouping at the railroad bridge, changing their destination from North Creek to "the first bar we could find," feeling "more like survivors than conquerors." [63]

Bob Masters and Clyde Smith described an overnight trip through the gorge that they did with four other boaters, including Ed Hixon. [64] Outfitted with seventeen-foot aluminum canoes, assorted gear, and food, the group left Newcomb "before the snow had melted from the slopes of Mt. Marcy." The two also leave the sense that not many people made the trip though the gorge, describing those on the trip as "one of the privileged few."

Two years later, in May of 1971, Redd Buck wrote an account of a canoe trip that he took through the gorge with the same Clyde Smith noted above. [65] As before, it was an overnight, starting from Newcomb and ending in North River. The group used aluminum canoes, as these boats were "more easily hammered out after colliding with rocks." The two boaters left Newcomb in the morning, with Buck commenting on how unimposing the river looked at that time, but that countenance soon changed with the approach of Long Falls Rapids. Buck commented that his perception of the river went from being "not threatening" to praying "to every conceivable deity for absolution." The two made it down to Blue Ledges, where Buck described the scene as defying description, with the "magnificent campsite" set before a ledge that rose hundreds of feet above the "tranquil pool" of the river.

Smith later published a book with a chapter that described the scenery and some of the motivation that he and some friends had for running the gorge. [66] The chapter was actually a compilation of several similar trips that they took over the years, not just a single trip. [67] Despite the risk of the trip, Smith returned to this part of the river "time and again to absorb its spectacular setting and enjoy the thrill of running its rapids," [68] much the same reason that Charles Farnum gave for his run in 1880.

Echoing the thoughts of many, Smith was quite descriptive of the scenery, contrasting the upper section with the Hudson below Albany. [69] In the upper section, one finds "a country of unparalleled beauty. Here the Hudson lives, breaths - and surges unmolested," with the Hudson Gorge run being a "supreme challenge" to boaters.

At Blue Ledges the enchantment with the wild scenery of the Gorge continued:

> Blue Ledge's dark hulk looms like a mighty sentinel in the fading twilight, its sheer face echoing a muffled from the Hudson. This is the throbbing heart of the Hudson - we have penetrated to its innermost sanctuary. A place of incomparable beauty appreciated more fully because of the effort it takes to get here - and the even greater effort needed to escape. [70]

Smith also described the feeling of taking a canoe through a rapid:

> Our canoe bounces over the waves and plunges into booming holes, then pops out again, spewing foam and spray. The sound of crashing water is deafening as it reverberates off the chasm walls. One moment we seem suspended in air, the next engulfed in a torrential immersion. Twisting and turning, we thread our way around monstrous boulders, past boiling whirlpools, and back into the corkscrew of thrashing waves. [71]

The Town of Indian Lake also had its bold adventurers. Pat and Joe Cummins recalled some of the local young people of the town tubed down the gorge during the late 1960s and early 1970s. [72] The tubers started out on the Indian-Hudson River junction, followed the Hudson downriver, and ended in North River. These trips were done during the summertime low water levels and took all day to complete. According to Pat, the groups fished along the way, relaxing and encountering some rock throwers from the Northern Frontier Camp. Joe said that the trips took about twelve hours and that they took out at the D & H Railroad bridge, leaving the deflated tubes there for another time.

Northern Frontier Camp, located on OK Slip Pond, began leasing land from Finch, Pruyn Paper in Glens Falls in 1965, holding their first boys' summer camp at that location during the summer of 1966.[73] A non-denominational church camp organization, Northern Frontier held camps in several other locations and was attracted to the OK Slip location by the remote and private setting. The camp featured many of the traditional programs of summer camps, such as swimming, boating, camp skills, and campfire programs, as well as Bible studies. Some of these programs eventually included overnight trips and, according to long time board member Bob McKenney, two of the campout spots were in the Hudson River Gorge.

One of these campsites was at the sandy beach on river right at Blue Ledges, and the other at the beach on river right next to where OK Slip empties into the Hudson. Bob also remembered day-long horse trips by trail to these locations. Keith McKenney, son of Bob McKenney and a former caretaker at the Northern Frontier Camp, also recalled a camp program that involved using the river.[74] Keith eventually became one of the first Whitewater Challenger raft guides on the Hudson in the 1980s.

Some of the Northern Frontier staff would trek to the river for their own personal outings as well. Jim "Bone" Bayse of Beaver Brook Outfitters spoke of the times that he, McKenney, and Shawn Frawley would play in the gorge during time off from Northern Frontier. They were employed as staff at the camp in the mid-1970s, with the Hudson River in their own "back yard". Bayse gave the summer of 1977 as the date for the following narrative:

> We got to know the Hudson pretty well during those
> summers. Working in the kitchen allowed us enough

time to finish up with the lunch chores, run the trail out to the Blue Ledges, jump in the river, and float down through the Narrows, Osprey Nest, and Carter's rapid before taking out and running up the trail to OK Slip Falls back into camp in time to start our dinner chores. Depending on the day, we would sometimes find logs to float on down the river, while other times we would practice a method we called "rump bumping." Rump bumping is floating down the river with your feet out in front of you, letting the soft part of your backside bounce off the rocks while using your arms to steer and stay afloat.

On days with more time, we would explore the river up to Cedar Ledges or down as far as the railroad trestle. In my time working at the camp, there would be occasions when the forest rangers would come into camp to ask for assistance in looking for reported lost hikers in the Gorge area. We were always more than eager to help. In fact, we enjoyed it so much that we formed our own group that we named "Hudson Gorge Search Rescue and Recovery." We never ended up involved with major rescues, but it was not unusual for us to find abandoned canoes or lost camping gear left behind from folks who thought that maybe a summer canoe trip down the gorge was a good idea. [75]

Not everyone who was aware of the upper Hudson River and the gorge during this period looked upon it as a great recreational resource. During the 1960s, record draughts in New York affected water resources across the state, resulting in state-wide water shortages.[76] New York City began looking at the Hudson River as a possibility to help supplement existing water sources by reactivating an existing water intake near Chelsea in Dutchess County. Phillips reported that New York City Mayor John Wagner, referring to the plan to reactivate the Chelsea facility, also felt that the water runoff from the Adirondacks could be "stored and later used".[77]

This was not the first time New York City and other urban officials looked upriver with dreamy eyes to the Upper Hudson region as a water supply area or for some type of dam proposal. In a publication called *The Argus,* with a date of April 10, 1872, surveyor Verplanck Colvin proposed utilizing Adirondack lake water to help provide for present and future water supply issues for Albany and other towns downriver.[78]

Mitchell gave a few details on Colvin's proposal.[79] Colvin suggested a stone dam be built on the upper Hudson at the confluence with the Schroon River near Warrensburg to secure water for the Hudson River valley. Colvin even suggested building a series of canals to supplement Hudson water with that of surrounding lakes. In a report dated 1907, the New York State Water Supply Commission outlined thirteen possible sites on the upper Hudson River that could act as practical water storage facilities, with several of these located in the Town of Newcomb.[80]

J.T. Fanning, in *Report on a Water Supply for New York and Other Cities of the Hudson Valley,* reported that water shortages at that time prompted a study of possible water sources for the New York City area in the Adirondacks.[81] Lake George was listed as a possible source to direct water by gravity down to the city. Because of its proximity to the Lake George area, "that portion of the waters of the mountain lakes and tributaries of the Upper Hudson might be so conducted as to reinforce the supply of Lake George." The Hudson River water was to be diverted by canal to Lake George, with a dam on the river to help direct the water into the canal, where it could be stored in Lake George.

In a remarkable statement, Fanning viewed the Lake George–Upper Hudson area as a blessing from God - that God had the forethought to design such a potential resource for New York City. Three years later, Fanning, in another report on New York City water supply problems, wrote that engineers were looking at the Upper Hudson region as "the most desirable source" of water for the growing New York City and Hudson Valley region.[82] Fanning also noted that recent surveys (probably Colvin's) showed that Adirondack lakes could be adapted as storage areas for water aqueducts.

Several floods in the Glens Falls-Albany area in the early part of the 1900s prompted the formation of the Hudson River Regulating District in 1923. The Board of the Hudson River Regulating District wrote a plan that detailed proposals to construct a system of dams to help manage extreme fluctuations of river levels.[83] The plan lists sixteen previous reports that spoke of dam construction on the Hudson and its tributaries, beginning with the McElroy Report of 1867 and up to preliminary reports to the district in 1922. Several are important to note, as proposals to dam the Hudson at Ord Falls, the Essex Chain of Lakes, Cheney Ponds, Boreas Ponds, and Thirteenth Lake could have significantly changed the Upper Hudson landscape seen today. Most of these proposals, too, would have flooded timber on state land, but the plan did not see that as a problem with the state's Forever Wild Amendment.

The district's written plan provided details for the proposals. The Ord Falls Dam would be located just above the falls, a few miles below Newcomb, concluding that the topography provides an "excellent opportunity for the creation of a storage reservoir."[84] Total acreage of the reservoir would be 5,960, flooding parts of the Town of Newcomb, Lake Harris, Rich Lake, and expanding Catlin Lake's shoreline. The reservoir would also reach up the Hudson almost two miles past were Newcomb Lake drains into the river. The type of dam and the materials to build it would be determined by the bedrock found at the site. An interesting note is that, in the eyes of the report, the major obstacle was the relocation of the state highway that ran through Newcomb, with little regard to the relocation of the residents of the town.

The Chain Lakes Reservior details are found on page twenty-seven, with the ideal location of the 100-foot-high dam to be on the Cedar River, about two miles upstream from the junction with the Hudson.[85] Compared to other proposals in the plan, such as the Ord Falls one, the Chain Lakes dam required the removal of only the hunting camps on Third Lake. The dam would flood out about 4,700 acres, including the Chain Lakes and Pine Lake, and reach up the Rock River several miles.

Other dams of note in the plan were the ones for the Sacandaga River at Conklinville and for the Goodnow River below Newcomb, both of which were eventually built. Several others not built were ones at Thirteenth Lake in North River, which would have raised the level there twenty-seven feet, and one on the Hudson at Lake Luzerne, just above Rockwell Falls and the junction with the Sacandaga. The plan also toyed with the idea of having dams at Rich Lake, Catlin Lake, at Lake Sanford in the Upper Works area, and twin dams on the Cedar River and the Indian River, with the Indian River dam to be located near the site of the present Lake Abanakee dam. [86]

In a prophetic proposal, as we shall see, the district plan also looked at a dam in the Hudson River Gorge to be 200 feet high and located 2,000 feet downriver from the confluence with the Indian River to take in portions of both the Ord Falls and the Chain Lakes Reserviors. [87] This dam and the reservoir were never considered as more than an alternative to the Ord Falls and Chain Lakes proposals, and not seriously considered then. It took forty years for that to happen.

The New York City dam plan of the 1960s sought state help in financing and coordination, with Governor Rockefeller authorizing the Water Resources Commission to study the problem and develop recommendations. [88] Schamberg reported that the date of this action was 1965, with the Commission issuing its report on December 19, 1967. The report proposed fifty-eight reservoir sites, including those in the Hudson River Gorge, as part of an overall plan to address water shortages. "The most apparent need now is for additional major storage reservoirs to ameliorate the most critical water problems and to develop the greatest potential benefits", the report is quoted as saying. Schamberg further noted from the report that the Hudson River Basin could meet future water needs by "direct withdrawal from the river" and "upstream storage". [89]

One of those "upstream storage" areas was to be the Hudson River Gorge. Several sites were proposed, with the most favored site being half a mile downstream from the confluence of the Indian and Hudson Rivers, [90] the exact spot proposed by the Hudson River Regulating District forty years before. The dam would be referred to as Gooley #1, for the Gooley Club located at the confluence of the two rivers, which would have been drowned by the reservoir water. The dam itself would be a three-quarters-of-a-mile long earth embankment dam, 200 feet high, with a concrete spillway 400 feet long located on the left bank, with a minimum discharge flow being 923 cubic feet per second (cfs).

Schaefer further noted that the dam would have created a reservoir over thirty-five miles long and would have required 16,000 acres of land, 14,500 of which would be flooded. [91] The Temporary Study Commission noted that of the 16,000 acres needed, 12,000 were privately owned, with approximately 170 homes in and around Newcomb needing removal and about eleven miles of State Route 28N needing relocation; in short, the Town of Newcomb would have been under fifty feet of water. [92] Needless to say, the Gooley #1 Dam would have had a huge impact on the area, both before and after construction.

Just as with the Hudson River Regulating District's plan of 1923, the Gooley Dam would have required the flooding of 3,000 to 4,000 acres of state Forest Preserve land, protected by the Forever Wild amendment of the state constitution. Schaefer noted that the Water Resource Commission felt that a constitutional amendment to proceed with the proposal was not necessary, as Article XIV had a clause allowing the building of municipal water supply reservoirs. [93]

Hennigan noted that the proposal was a complete surprise to the public, as there was no public input or discussion. [94] The scope of the proposal and its potential impact was treated as a serious threat, with opposition widespread. [95] The Adirondack Hudson River Association was founded to oppose the Gooley Dam and was structured much like the group that led the successful opposition to the Panther Mountain Dam proposal on the Moose River in the late 1940s. The group formed a similar strategy, with the ultimate goal being to get legislation similar to the Stokes Act of 1950 that banned the dam on the Moose River. The group managed to arrange public meetings to publicize the issue and the group's position, had a film made on the issue, and lined up key politicians who supported the position of the group.

The Schenectady Chapter of the Adirondack Mountain Club (ADK) voiced opposition to the project as well. In the September–October issue of the ADK's magazine, *Adirondac,* the Chapter reported on the proposal, its costs, and its implications. [96] The essential argument of the article was that water usage policy in New York City at that time encouraged wasteful use and that the dam would do nothing to curb this. For the Adirondacks, the destruction of the scenic gorge and various upriver sections for a policy that would continue wasteful practices was not justified. The article also pointed out that the Hudson River had no protection under the federal Wild and Scenic Rivers Act, suggesting that similar protection was needed for the Hudson.

In an editorial dated February 24, 1969, the *New York Times* also stated its opposition to the project. [97] The paper sided with the argument, put forth by the Adirondack Hudson River Association, that the dam was not needed when other solutions were available. The *Times* felt that drawing fresh water from the Hudson below Albany, along with water metering and usage of desalinization technology, would have been more than adequate to meet the city's water needs.

In an effort to respond to the strong opposition to the project from a wide cross section of interests, a bill was proposed in the New York State Legislature to ban the Gooley Dam. Schaefer reported that the bill was introduced by Senator Bernard Smith of Northport and Assemblyman Clarence Lane of Windham, with co-sponsership coming from Senator Walter Langley of Albany and Scholarie counties, all three Republicans. [98] Support amongst other legislators and passage of the bill, though, was not assured. A chance meeting between Schaefer and a friend of a key legislator produced a meeting with this politician, who promised support. Several days later, the bill was passed by the NYS Senate 53-0, and then by the Assembly 121-0.

Schaefer reported on final passage of the bill on April 17, 1969, with additional parts of the upper Hudson River being protected. Several days after passage of the bill, Governor Rockefeller signed the bill into law. While the Gorge was protected from the Gooley Dam, development threats to the upper river and the gorge remained.

In an editorial supporting the proposals of the Temporary Study Commission, the *New York Times* reported on plans by Finch, Pruyn to subdivide and sell forty building lots on the land they owned at the confluence of the Indian and Hudson Rivers. The *Times* editorial supported the protective proposals as a way to prevent development like that proposed by Finch, Pruyn. Sale of these lots, the *Times* felt, might encourage other such development along a stretch of river whose value lay in "its wild character, its freedom from the presence of man." [99]

Another bill passed at that time by the legislature directed a commission to be established to study the water needs of the downstate population. [100] In signing this bill, Governor Rockefeller noted the water resource problems for this area and called for additional water resources to meet the need. Newcomb residents saw this bill as the governor trying to appease both sides of the water issue, as the specter of the Gooley Dam continued to haunt the area. Paul Schaefer, as did the Adirondack Mountain Club, saw the need for additional protection of the upper Hudson River area from the state legislature and the various water commissions in order to put the Gooley Dam ghost to rest. [101]

Such action was taken in 1972, when Assemblyman Glenn Harris and Senator Bernard Smith introduced a bill to create the New York State Wild, Scenic, and Recreational Rivers System (WSR). Drafted by Pete Payne Jr., the bill gave protection to 180 miles of rivers in the state, primarily in the Adirondacks, with direction for the newly created Adirondack Park Agency to make proposals for the inclusion of other rivers. [102] Of the 2,000 miles of rivers in the Adirondacks, about 1,000 were studied for inclusion; by 1986, the original 180 miles had expanded to 1,238.

Modeled after the federal Wild and Scenic Rivers Act, the WSR bill stated the New York legislature found that many of the state rivers "possess outstanding natural, scenic, historical, ecological and recreational values" and that certain types of development would deprive future generations a chance to enjoy these qualities. [103] The WSR act established river protection in three different categories, with provisions for the inclusion of additional rivers in the future.

Specifically, a *Wild* designation meant that the rivers or river sections needed to be at least five miles long, be half a mile from the nearest public highway, be managed as a wild area, be free of dams, and have no motors allowed on the river corridor. *Scenic* designation had limited road and development intrusions, no dams, no minimum river length, and riverbed management geared toward preserving and restoring natural scenic qualities. *Recreational* rivers would be readily accessible by road or railroad, contain development in the area, and allow some dam building.

The ten and a half miles of the Hudson River between the Cedar River and the D&H railroad bridge just before the Boreas River confluence was designated Wild, with the nine-mile stretch between Newcomb and the Cedar and the four-mile section from the Boreas to the hamlet of North River designated as Scenic. The other fifty-eight and a half miles of the Hudson received the Recreational designation. [104]

Public support to shelve the Gooley Dam helped create a similar base for the passage of the WSR Act. [105] As part of this campaign, the Adirondack Hudson River Association created a documentary film on Adirondack rivers, thinking that the public needed to know where these rivers were, what parts would be protected, and why they needed protection. The film, done in large part as a master's degree project of Fred Sullivan from Glens Falls, documented wild and free-flowing Adirondack rivers, some to their source in remote locations.

One of the river runners in the group was Pete Payne Jr. of Wilsboro, who said that while the film contained footage of the Hudson run, other rivers were also featured. [106] Payne also noted that although the group completed the run through the Hudson Gorge successfully, the trip was not without incident! The film helped solidify the rationale behind the need for river protection, pointing to the need for legislative action such as the WSR Act, and helped ensure the bill's passage and signing into law in 1972.

Hudson recreational runners of the 1960-70s knew the river and made the recreational potential of the Hudson River Gorge well known amongst a growing network of river runners and the general public. Ed Hixon commented on this effort, that the role of these boaters was not only in the opposition and acts of protest (such as survey stakes for the dam disappearing into the river) that they helped generate, but also in the notoriety these boaters and early rafters brought to the Hudson River Gorge. [107] People came to know about the upper Hudson River and the gorge as a result, making the recreational and secinc potential of the river a primary value. Because of their efforts, they helped save the gorge from being flooded by the Gooley Dam, and it's wild character being developed beyond recognition, allowing river runners to continue to ply their craft forty years later. *All present-day users owe a debt of gratitude to this past generation of Hudson river runners and activists.*

With protection of the Hudson River in a wild and scenic condition and the free- flowing status of the river established rather firmly, recreational boating on the Hudson from Newcomb to North River continued to grow during the 1970s. Several articles published in the *American Whitewater Affiliation Journal* and *Adirondack Life* helped prepare adventurers for the trip. Cooney kayaked the Hudson River Gorge in early June of 1970, prompting him to study runable water levels on the river. [108] The study was aimed at helping boaters predict when the best times to make the run were. Not surprisingly, the period from April to May provided the highest levels, with May having the best all-around levels, using three and a half feet on the North Creek river gauge as the minimum runable level. Cooney did see some runs possible in August, but with a very short timeframe.

Adirondack Life published an article in 1979 by Bernard Carman that briefly described the trip through the Hudson River Gorge. Carman listed the put-in as Newcomb, the trip length as twenty-seven miles to North River, and that it would be best done as a two-day trip, with an overnight at Blue Ledges. While Carman did list the trip as "beloved" by some boaters, he described it as a potentially dangerous trip for the unprepared or for those who did not realize the magnitude of the trip. As Carman said, a canoe trip through the gorge required "proper preparation, suitable equipment, and a fair amount of expertise." [109]

Zwick provided some guidance as to what to bring for a fast-water canoe trip. A standard aluminum canoe was acceptable for all but the roughest water, as it held up well in minor collisions and scrapes with rocks. If possible, a cloth cover fitted over the ends helped keep water out and made for less bailing. Each canoe should have six to twelve feet of rope attached near the stern, freely dangling in case of an upset. An extra paddle should be lashed to a thwart, along with a bailer and extra clothes, food, and a map, which should be double-bagged in plastic and securely held to the thwarts. A PFD was listed as a "wise precaution" and a wetsuit was recommended. [110]

Clyde Smith gave practical insight into the paddling method that open canoeists used in a rapid. [111] The canoes went through one at a time, with the other paddlers on shore where they had a better chance of providing help to any canoe that might overturn. As the canoes went through the rapid, they would backpaddle in order to retard the forward movement of the canoe, which helped prevent large waves from filling the boat with water.

While the popularity of recreational river running on the Hudson River from Newcomb to North River increased during the 1970s, so did the number of search and rescues. In the period between 1975 and 1979, Department of Environmental Conservation (DEC) forest rangers reported two fatalities and six major rescue operations of river runners in the gorge. An *Adirondack Life* article outlined how DEC personnel adjusted their safety plans to meet the increased usage and concluded with a list of guidelines for potential river runners, including the recommendation that closed deck boats be used in the gorge. [112]

A Hudson River trip that had implications for the next generation of river runners was a kayak trip in the spring of 1978 by the Appalachian Mountain Club. Among the participants was a kayaker named Wayne Hockmeyer, who ran a raft company in Maine and heard of the Hudson River as a whitewater run the year before in 1977, probably from several sources, including Indian Lake resident John Monthony. [113] Hockmeyer completed the run and saw the potential for commercial rafting to take place, returning the next year for that very purpose.

Dr. John Rugge running the Hudson River Whitewater Derby.
Larry Wilke photo

Cedar River put-in for a Hudson Gorge
overnight canoe trip, April, 1973.
Ed Hixon photo

Meal time on the Hudson River
Left: Liz Smith cooks dinner at the Cedar and
Hudson River confluence campsite, 1973.
Right: Liz and Clyde Smith have lunch on river, 1973.
Ed Hixon photos

Clyde Smith lines a canoe around the Narrows, April 1973.
Ed Hixon photo

Clyde Smith and friend running 3rd Hole in
Harris, Hudson River, April, 1973.
Ed Hixon photo

Recreational rafters in the Narrows, 1976.
Clyde Smith photo

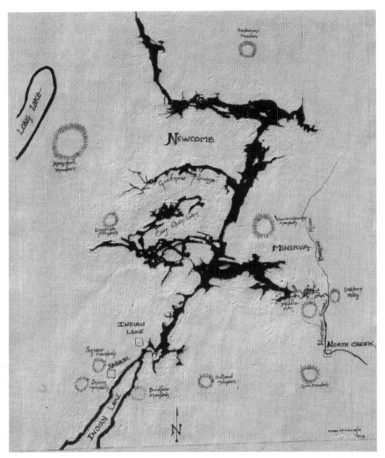

This drawing shows the potential impact
of a dam in the Hudson Gorge.
Mark McMonagle artist

Commercial Rafting: In the Beginning

With the popularity of river running growing in the west, several budding raft companies began to look for rivers to run in the east. In 1963, the Youghiogheny in Pennsylvania was first rafted commercially and in 1965, rafting in West Virginia began with a run of the New River.[1] Rivers in North Carolina began to be run in 1971, Maine in 1976. As outfitters looked for other rivers to run in the east, the Hudson River became an attractive possibility due to its wild setting, Class III-IV rapids, proximity to urban areas, and name recognition.[2] The popularity of rafting on the Hudson grew quickly and was reflected by the increase in the number of raft guests and in the number of outfitters.[3] This popularity proved to be a management problem as well, with rafting on the Hudson almost becoming a victim of its own success. Even so, these early commercial outfitters faced the problem of establishing both themselves and an industry along with acceptance by the local townships. As a testament to their success, whitewater rafting continues to be a thriving industry and an important part of the economic and social fabric of the region, continuing a legacy of river running in and around the Hudson River Gorge.

As to who was the first river runner to use an inflatable raft in the Hudson River Gorge is, like many other "firsts," something that may never be known with any certainty. God may know, but chances are, not us. Commercial rafting in the gorge was the same way; who exactly the first river runners that were paid money to guide the people who paid them and who these payers and payees were will probably be something known only to God, too. The first commercial runners of <u>record</u> are a little more certain. As always, though, rafting in the Hudson Gorge and the east did not happen in a vacuum but occurred in the context of national trends.

In the west, Bennet cited Julius Stone as having run the nation's first commercial river running trip in 1909, running the Colorado through the Grand Canyon.[4] Staveley gave some more details of the trip that started on September 12, 1909, in Green River in Utah. Stone built four boats for him and his friends and hired pioneering river runner Nathan Galloway to help guide the group down to Needles, California, arriving there on November 19, 1909.[5]

Western rivers were run commercially on a regular basis by the mid-1930s, with two of the earliest attempts made by Bus Hatch and Norman Nevills. By 1936, Hatch and his friends were running ten-day trips at the cost of $65 per person on the Green River.[6] Hatch and his relatives had been running rivers in Utah since the late 1920s in wooden boats. As his reputation grew, his services as a river runner became more in demand by "surveyors, engineers, fishermen, hunters, and just plain thrill seekers".[7] Hatch realized that river running could be a profitable business and started the first commercial river running company, according to the Hatch organization.

Quist cited how Nevills began running trips down the San Juan River in the 1920s with guests from the family lodge in Utah.[8] Staveley wrote that by 1936, Nevills was regularly running commercial trips on the San Juan.[9] Staveley also cited that a film made of the trip and released to universities in California resulted in an increase of interest in river running.[10] In 1938, Nevills made another "first" commercial raft trip - depending on who you ask - down the Colorado through the Grand Canyon with a great deal of publicity generated by the trip. Clips from the *New York Times* demonstrated a national concern for the welfare of the trip participants due to high water levels from recent rains. Nevills made it through and his raft business expanded from there. Commercial river running in the west continued to grow as more river runners set up outfitting businesses on other rivers, such as the Green and the Salmon.

While running western rivers became increasingly popular, outdoor recreationists looked at eastern rivers to run. Gaines cited the beginning of commercial rafting in the east to be 1963, when Karl Kreuger and Lance Martin ran the Youghiogeny in Pennsylvania and formed their own raft company. [11] Schmale confirmed this as well, saying that several of these runners then began to branch out looking for other eastern rivers to run. [12] In 1964, Jon Dragan, who worked with Kreuger and Martin, came to the New River area of West Virginia and started a raft company there. Gruspe cited the year of 1968 as the year that Dragan and his brothers began to run the New River commercially. [13]

As the industry was in its infancy, they had to scrape together rafts and equipment, borrowing money from relatives after being turned down by skeptical banks. The group started with military surplus rafts and pick-up trucks, with each river runner chipping in $10 or so for supplies. Base camp was located between the upper and lower runs of the New River so customers could raft both sections. That first year, the Dragans played host to up to eighty river runners, with the brothers eventually forming Wildwater Unlimited.

Other eastern rivers soon found themselves playing host to a new generation of river runners, with Wildwater Unlimited starting to raft in North Carolina in 1971[14] and Whitewater Challengers in Pennsylvania on the Lehigh in 1975. [15] Of particular interest to this book was the beginning of rafting in the state of Maine, the province of Ontario, and the Sacandaga River in New York. Wayne and Suzie Hockmeyer started to run the Kennebec in 1976, [16] eventually expanding to run other Maine rivers such as the Penobscot and Dead. In 1975, Joe Kowalski and his friends formed Wilderness Tours to raft on the Ottawa River in Ontario, Canada. [17] Bill Cromie and his business partner, Rusty Brust, began to run the Sacandaga River near Lake George, New York, in the late 1970s. [18] All five would play important parts in the beginning of commercial rafting on the Hudson.

Although the Hudson River was not well known as a commercial raft run in the 1960s into the early 1970s, it was well known for its whitewater. The Hudson River Whitewater Derby, run in the North

River-North Creek area, is a slalom and downriver race held annually since 1958.[19] Started by Roland Palmedo, who saw the potential for such an event, the Derby quickly gained popularity, drawing participants and spectators nationwide. In 1967, Senator Robert Kennedy participated in the Derby after running the gorge the day before in an effort to draw attention to river issues.

By 1975, the Derby was well known to whitewater boaters nationwide as Jack Hope, in his book *A River For the Living,* referred to the Derby as the country's most popular whitewater race and competition. [20] Thus, with at least part of the Hudson known for its whitewater by the mid-1970s and the business of rafting expanding in the east, it did not take long for the Hudson to be seen as a commercial run.

John Monthony of Indian Lake, who ran a marina in the area as well as being an outdoor guide, was one of the first to think that the Hudson could become a successful commercial run. In an interview with *Barkeater,* Monthony told how he had been rafting the Hudson since the early 1970s, taking a few people downriver. [21]

His son Kim talked about one of those trips, saying how Monthony got a raft in the early 1970s that he could take down the gorge. According to Kim, John didn't know that much about running a river except what he had read in a book. Like the groups from Newcomb a few years earlier, Monthony organized trips for local friends and associates, including Elmer Norton and Dane Cole. The major goal of the trip for John was just to stay off the rocks, but on one trip, Elmer helped to detract from that goal by falling out in the Narrows and almost drowning. [22] Cole stated the reason for the trips was not necessarily to run the river for whitewater, but more as a means to fish the river. In the next few years, Monthony organized other raft trips down the gorge and began to visualize the potential of the gorge as a possible commercial trip. [23]

Monthony's wife, Janet, referred to him as an "instigator" in reference to the beginning of Hudson rafting. [24] Monthony tried to make a commercial venture out of the run, but did not find much support for it, as the feeling was that "no one would pay to go down and get scared to death. It would be idiotic." [25] Monthony and his son Kim eventually became one of the outfitters that operated on the Hudson in 1983 as Indian Lake Outfitters, using two rafts. While their base was in Indian Lake, their take out was at Toag's Bed & Breakfast in North River, where they had a meal before returning to Indian Lake.

In the summer of 1974, as part of a scouting mission of eastern rivers, Ken Powley ran the Hudson, along with his wife Penny and friend George Stefanyshyn. [27] The crew began their river trip in Newcomb, making it to North River just before night after a long day. Not only was it long but it was cold, leading Powley to rule out the Hudson as a commercial run, at least for the time being. [27] The next year Powley began to run the Lehigh River in Pennsylvania, forming the company Whitewater Challengers.

In 1975, Tim Record and his cousin started running commercial trips on the Hudson. Tim had approached the DEC about these trips, with the DEC sending him an okay in the form of a letter. Record went on to be one of the original eight outfitters on the Hudson, as American Outfitters. [28]

John Monthony also played another important part in the start of commercial rafting on the Hudson. According to a phone conversation with Monthony's son Kim, John brought the potential of the Hudson River Gorge as a raft trip to the attention of an up-and-coming raft outfitter in Maine. [29] Wayne Hockmeyer's Northern Whitewater Expeditions ran the Kennebec River in Maine starting in 1976. But with the Maine winter ski season ending in March and the Kennebec rafting season not starting until June, there was always a desire to fill the two-month gap in between. Thus, with a blank two months of calendar time, any opportunity to fill the gap was welcomed.[30]

In the spring of 1978, Hockmeyer came to look at the Hudson as a possible run, starting on the Indian River. [31] Kayaking the same gorge run by so many other river runners since 1849, Hockmeyer quickly realized the potential of the Hudson River as a commercial whitewater raft run. After the run, he made plans to return to Indian Lake in 1979 with rafts, staff, and equipment for a training trip, and to further explore the Hudson River potential with local people. For that 1979 trip, the Northern group stayed in Chestertown, [32] but eventually set up a base at the Lone Birch Motel in Indian Lake when they returned for a full season in 1980. While there in 1979,

Hockmeyer also initiated contact with local people to talk about the potential for commercial rafting, as evidenced by Indian Lake Town Board records of May [33] and September [34].

Meanwhile, up in Ontario, Canada, Joe Kowalski, who had already run the Youghiogeny River with one of his college professors, started to run the Ottawa River with his new company, Wilderness Tours, in August of 1975. [35] As the business grew, Kowalski, like many others, looked for other runs to round out his season. Like a beauty parlor or a favorite fishing spot, it is hard to keep secrets in the whitewater world. When Kowalski heard about the Hudson River as a possible spring run, he went to look at it in the spring of 1979 as well.

On the home front, after taking a trip down the Cheat River in West Virginia, Bill Cromie of Albany and his friend, Rusty Brust of Corinth, became convinced of the potential of the Adirondack region for whitewater recreation. [36] After investigating the potential of several rivers, they felt sure that the Hudson, amongst others, were great runs. In September of 1978, they bought a Udesco raft, formed the company Adirondack Wildwaters, and took thirty-five people down the Sacandaga River one weekend. From that success, they awaited the coming spring season on the Hudson and Sacandaga Rivers.

During the late 1970s, other local river runners began to look at the Hudson as a potential commercial run. In an article in the *Hamilton County News*, Pat Cunningham stated 1979 as the first year his company ran the Hudson commercially, although there was no specific date given. [37] On a personal basis, Cunningham was involved with the Northwoods Club Hudson raft trips of the 1950s that Hallie Bond spoke of in her book on Adirondack boats. [38] During a personal interview, Cunningham confirmed those trips and mentioned the Foseburgs - of previous Hudson fame - having been involved with them. [39]

In the Town of Indian Lake, Hockmeyer found people with a similar problem: what to do between the end of ski and snowmobile season and the start of the summer season? Like many towns in the Adirondacks, Indian Lake is dependent economically on the influx of tourists during the year. [40] Winter season reflects strong visitor numbers, as do the summer and fall, with a two-month gap between the end of winter in March and the beginning of summer in June.

As the Hudson River's potential to fill this gap became apparent, several local business people in the town became interested and supportive. [41] John Starling, who formed Adventure Sports Rafting, said, "Before the river rafting caught on, there was nothing going on here in April and May." Lorraine Moore, who ran the Lone Birch Motel, concurred, saying "Before rafting there was nothing - everything was closed up." Bob Geandreau, who operated a colony of tourist cabins, also supported the idea of rafting to fill the two-month void and became a valuable contact with the Town Board, as president of the Indian Lake Chamber of Commerce. A great match it would prove to be.

The exact date, though, in 1979 when these commercial outfitters first ran the Hudson River Gorge had been lost in the course of thirty plus years. Records are scarce, as are firm remembrances! That being said, there is hope in matching the descriptions of the environmental conditions that were remembered with weather conditions recorded in local newspapers and river level archives from the United States Geological Service (USGS).

Not much happens on the Hudson before April, as ice can still be on the river into late March; even the log drives didn't start much before then. Most outfitters were still in transition mode from ski season at the end of March, so a weekend before April was highly unlikely. Conversely, Indian Lake Town Board records indicated that Northern Whitewater ran the Hudson before the Town Board meeting in early May. [42] Thus, the most likely dates were sometime in early April of 1979, and most likely on a weekend.

Bill Cromie did a trip on the Hudson on the April 7th weekend. [43] According to his recollection, they put in at North River on April 5th and floated down to Riparius, commenting about the beauty of the ride but feeling the rapids were not big enough for a commercial venture. The very next day, April 6th, they did the section from Riparius to The Glen and felt that, while it provided more impressive rapids, they still considered it a good "plan B" in case of too-high water in the gorge. The April 6th date, though, meant that they rafted in the midst of a major winter storm. Cromie also recalled another trip on the Hudson that April, where he did run the gorge. The level Cromie mentioned for his first Hudson Gorge trip matched with the USGS archives for an April 14th date, [44] which also confirmed the timeline for the trips on the previous weekend.

The *Hamilton County News* reported on a huge snowstorm on April 6th, leaving almost a foot of new snow in parts of the area. [45] The *Glens Falls Post Star* gave more details of the weather that weekend, reporting that not only did it snow, but there was also significant wind. The April 6th edition of the *Post Star* said that the extended forecast for the New York area was for snow, as a large low pressure system was moving across the Midwest, bringing snow and high winds. [46]

A detailed forecast in the April 7th edition reported on the impact of this storm, with near hurricane force winds in Wisconsin, Michigan, Ohio, and southwest Ontario Thursday into Friday. The report concluded with a forecast for Saturday, April 7th, of partly sunny skies but with cold, blustery conditions with temperatures in the high 30s to low 40s. On the forecast page, a high wind warning remained in effect for Friday into Saturday, with the forecast for Saturday, April 7th, being "cloudy with occasional flurries," highs in the mid 30s. [47]

By contrast, the *Post Star* reported on much different weather in the area for the weekend of April 14th. The general forecast for the area in the Saturday, April 14th edition on page one was for breezy conditions and a chance of rain, with highs in the low 50s. The longer forecast on page six gave more details, with the National Weather Service saying that rain had begun to move north from Pennsylvania, predicting a "solid day of rain" on Saturday the 14th. The ridge of high pressure that brought "pleasant weather" the last few days was moving east toward New England. The specific Adirondack area forecast for the 14th was for breezy conditions with periods of rain, high in the 50s; the percentage of rain was 80%. [48]

The April 7th forecast matched up with Joe Kowalski's recollection of the day he first arrived on the Indian River, saying that there was "lots of snow on the ground and on the road", with the weather being "overcast and cold with a few sunny breaks." [49] Wayne Hockmeyer also remembered overcast skies the day he first arrived in Indian Lake to run the Hudson, as well as the deep snow. [50] This adds credibility to April 7th being the day these two first rafted the Hudson Gorge from the Indian River, as well as Kowalski's later review of the 1979 calendar and stating that "it looks like Saturday April 7, 1979." [51] With little reason to doubt, Saturday, April 7, 1979, seems to be the date Hockmeyer and Kowalski began to run the Hudson River Gorge, ushering in the start of commercial rafting as an industry - that is, day-long trips through the Gorge that start on the Indian River - with the staff trips these two did. A full season would begin the next year, as we shall see.

As such, the USGS archives of the North Creek gauge measured the river level that day as being 4,220 cfs, making it in a high five to low six foot level. [52] Thus, conditions on that day of rafting were a medium to high river level with cold temperatures, not much sun, and some lingering wind. With bucket boats being the standard for that time, the rafters spent a cold but exciting several hours on the Hudson.

Interesting stories of that first year exist from several of these river runners. The first head-to-head "meeting" on April 7th between then-competitors Kowalski and Hockmeyer proved a memorable one for both men and makes for a good guide story! *So there they were,* as Kowalski remembered, packing up rafts and gear, driving five to six hours to the put-in on Chain Lakes Road in Indian Lake, and finding knee-deep snow from the storm the day before to drag rafts through. [53] While they struggled to get rafts to the put-in, Kowalski remembered a truck coming down the Chain Lakes Road with an attached trailer and a raft on top of the trailer - a yellow raft with the word "Northern" printed on the side. What happened next could have meant the end of Canadian-American relations as we know them today!

Put nicely, Joe described a "drop-dead gorgeous blond." referring to Suzie Hockmeyer, in the passenger seat [Alan Haley was in the seat, too, JTD]. Sitting next to them was an outrageous person in the driver's seat who rolled the window down and, seeing the Wilderness Tours raft, muttered how he could not run any river without running into another outfitter. Put another way, Joe recalled that the truck "pulled up beside him and the driver unleashed an expletive-laced tirade about having to share the river,"[54] that driver, of course, being Wayne Hockmeyer.

In a fond rebuttal years later, Wayne said that Joe "loves to tell people about the madman he met on the Hudson."[55] Like Joe, Wayne came down from Maine to look at the Hudson as a possible commercial run. Driving the snowy roads from Chestertown the day after a major snowstorm and turning down a lonely Indian Lake back road, Wayne came upon the Wilderness Tours group trying to make it to the put in through the snow. Recognizing Joe as the "guy who was following me around" on the other rivers he was running, Wayne felt that he was doing the work to look into these rivers while Joe was tagging along. Despite Joe's river background on the Ottawa, "none of this mattered to me when I met Joe at the put-in," Wayne remembered years later. All Wayne saw at that time was a copycat who was following him around, investing minimal time and effort.

In his rebuttal, Wayne confirmed the "explative-laced tirade" Kowalski spoke of. "It is very funny now. He is a close and dear friend," Hockmeyer later said of Joe, telling how the two ran the Grand Canyon together (a photo in the Northern base in Maine shows that, on one occasion, the two were even in the same dory running Lave Falls with Colorado River legend Martin Litton separating them!) and often ski together. Thirty years later, though, Wayne still feels the need to defend himself whenever the subject comes up of his and Joe's first meeting on a snow-filled back road in the Town of Indian Lake on an overcast day in April of 1979, an event which helped spawn the next generation of Hudson river runners and *their* stories.

Bill Cromie had an up-close and personal first encounter with the Hudson Gorge in 1979.[56] On the weekend of April 14th, Cromie and his business partner, Rusty Brust, put their raft on the Indian River below Lake Abanakee, rode the Indian to the Hudson River, and followed the Hudson down to North River. Cromie described the beauty of the Indian River, with "rapids simple, but the scenery was beautiful, and we were accompanied by three deer." At the junction with the

Hudson, Cromie described the water flow as "brisk," with the scenery down to Blue Ledges as "spectacular."

On the shore, ice and snow were still on the banks, icicles dangling from the Blue Ledges, and ducks flying overhead. Cromie reported that the level was 4.5 ft., and while the level could prove a challenge to canoeists, rafts would find it "reasonable," with minimum effort needed to make it down. USGS archives recorded the level at 2,000 to 2,500 cfs, confirming the date as April 14th. [57]

Cromie told of a personal encounter with the river at a ledge drop after Harris Rift [probably Greyhound or Fox Den], describing it as

> ...one ledge that was very precipitous and again caught us off guard as the suck hole backed the raft into it and I was dumped into the water. Needless to say, this was quite a shock, as the temperature had dropped and we had small snowflakes in the air. The initial impact of hitting the water left me breathless and produced a rather intensive hyperventilation that I found uncomfortable. My wetsuit served me well as I adapted to the cold promptly and was able to move toward the raft of my own volition. I was also impressed with our life jackets, which very promptly brought me to the surface and provided very high flotation. Rusty and Pat [Bill's brother, JTD] pulled me in. [58]

The trip was completed and considered a success with Cromie and Brust, like Hockmeyer and Kowalski, making plans for the next season, including attendance at the important February, 1980, Indian Lake Town Board meeting.

Still in its infancy compared to what it would soon become, rafting didn't seem to gain much notice in 1979 with many in the local community. The minutes of the Indian Lake Town Board recorded that at the regular May meeting, Bob Geandreau reported on what Hockmeyer's Northern Whitewater Expeditions did that April and the publicity that the town would get as a result of rafting. [59] Thus, the minutes indicated that Hockmeyer contacted local people about the commercial potential of the run while there in early April. Geandreu noted that the Town would have to plow the Chain Lakes Road in order for the rafters to get to the put-in. The major concern that the Town Board had was the amount of insurance that Northern carried and the liability of the Town for providing releases.

The minutes of the September, 1979, meeting recorded that Geandreu asked that the Town Board approve raft trips on the Hudson River by Northern Whitewater Expeditions. A letter from Northern presented at the meeting indicated that they carried $500,000 in insurance and included the Town of Indian Lake. Northern was also willing to pay the Town $500 for extra plowing to the put-in, indicating Hockmeyer's desire to work with the Town to make the trip work. The minutes record that the town attorney, Ed Stewart, saw no problem with the legal aspect of the Town's involvement with rafting. [60]

All this effort on Geandreu's part underscored the important role he played in the establishment of commercial rafting in Indian Lake. John Vorhees, who was on the Indian Lake Chamber of Commerce Board at the time, credited Geandreu with a leading effort in the establishment of commercial rafting on the Hudson River. [61] Geandreu, who owned a colony of rental cabins, knew the importance of the tourist trade to Indian Lake. While some were only able to see rafting as an adventure, Geandreu saw it as a business and a real long-term boon to the local economy. He became "the political spearhead" for rafting and was the one who "talked the board into really getting behind it." As such, Geandreus' name appears in the Town Board records as a prominent advocate for rafting, as well as being the lead person on several written Indian Lake Chamber of Commerce documents about rafting. Lorraine Moore also seconded this observation, saying Geandreu was the lead person in working with the Town Board on behalf of rafting. [62]

There was very little interest paid to commercial rafting on the Hudson by the *Hamilton County News* (*HCN*) that year as well. All through the month of April, there was no mention of rafting in any feature articles and no advertisements for rafting. An advertisement for the Town of Indian Lake in the *HCN* Hudson River Whitewater Derby supplement that year did not list rafting among the attractions and activities that Indian Lake offered tourists. [63] The supplement had two articles by Sheila Satterlee on rafting in general, with one describing what it was like to raft [64] and one on how popular rafting had become. [65] Neither specifically mentioned rafting on the Hudson River.

Before rafting on the Hudson River could become commercially feasible, though, the problem of accessing the gorge had to be addressed. The outfitters that did the run in 1979 realized that in order to make the run a commercial success, the Hudson had to be accessed from the Indian River. The additional distance from Newcomb would take too much time and the water levels in the Cedar River were unreliable; securing water releases for the Indian River access from Lake Abanakee was crucial.

Through 1979, though, any trip down the Indian to the Hudson involved a certain degree of chance that the Lake Abanakee dam would be open. Or one could track down the Town Water Department to ask for a release, as scheduled releases for the purpose of rafting were not established. [66] For rafting to be marketed to paying guests, there needed to be a little more certainty.

The Lake Abanakee dam itself was completed in November of 1951, [67] with the Town of Indian Lake making releases from the dam in order to maintain water levels on the lake. [68] Rick Fenton wrote about a conversation he had with former Indian Lake supervisor, Dick Purdue, in 1991 about the releases and recorded it in a handwritten notebook. Purdue said that "Before rafting, releases were made in response to fluctuating Abanakee levels" as well as any water released from upstream at Indian Lake. [69] The Town needed to maintain a minimum level in Abanakee to cover water supply intakes, and even with a newer pump system, there was still a concern for certain water levels to be maintained on the lake. Such a concern explained the interest the Town Board always had in establishing certain criteria for maintaining water levels in Abanakee during releases for rafting.

Fenton mentioned that outfitters who ran the Hudson in 1979 - presumably Wayne Hockmeyer and possibly others - first approached the Indian Lake Chamber of Commerce about having regularly scheduled releases, probably while they were there in April of 1979. [70] This explained Bob Geandreu going before the Town Board in May and September that year to report on the rafting activity of that year, setting the table for the important February, 1980, Town Board meeting where a full-fledged proposal was made by several outfitters requesting a regular schedule of releases from Lake Abanakee to facilitate raft trips.

An article on page twelve of the *Hamilton County News* reported on the February meeting, when the rafters addressed this realization. The board heard "presentations by four whitewater outfitters" who planned to have raft trips on the Hudson River between "April 10 and May 31". [71] Bob Geandreau introduced the outfitters to the board and the outfitters presented their raft plan, including how it would impact the local economy. The board agreed to release water for "one-half to one hour per day each morning" during the season to help insure a successful trip down the Indian River to the Hudson River. The board also placed several conditions on the releases, with an eye toward limiting the Town's liability and the potential effects of the releases on Lake Abanakee water levels.

The Indian Lake Town Board minutes fill in some of the details of this historic meeting. [72] The minutes recorded that "several men" were present to ask the Town to release water on the Indian River to facilitate raft trips on the Hudson, which would help extend their raft season. The record lists three of the men specifically: Wayne Hockmeyer of Northern, Jay Schurman of Unicorn Rafting, and Joe Kowalski of Wilderness Tours. The outfitters sought to access the Hudson by way of the Indian River and needed a release of water from Lake Abanakee to do so. They estimated that there would be between 100-125 people per weekend from April 10th-May 31st. To avoid liability to other users of the river, notices of the schedule of releases were published and posted.

In response, Ernie Blanchard, who was the head of the Water Department for the Town, said that the dam could be opened on such a schedule and Tom Mahoney, Highway Superintendent, said that the road to the put-in could be maintained to facilitate access for rafting. Councilman Dominic DeFilippo wanted assurances that taxpayers would not bear the cost of repairs to the dam in case of a breakdown caused by the releases and that the releases would be "compatible" with fishing. Wayne Hockmeyer answered by saying that the rafters would be bused in and then the buses would leave, that the outfitters would police the area, and that the outfitters would help pay the costs of any breakdown of the dam. Two of the outfitters eventually operated a base in the town of Indian Lake, with Northern at the Lone Birch Motel and Wilderness Tours at the Adirondack Trails Motel and the American Legion. [73]

The board approved the proposal, with Councilman Bob Gates offering the following resolution, which was seconded by Councilman Herman Hutchins and carried unanimously:

> Resolved that the Town of Indian Lake will maintain Chain Lakes Road and provide regular daily releases of water from the Lake Abanakee Dam for a period of from one-half hour to one hour a day for the period of April 10 through May 31, 1980 for the purpose of facilitating the use of the Indian River by outfitters taking people on river tours provided that prior to March 15, 1980 the outfitters
>
> 1. Provide satisfactory evidence that Indian Lake is an additional insured on their insurance policy in the amount of $300,000.
>
> 2. Demonstrate that their insurers are qualified in New York State.
>
> 3. Agree to clean up any litter resulting from their activities.
>
> 4. Agree to obtain waivers of liability from all customers.
>
> 5. Erect signs at the Abanakee Dam clearly warning of the planned releases of water.

> Resolved further that the planned releases of water be
> advertised by the Town Board in the *Hamilton County
> News* for two (2) weeks preceding the beginning of
> river activities.
> Provided further that the Town Board reserve the
> right to terminate planned releases of water at its dis-
> cretion. [74]

This became the first agreement between the town and the raft
outfitters who ran the Hudson River, setting the framework around
which raft trips were scheduled and operated even thirty years later.

Several personal accounts exist from the early years that help
describe what it was like to raft on the Hudson at that time from a
customer's perspective and perhaps can give a sense of what it was
like those first few years. One of the first accounts of the river trip
itself was published in the *Hamilton County News* and read more
like an advertisement for Hockmeyer's outfitter. [75] The article talked
about how the Hudson River trip gave a similar raft experience as on
western rivers.

According to the article, the "thrills" of riding western rivers in
a raft had "met their match," as crowds of Hudson rafters had taken
the ride. Trips were taking place for the second year and the turn-
out was "superb," with further trips planned through mid-May. The
trip started out just below the Lake Abanakee dam, with a release
that gave the rafts "a good start." Lunch was at Blue Ledges, with
the trip continuing from there to North River with wetsuits, PFDs,
and paddles provided. All reports were that it is "a superb trip from
start to finish, with beautiful scenery." The article also happened to
include a note to contact Wayne Hockmeyer for more information!

Two years later, Jim Briggs gave a more detailed account of how
the day progressed in the *Hamilton County News*:

> The customers begin to arrive about 8:00 am but the
> Lone Birch Motel has been busy long before. Rafts and
> related paraphernalia are being loaded on trailers. A
> line has formed at the Motel's garage where customers

are being fitted for wetsuits. An army tent has been erected so the rafters can change into their wetsuits. They emerge looking like frogmen with neophrene booties instead of flippers... Shortly everybody is fitted and the rafters-to-be gather around as the head guide or fleet admiral gives instruction. [76]

The talk consisted of instructions on what to do in case rafters fell into the river and other general safety instructions. Mason Smith, in *Adirondack Life,* gave more details of the Northern pre-trip preparation and safety talk, including authentic Maine dialect:

We had been advised to wear bathing suits under our clothes. In the dressing tents we pulled on good new wetsuits with full sleeved jackets. Some of us bought wetcell booties too, to wear under the sneakers which are required in the fabric bottomed boats. Over the suit the company's brochure advised wool sweaters and a shell or anorak and a wool cap and gloves...

There was going to be a "lectua" first as the Mainiacs pronounced it. Charlie Hathaway seemed to be the head guide. He stood up on the flowerbed. He was holding a clipboard which he occasionally swung up but didn't really look at. His speech contained information of importance which the ho-hum recitation would deny: how to catch our neighbors when they got knocked out of the raft. How to float and how to breath when they didn't catch us. Then he said "We do naught take you down the riva. You take yourselves down the riva." And he told us how we would be sitting without attachment of any kind upon the round inflated sides of the raft leaning overboard to paddle. "Reach out, grab a piece of the riva, and pull it toward you." Each raft would have an experienced guide in the stern, and he would shout commands, and the safety of our trip would depend on our executing them, because we and our paddles were his only means of controlling "where the raft is in the riva."

He said, "Now I have to read you a statement for our insurance company." He didn't read it His eyes wandered skyward as he droned it out. "People have been and will be hurt on float trips with this company. This company assumes no liability whatsoeva." Good, nothing to worry about, let's go. He divided us into groups and assigned each group to a boat, and we climbed into a nice old Canadian Blue Bird school bus, painted conservation green, that would take us to the put -in. [77]

Reporter Mike Houston provided an excellent description of riding the rapids on a raft trip with Bill Cromie's Adirondack Wildwaters in an article in the *Utica-Observer Dispatch*:

We screamed some more and I turned around to see how the rafts behind us handled the exhilarating experience. As if by command, another mighty stretch of rapids was upon us, tossing me quickly to the floor. The two men in front of the raft greeted its frothy power with their faces. We laughed and yelled loudly, like children on their inaugural roller coaster.

The feeling made any amusement park ride seem petty. This was Mother Nature, the real thing. We were all wet – the raft was already filled with water above our ankles – but it didn't matter. I no longer felt cold...I felt alive.

The raft lifted into the chilly air, and suddenly those sitting up front were much higher than the rest of us. The swirling eddy sucked the back of the raft down for a second, then spit it out for its next challenge. The raft hit another set of rapids and lifted again, giving us the feeling that it was going to split. It didn't, only jettisoned us ahead for some more merriment amidst loud shouts that we were lost in the dense forest.

We bailed water from the raft and headed down a river bolstered by scenery too beautiful for a post card. [78]

After paddling some and seeing trees, ravens, steep-sided ledges, and no houses, Houston commented:

No one spoke. We only gazed and absorbed... The brisk weather and grey skies seemed to accentuate the pristine scenery and highlite the individual senses. It seemed like a December day, but it smelled green, like spring was in the offing. For a moment, I was glad it wasn't warm and sunny. It probably would have detracted from the beauty. [79]

One of the traditions that Wayne Hockmeyer brought with him to the Hudson was that of the "Maine Guide Lunch," where the guides stopped the trip and cooked lunch for the guests. [80] When Hockmeyer first started running the Kennebec, the trip motored across Indian Pond to Harris Dam, where the Kennebec run starts, with the trip stopping at the dam for lunch. A *Yankee* magazine article by Mel Allen listed the menu of the trip as steak, roasted potatoes, roasted onions, and steaming coffee, all cooked over an open fire. [81] Northern guide Alan Haley confirmed this as the menu on the Hudson, with the trip stopping at various places - most notably Blue Ledges and the confluence of the Hudson and Boreas Rivers. [82] As it was a full cookout lunch, the whole process took almost one hour to complete. By contrast, most lunches on the Hudson in 2014 are pre-made and are done in less than thirty minutes.

Several other outfitters followed suit and had lunch out on the river, with the menu and location varying depending on the outfitter.

In an article in *Adirondack Life,* Alice Gilborn talked about the lunch stop on her trip with Pat Cunningham's Hudson River Rafting:

> At 11 am we pulled out for lunch on a bank opposite a towering wall of blue-grey rock. Blue Ledge. This was Cunninghams's particular stopping place, chosen by prior agreement among the outfitters. (At least one outfitter does not stop at all, preferring to run straight through and reward his customers with lunch at the end of the trip) A pair of ravens, whose nest we could see in a crack, wheeled and called above us. I had trouble standing on firm ground and for the first time felt a chill through my damp covering.
>
> Pat planted a stick in the sand at the edge of the water. He gathered a few pieces of wood stashed behind a tree, then built a fire on the ground against a rock to warm water for soup and coffee. Welcome as the fire was on this cold day, Pat does not always make one... Our meal was also floated in: cold cuts, bread, cheese, nuts, fruit and candy bars sealed in a watertight bag lashed on the raft. All the time Pat kept an eye on his improvised gauge, and since the river shrank steadily away from it, we did not linger long. [83]

By 1987, this changed for Cunningham to a lunch of GORP (good ole raisins and peanuts) and hot chocolate, with the hot meal after the trip. [84]

Other companies also tried the extended lunch stop, with mixed reviews. Wilderness Tours tried the on-river lunch during their first year, but abandoned it by their second year, opting instead for an after-trip meal at the Indian Lake American Legion. [85] By 1982, Jim Briggs reported that Wilderness Tours gave a big breakfast and a hot meal after the trip.[86] Eastern River Expeditions had a steak cookout after the trip at the cabins in the back of Marty's in Indian Lake. [87]

Unicorn began with a similar lunch as Northern, stopping at the confluence of the Boreas and Hudson Rivers or at OK Slip Brook. [88] Hank Rose, who guided for Unicorn, noted the problem of guests getting cold with a prolonged stop, noting, too, that when there was still snow on the trees, the meltwater dripped into the potato salad! [89] The Unicorn brochure also listed lobster lunch for their Maine trips, but steak on the Hudson, with side trimmings and both dutch oven deserts and old fashioned ice cream makers. [90]

Company brochures also give information on lunches. In a brochure dated 1982, Whitewater World did not show a menu but mentioned they have a "streamside lunch break" on their trip. [91] Wilderness Raft simply listed a riverside lunch, but no specific menu items. [92] Adirondack River Outfitters (ARO) offered a "hearty and nutritious shore lunch with an open fire and warm beverage" for both their Hudson and Moose River trips and a "warm beverage and light snack" after the trip. [93]

The common complaint about an extended lunch out on the Hudson River during April was that it made guests cold. Guide Lori Benton [94] went on her first Hudson trip with her Girl Scout troop, doing the run with Northern. She gave an account of a Northern lunch break. The group stopped "at the confluence of the Boreas River and they first started a fire brewed coffee in a big old pot and threw some eggs in, we were freezing!! Did I mention that? They cooked steaks on the open fire and we were grateful to have them, but more anxious to get on out of there". Jay Schurman of Unicorn eventually concluded that extended lunches at that time of year were not such a good idea.[95] The DEC didn't think so either, as by 1985, they prohibited the cookout lunches due to the environmental impact.

Another view of the rafting experience of that time was found in a survey done in September of 1983 as part of the information gathering for the Unit Management Plan by the DEC. Dick Cipperly mailed out a survey to rafting guests, asking about the experience the individual had. [96] Included were questions pertaining to the use of the land and the number of rafters, as well as conditions, personal impressions, and profiles. Over sixty surveys were returned, with several having personal comments written on the back. The survey provides an excellent snapshot of the rafting experience at that time.

Most of the forms list April, 1983, as the date of the trip, with some listing May, while others weren't sure. All nine outfitters were represented, with Unicorn and Wilderness Tours having the most returned forms. Respondents gave a variety of weather conditions for their trip, with the most predominant weather feature mentioned being cold, either by itself or in combination with other features on forty-four of the forms. In a later question, most said that even though they were cold, they enjoyed the experience. Group size varied from one to eighteen; the number of rafts on a trip ranged from one to eleven.

There was a fairly even split between experienced rafters and newcomers, with most saying they had heard of the trip from a friend. When asked what they enjoyed most about the trip, forty-four said it was the natural beauty of the gorge. When asked if they thought that there were too many people on the river, forty-eight said there was just the right amount, with eleven saying that there were too many. Personal comments on the back of the forms varied, with most complimenting the individual guides and the organizations. Several comments said there may be a need to place a limit on the numbers allowed on the river. [97] More on that in a later chapter.

The raft experience did not always end when the rafts and guests returned to their bases. With the adrenaline and testosterone still on full throttle, many raft guests and guides relived their river experience in downtown Indian Lake at the Oak Barrel and/or at Marty's. The atmosphere was, as Wayne Failing described it, "the wild, wild west," with guides and guests hanging out in groups like the Jets and the Cribbs from the musical *West Side Story*. [98]

In the Oak Barrel, as it was known then, owners Tom and Cathy Scully eventually showed video that Tom shot on the Indian River from a point just downstream from the present day Photographer's Stand, where trip photos are often taken. Other activities at the bar, though, were not always as sedate as watching videos! Gary Staab recalled pile-ons, whipped cream incidents, women flashing, and a general party atmosphere.

In one incident Staab described stuffing one guide of small size in a decorative canoe that hung from the Oak Barrel wall, strapping him down, and leaving him for the night. [99] Wayne Failing remembered another instance when a guide was hoisted to the ceiling using rope and carabineer and left dangling. When Cathy Scully came out from the kitchen and saw the guide dangling from the ceiling, Failing remembered her shaking her head in both amusement and amazement before returning to the kitchen. [100]

Wayne Hockmeyer retold an interesting story of one of his guides riding a bike down Main Street of Indian Lake on the way to the Oak Barrel. He described it as follows:

> When you went into Indian Lake on Friday and Saturday it was the wild west. I remember one night we got done with the trip all our guests were going downtown and by now Marty's and the Oak Barrel both were full. I remember that we (the Northern staff, JTD) were just going to town. We were walking in and I remember Carl Otley (a Northern guide, JTD), an older guy about 50, we called him Charleton Heston because he looked just like him, had tied one with his Pina Collates. We had come into town and he comes peddling behind us on a bicycle to catch up. I don't know whether he borrowed it from Lorraine (Moore, JTD) or what, but he comes into town in the middle of the road and he's weaving all over the place in traffic. I was screaming at him, I go "We know he's gonna be killed!" I'll never forget it because we were all chasing him down Main Street and he's weaving like a drunk and there's traffic, not a lot, but cars are coming. We were all chasing him to catch him. We finally catch him and pulled him off his bike. We got him into the Oak Barrel and he fell asleep on the bar. It was crazy and we had crazy people coming in. [101]

Some of this party and relaxed feeling spilled over into the morning of a trip, as Staab remembered practical jokes. On one occasion, a raft company arrived at the put-in for a raft trip to find their rafts nowhere in sight. Another group of guides from another company took the rafts and put them in the water. In another instance, a raft company came to the put-in only to find one of their rafts dangling from a tree as a response to a previous joke. Staab did note that, despite the jesting, rafts were never maliciously tampered with or deflated. [102] It is interesting to note, too, that, according to the recollections of the Town Judge at that time, Ken Cannan Sr., there was not a corresponding increase in the number of cases or tickets due to rafters brought before him.[103] River runners had a good time, but, overall, it did not seem to get out of hand. Some of the townspeople resented the corruption of their peaceful town and bar, but others joined in the party. [104]

The popularity of commercial rafting on the Hudson grew quickly. In his first full year of rafting the Hudson, Hockmeyer reported having between sixty and eighty people per day, figuring the total for the year to be several hundred. [105] These numbers rose to hundreds per day, as Gilborn reported that one outfitter reported almost 400 on one day in 1981. [106] Hockmeyer estimated that the total numbers of guests by 1982 was between 4,000 and 5,000 per year, along with numerous private rafters, kayakers, and canoeists.[107] As there was no Town personnel taking records during the first few years at the put-in ramp, accurate attendance records are scarce.

Ben Woodard, who was the on-river assistant ranger at that time, provided one of the first snapshots of the numbers of early river runners and private boaters on the Hudson, based on personal observation. Woodard listed the outfitters he saw, along with the number of rafters each had, for two weekends in May of 1982. He also included the numbers of private boaters he saw and problems he observed.

For the May 1-3 weekend, he listed several outfitters having trips, with numbers totaling 345 on May 1st and 396 on May 2nd. Both Northern and American River Expeditions had overnight trips that weekend as well, with those numbers being ten and eight respectively. Private boaters numbered from fourteen on May 1st to forty-one on May 2nd. The next weekend Woodard recorded was May 7-9 and it showed a similar trend, with numbers for individual outfitters ranging from nine to eighty, with 409 total on May 8th, 400 plus on May 9th, and private boaters up to sixty-four. [108] While these records may not be complete, they showed that by 1982, there were some very busy weekends on the Hudson.

In 1983, when the Town began having Barry Hutchins at the put-in, [109] a more complete and accurate record became available, although only for the period from April 9th to May 8th. Weekends continued to be large, as shown below:

*April 9-10: 469, 206

*April 15, 16, 17: 9, 734, 512

*April 22, 23, 24: 113, 709, 383

*April 30, May 1: 693, 151

*May 7, 8: 493, 190

*Town of Indian Lake 1983 Raft Attendance Records [110]

The number of outfitters grew as well, going from the nine listed on Woodard's 1982 observation to eighteen listed on the 1983 sheet, including Whitewater Challengers, who did not run until fall of that year.

While 1984 records could not be found, 1985 showed an even larger growth in numbers and outfitters:

*April 13, 14: 788, 611

*April 20, 21: 998, 634

*April 27, 28: 1031, 737

*May 4, 5: 1001, 667

*Town of Indian Lake 1985 Raft Attendance Records [111]

The number of outfitters had also grown to twenty-three by then.

One of the major influences in the large increase of Hudson rafters was the publication of an article in the *New York Times* that
described the trip. [112] The article, by William Wallace, in the May
17, 1982 edition, described how rafting had grown in several eastern states after flourishing out west. Several of the more popular
eastern rivers that are run commercially were mentioned, including
the Hudson in New York. In the context of a raft trip on the Hudson,
Wallace described several aspects of a raft trip, including gear, price,
and season. He also mentioned how risk seemed to be a motive for
many to participate in certain outdoor activities and that rafting
gave a good mix of risk and safety. [113] Thus, a person could have an
exciting and adventurous trip while knowing that there was some
measure of safety woven into the adventure.

With the ability of the *Times* to reach a large metropolitan audi-
ence, the article helped to popularize rafting and make known the
availability of a major whitewater river trip within close proximity
to the New York metropolitan area. This potential also proved to be
a threat to some of the established Hudson outfitters, as other raft
companies, who marketed to the New York-New Jersey area, looked
to add the Hudson River to their schedules. More on that later.

By the mid-1980s, rafting on the Hudson River had attained a
great degree of notoriety. In 1987, *Canoe Magazine* rated the Hudson
trip as one of the top ten raft trips in the United States. [114] In 1986,
the New York State legislature declared Indian Lake to be the
Whitewater Capital of New York. The first advertisements for rafting appeared in the *Hamilton County News* in April, 1982, [115] with
Adirondack Life featuring advertisements for several outfitters in
the May/June 1982 edition. [116] The American Motel in North Creek,
located on the present-day Cooperfield Inn site, began to offer special
raft packages to guests. Local musicians Mitch Frazier and Mike
Leddick were featured performers in North Creek during raft season. [117] Truly, rafting on the Hudson River had shifted out of low gear
and was accelerating up to highway speed!

While the numbers grew for commercial rafting, problems and
concerns grew as well with regards to the impact the industry was
having on the town of Indian Lake. One such problem was that

although rafting had been greeted with open arms by many in Indian Lake, some were not so thrilled. When the Town Board published and made known its intention to provide releases from Lake Abanakee for rafting, some residents expressed concern. An article in the *Hamilton County News,* dated March 12, 1980, reported on the Town Board meeting of March 3rd when the board discussed two letters expressing concern over the proposed releases. The board agreed that there would be no noticeable effect and that the Town would monitor releases to guarantee no adverse effect on the lake. [118]

Gilborn cited concerns of anglers who plied their craft on the Indian River. The Town Board heard from several anglers "who claimed to have been swept off their feet by the sudden release from the dam". [119] A sign at the dam gave the dates and times of the releases and Ernie Blanchard, who opened the gate, checked to see if there was anyone downstream before raising the gate. Ernie, according to his daughter, Autumn Blanchard, went so far as to patrol the Chain Lakes Road to check for and warn anglers of the release before he opened the dam. [120]

Indian Lake Supervisor Barry Hutchins remembered having to represent the views of the local fish and game club, as its president, while seeing the potential rafting had for the town. [121] Both Hutchins and local retired log driver LeRoy Spring were on hand at the May 11, 1987, Town Board meeting, representing Indian Lake-Blue Mountain Lake Fish and Game Club, to express concern of the effect of weekday releases for rafting. [122] This continued to be an issue, as Jennings reported in the *HCN* that Spring expressed concern that the releases for rafting were exposing some pike spawn and might have been a shock to fish. Spring claimed that there appeared to be a ten-inch drop in the lake level after a release. Jennings reported that the DEC failed to follow up on a proposed study of the effects of releases. The Town Board approved an increased stocking of fish to compensate. [123]

Ellen Craig reported that in 1992, the DEC conducted a thorough fish population study, catching and netting fish to record their size, health, and the diversity of species. At the Town Board meeting on March 19, 1993, senior DEC biologist Rich Preal was on hand to present the results, saying to the assembly that declining pike populations were due more to natural conditions than the releases for rafting.

Preal told the board - and an interested crowd of about twenty-five - that it was not uncommon for a dammed river that created a reservoir like Lake Abanakee to see excellent fish growth for the first ten to fifteen years after the impoundment was in place, only to see this growth rate level off and decline as the aquatic life adjusted. Thus, while some fish loss might have been attributed to rafting releases, "the natural change in nutrient conditions in Lake Abanakee is a bigger factor," and similar bodies of water had experienced the same pike problems as Lake Abanakee. Preal also cited the 1975 Lake Abanakee fish study, also done by the DEC, which found that the "pike population was not large and growth of the species was not good" even before the start of commercial rafting in 1980. In short, as the nutrient levels in a lake go, so does the fish population. [124]

The effects of rafting on Hudson River fishing was once again raised recently by Jim Nash, as he felt that releases for summer rafting were stressing trout populations past their safe point, reducing the ability of the river to sustain a viable trout population. [125] Mike Hill reported on a study that disputed Nash's claim. [126]

In the study, conducted by researchers from Cornell University, a combination of temperature readings and tracking of trout with implanted transmitters was used to monitor trout movement to see if trout found the cold water pockets they needed. The group found that the Indian and Hudson Rivers were warm to begin with, and as such, "are not a great summer habitat for trout even without the releases". The complete study, authored by Baldigo, Mulvihill, Ernst, and Boisvert,[127] can be reviewed at http//pubs.usgs.gov/sir/2010/5223.

One of the ways that outfitters addressed local anxiety over rafting early on was to institute a local's day when local residents could run the river with an outfitter on selected days for a reduced price. [128] Many Indian Lake residents took advantage of the offer, with the program continuing on for many years after. As of 2012, Adirondack River Outfitters still advertises a local's day in the *Adirondack Express*.

A unique way of building relations with the town residents and educating them about rafting was a school program put on by Eastern River Expeditions. Here the outfitter visited the Indian Lake School and did a presentation to students on rafting. Eastern manager Joey Fabin outlined the content of the program as dealing with raft safety, equipment, proper paddling, and general procedures. [129] A photo in the *HCN* showed students dressed in PFDs and helmets, sitting in a raft and being instructed on proper paddling. [130]

Including the town in the rafting process and compensating them for the effort of providing releases was part of the plan that Wayne Hockmeyer had from the beginning. Following a formula that had proved successful on the Kennebec, Hockmeyer felt that including the town and its residents in the business of rafting made good sense, and part of that inclusion was compensating the Town for the releases. [131]

The proposed compensation was based on the number of guests for each outfitter and helped the Town with the cost of managing the releases and, eventually, the maintenance of the access site. This was important regardless of "who owned the water," as "it was a good deal" for all. As Hockmeyer pointed out, the Town provided a service that allowed the existence of the raft business. Hockmeyer proposed this fee as early as March, 1981, at a Town Board meeting. [132] By March of 1982, the Town Board voted to charge outfitters a $2-per-rafter fee, to be collected in four payments. [133] While some of the outfitters objected to this fee, most were open to it.

Among the other issues that appeared was a concern about littering in the gorge. Gilborn expressed this, seeing the possibility of litter along the river corridor. [134] Proskine, though, wrote in his guide book about the river being very free of litter, with the rafters doing an excellent job of keeping the river shores clean. [135] Jay Schurman expressed awareness on the rafters part to keep the river clean, saying, "Part of the package we sell is wilderness". Gilborn also quoted Pat Cunningham expressing a similar view when he said, "Everything that goes in, goes out. If not, we cut our throats." [136] Dick Cipperly of the DEC remembered concerns for the impact of on-river cook-out lunches from concerned citizens who hiked into Blue Ledges.

The eventual solution was that these lunches were eliminated by the DEC by 1986. [137]

Supervisor Dick Purdue stated that the quality of the available guides was an early concern. [138] Many out-of-state outfitters brought a core of their own guides, supplementing them with local people. Outfitters from the area, of course, filled their staff with local people. However, in order to guide on the Hudson at the time, the only thing needed was a license that could be picked up from a local DEC forest ranger for a few dollars. As Michael Whiting of Whitecap Rafting, based at Friends Lake Inn, described it, "a licensed guide could mean that a person only filled out a DEC application." [139] Also, Ken Cannan Sr., the Town Justice at the time, reported that often guides shared one license amongst several of them. [140]

That being said, the fact that there were several near-misses on the river led some to believe that more than just a $2 piece of paper was necessary to improve the quality and safety of the guides on the river. With rangers reporting back to the DEC concerning river conditions such as these, licensing was soon on the DEC radar screen. [141]

In response, many of the companies provided training for their guides, such as that provided by Northern Whitewater Expeditions. Guide Lori Benton remembered going to Maine one summer as a teenager to train as a raft guide for Eastern. The course was two weeks long and cost $200. [142] Guide Doug Cole remembered having to train new recruits from scratch. [143] Unicorn advertised several guide training workshops in their 1982 brochure, including one specifically for women, all of which took place in Maine. Participants received training in "the fundamental skills of reading whitewater and maneuvering rafts, emergency procedures, equipment maintenance, wilderness cookery, and the finer points of guiding safe, enjoyable raft trips." The cost ranged from $375 to $420 per person, with the minimum age listed as twelve. [144]

Jim Briggs reported on a guide training program put on by the Cornell Cooperative Extension Office. The program included training in safety and first aid, "techniques of tourist hospitality," and Hudson River ecology and geology. The course was sixteen hours total and was offered over two weekends. Graduates were referred to outfitters and were able to go right into river training, having attained a common pool of skills and knowledge. [145]

Another *HCN* article by Briggs detailed other topics covered in the guide training. The first week of the program began with an introduction and a rationale for the course, going on to cover the history of the Hudson River Gorge given by Hallie Bond of the Adirondack Museum. The ecology and geology of the region was given in separate sessions. The second week of the program covered a discussion of how to read the river and whitewater techniques, given by Jerry Marquis of Wilderness Tours. There was also a presentation on elements of tourism and the promotion of the region. DEC forest rangers taught a session on search and rescue procedures and Mark Malcoff presented a video on cold water survival. Participants were charged only for the course materials and the coffee that was provided. A note at the end of the article stated that the course was not required, but attendance could help participants pass the guide exam that would be part of the new DEC guide licensing program. [146]

The DEC looked at revamping the guide license program as early as 1982. A DEC memo dated June 10, 1982, mentioned the formation of a "guide licensing committee" that would look at "determining credentials for water related guiding". [147] A response to the 1982 Gilborn article in *Adirondack Life* from Tom Monroe of the DEC also indicated the desire of the DEC to "initiate a close examination" of whitewater activity and its impacts, and that the DEC would work with outfitters on the licensing issue. [148] Thus, while regulations from this examination would be large in scope, the process would also zero in specifically on the quality and training of guides.

The newly formed Hudson River Professional Outfitters Association (the Association) was interested in this examination and any regulations that might affect the budding raft industry collectively and individually. The body of an Association letter written by Wayne Hockmeyer outlined the position of the Association on several key issues under consideration by the DEC and the Guide Regulating Committee. [149] The letter centered on outfitter representation on the committee, new requirements for guide licensing, and safety regulations for running the river. The need for safety regulations should be viewed in light of the "Black Sunday" incident on the Hudson less than a month before, where a major search and rescue operation took place for two missing rafters.

The other positions Hockmeyer detailed were the concern of the affects of certain licensing proposals on the guides themselves, such as having guides take physicals, fingerprinting, criminal background checks, and written exams. The Association felt that because of the short season and the hardship that some of the proposals would place on guides and would-be guides, such regulation could affect the quality of the guide in the raft and, as such, the guests' experience. Hockmeyer concluded the letter with a statement of assurance that the interests of the Association would be well represented by Mark Brown of the DEC, to whom the letter is addressed.[150]

A note from Bob Geandreau in the corner of the Hockmeyer letter indicated that Hockmeyer was at a meeting in Lake Placid several weeks earlier, demanding that he be on a committee, probably referring to the Guide Regulating Committee. The corner note begins by stating that Tom - presumably Tom Monroe of the DEC - saw Wayne at the Lake Placid meeting trying to get on the Regulating Committee. In the second line, Geandreau stated that he felt that Monroe was someone that would help ensure a favorable committee outcome. [151]

A follow-up letter dated May 24, 1982, written by Geandreau and addressed to Hockmeyer, tried to assure Hockmeyer, and the other outfitters, that the Town had the outfitters' best interests at heart and that the people involved with the process would be able to produce a favorable document for rafting. The letter seemed to have been written in response to Hockmeyer's appearance in Lake Placid and his demand to be on the committee. [152]

By 1986, the DEC overhauled the entire guide license program, making it mandatory for guides in several outdoor recreation activities to have a DEC-issued license. The need to overhaul the licensing program probably had as much to do with the overall proliferation of these activities in general as it had with increased rafting numbers. New state regulations now stipulated that guides be "well trained in their skill, as well as first aid, CPR, and cold water rescue". [153]

The *HCN* reported that under the new system, there would be six categories of guiding: hunting, fishing, camping, hiking, canoeing, and whitewater rafting, with the DEC establishing guidelines for each category. There would be an exam as well as a fee for a permanent license, which was good for five years. Candidates for a license also had to show proof of passing a physical exam and have current first aid and CPR certifications. [154] The revamped program became the framework around which guides are licensed today and provided a minimum standard of qualification for each category.

New regulations such as these were not welcomed by all, as Hockmeyer outlined in his letter to the DEC in 1982 on behalf of the Association. While some of the specifics have already been mentioned, several of the points will be reaffirmed. Primary for Hockmeyer was that in order for the core of Northern guides, on which he depended to legally guide the Hudson, they would have to make the ten-hour drive from Maine just for the hour or two it took to complete the exam. Other out-of-state outfitters, such as Wilderness Tours, also faced this daunting task of having their guides travel to New York to take the exam, validate their physicals and certifications, and pay the fee, putting out-of-state applicants at a disadvantage. Hockmeyer saw this as needless overreaching through regulation by the DEC, as up to that point, the feeling was that the outfitters themselves had done a more-than-adequate job of policing and regulating the growing industry. [155]

Hockmeyer pursued this in his letter to the DEC dated October 15, 1984, on the overuse issue. In the sections of that letter that deal with guides and outfitter licensing, Hockmeyer raised the question of the validity of written tests producing competent guides, feeling that "only on-river testing is a fool proof method." He also went on to say that such a method was not practical due to the high number of candidates to be given this opportunity and that, given the lack of fatalities up to that point, "one would have to question whether such an expensive, involved procedure is really necessary or desirable." He concluded by suggesting that the outfitters be licensed and charged with determining the competency of guide applicants and then be held responsible for their guides' performance. [156]

Equipment in the early years of rafting on the Hudson was generally the same as it is now, with a few differences. One of the most prominent differences were the rafts, which had solid rubber floors and were commonly called "bucket boats". Stops were necessary after each rapid to bail the water out using plastic buckets, with crews spending several minutes in the process. Whitewater Challengers guide Linea Newman recalled that bucket boats were great in high water because the extra weight of the water in the raft made them more stable going over big waves. [157] The very fact that the raft was filled with water, though, made it more difficult to steer, as the increased weight pushed the raft deeper in the water, creating more resistance. Newman also recalled that it was not uncommon for rafts to miss an eddy stop at high water as a result of the steering challenges. Challengers guide Tom Ebert, on the other hand, fondly recalled using the bucket boats. [158]

One of the more unique rafts used on the Hudson at that time was the Metzler, used by Pat Cunningham's operation. Not only was it a self-bailer, meaning that the floor allowed water to drain out, but it featured a wooden rudder, called a "tiller," which was attached to the rear of the raft and used by the guide to steer, much like the large wood rafts on the lower Hudson in the early days of logging. Several photos in the Gilborn article showed this setup very clearly, with the long-handled rudder attached in the stern with the turned up ends of the tubes. The guide stood in the rear and pushed or pulled the handle. [159] The Metzler was short-lived on the Hudson, as by 1985, photos in Gargan's *New York Times* article showed Pat Cunningham guiding a traditional type of raft using a guide paddle to steer. [160]

Typical of the 1980s were inflatable tube rafts ranging from the twenty-foot ones used by Northern to the shorter fourteen to sixteen foot rafts. As with today's rafts, these tubes encircled the thwarts, which provided both seating for guests and shape and stability from side movement. A non-inflated, flat piece of rubber attached to the bottom acted as a floor. Photos from Gilborn's article showed safety lines encircling both the Metzler and other types of rafts. [161]

Andy Leblanc, who guided for Adventure Sports in the mid-1980s, remembered that helmets at that time were optional. [162] This explained how some photos showed rafters with helmets on each person. Most of the time, both guests and guides had no helmets. Eastern River Expeditions required guests wear helmets, [163] as did WILD/ WATERS, [164] and a 1984 photo of an Eastern raft showed this. [165] It is a curious thing that helmet usage was not more common, since one guest in 1984 fell out of his raft and hit his head on a rock on the Indian River near Gooley Steps, as reported in the *HCN*. [166]

Paddles varied as well, with wood paddles being used the by guests shown in the Gilborn article in photos on page thirty and thirty-two. Other photos on page thirty-two showed white shafted paddles with red t-grips in the end of the raft (possibly a guide paddle) and a group of aluminum shafted, black t-gripped paddles in another. [167] Similar paddles were shown in the photos from an article in the April, 1985, edition of the *Utica Observer-Dispatch*. [168] Page twenty-six of Mason Smith's article in *Adirondack Life* showed a white shaft and white blade for both guide and guest. [169] A *New York Times* article did show Pat Cunningham using plastic paddles. [170]

River attire varied from photo to photo, with Mason Smith giving a list of what was worn. Northern gave out two-piece, full-length top and bottom wetsuits with wet cell booties to be worn inside sneakers, which were required for the fabric-bottomed rafts. Under the wetsuit, a bathing suit was recommended, with a wool sweater and shell jacket to be worn over the wetsuit. A wool hat and gloves completed the ensemble. Smith also reported that rubber bands were used as glass straps for eyeglasses. [171] An article by Silk recommended a wool or polypropylene sweater be taken along with a hat and gloves. [172] Everyone always wore PFDs.

An article in the *Utica Observer-Dispatch* also had a list of required or recommended clothing, starting out with long underwear - preferably made of polypropylene. A wool hat was listed, as water spray can run across a person's head and helped keep that area warm. Lip balm was also recommended to help the lips from chapping. Water repellent gloves, such as latex dish gloves, were suggested to keep the hands from too much contact with the icy water.

For the feet, wool socks and water-repellent socks were recommended, along with sneakers or waterproof footwear, as not every company provided rubberized footwear. It should be noted that with the use of bucket boats, the feet were always the most challenging to keep warm, as bailing never completely emptied the boat, meaning the feet were always in cold water. Eyeglasses were to be strapped in order to secure them to the head. A dry change of clothes was recommended, as well as a towel to dry off with. [173]

Pricing for a raft trip and what was included in that price varied amongst the outfitters. Advertisements for three outfitters appeared with Gilborn's article in *Adirondack Life*, with the ones for Hudson River Raft Company and Adirondack River Outfitters giving no price. [174] Adirondack Wildwaters listed a price of $35 per person for weekdays and $45 for the weekends, and advertised for trips on the Sacandaga but with no price listed. Adirondack Wildwater eventually operated out of the Wilderness Lodge off Big Brook Road in Indian Lake, offering a meal back at the Lodge after the trip. [175]

A *New York Times* article by Stanley Carr listed a $55 weekday price and a $65 weekend price for Whitewater Challengers, along with an $80 price for the Moose and a toll free number to call for reservations. [176] Guide Bob Wolff recalled that Challengers first did a spaghetti dinner after the trip at the American Motel in North Creek before having a cookout meal at the Challengers base. [177]

Several brochures dated 1982 gave some good details on price, age limit, and meals served. Unicorn listed a $50 price for the Hudson trip for weekdays and $65 on weekend, with a minimum age of fourteen, with the season listed as being from April 3rd to May 9th. Unicorn's overnight trip had a price of $130, with specific weekend dates.[178] Wilderness Rafting Expeditions listed a price of $59 for both weekend and weekdays, a $9 wetsuit rental price, and a minimum age of twelve for all trips. [179] Adirondack River Outfitters did not list a minimum age, but listed a price of $40 for weekdays and $50 for weekends. [180] Pocono Whitewater World listed a price of $50 for weekends and $45 for weekdays, and a minimum age of fourteen. An interesting marketing piece in the Pocono brochure mentioned the "little known Hudson River Gorge – the same thrilling new river fun sport you've seen on TV – is now waiting for you in the nearby Adirondacks." [181]

The clientele and guides of the day were typically male, with Northern's Kathy Barckley being one of the few women. Starting out as a guest and then becoming a guide, Barckley remembered fitting in well with the Northern crew at the Lone Birch Motel. She remembered driving to Indian Lake on weekends from Rochester, New York, and enjoying the scenery and the comradery of other guides. She even mentioned that she, at times, got free drinks because she was a woman. That being said, she also remembered the concerns that some male guests had over a female guide. [182]

Gilborn gave a good summary of the clientele of the early years, with guests ranging "from age 16-60 and have come from all parts of the Northeast. On the average they are in their 30's in good physical condition" with guests coming from "parts of New England, New Jersey, New York, and Canada." [183] Reporter Steve Silk, described river runners as being "more than 12 years old," with most participants "in their mid 20s to mid 40s" and occupations as diverse as "secretaries to ski bums." [184]

Guide Bob Raferty, who now owns Adirondack Raft Company, added some more descriptive terms, saying, "we had a rough bunch of firemen and cops from the cities... There was a macho attitude and a lack of women." [185] Michael Whiting gave a general description of the average raft guest as well, saying how they came from all walks of life, with many of them following the melting snow from the ski centers to the river. While the core group were business people and professionals, Whiting stated that there was a broad range of people interested in rafting, with an age range from teens to sixty-five. [186] Some guests were so adrenaline driven that Wayne Hockmeyer and Jay Schurman offered trips on the Moose River at times, as well as the Hudson, as Wayne put it, "for the crazies" and the "firemen, bachelor party groups." [187]

Marko Schmale of Whitewater Challengers remembered this about the river runners of that day:

> The clientele tended to be very gung-ho. They didn't care if there was ice on their lifejackets and it was freezing cold; they just weren't whiners. They were

in for the adventure. People would recite lines out of "Deliverance" regularly and say how hardcore they were because they were going rafting. At the time, rafting was that much of an adventure. A lot of the groups at the time were bus groups of cops and firemen from the New York City area. They would get on the bus in the city at 3 in the morning, ride up the Northway, drink cans of Bud all the way up. They would arrive pretty under the weather and we would be expected to take them rafting. Some of them slept on the bus, though. They were mostly male, very macho, but that was what people were expecting; it was the 80's, a little different time. It was a huge party. Very few young people as in teenagers; they were mostly 20-30's and very few women.

It was a younger group and hardier, too; if it was freezing cold, it didn't matter. Although it didn't matter in the morning for many of them, as I have heard through the years at trade shows, it was the coldest that they had ever been in their lives. If I had a nickel for everyone who came up to me at a trade show and said "that whitewater rafting on the Hudson was the coldest I ever was". And there were some cold trips! The fact that we had bucket boats and we didn't have synthetic clothing didn't really occur. Balclavas? Neck warmers? We didn't even have mitts! Feet were in water constantly in the bucket boats and that water was cold. [188]

It is interesting to note though that despite the overwhelming majority of rafters seen as testosterone-driven men, there was a significant representation of women. In photographs provided by Lorraine Moore of Lone Birch Motel, close to half of the guests pictured were women. Lori Benton remembered her first trip with Northern, going with a group of teenage Girl Scouts, and then becoming a "river groupie," hanging around with Eastern at Marty's because they had three to four female guides. [189]

Every indication is that the initial season of commercial rafting on the Hudson in 1979 was short, occurring only during the month of April, as those who ran it did so more as an exploratory and training trip. As the February, 1980, agreement indicated, the season that year would run through May. [191] Gilborn indicated in her article that there were a limited number of fall water releases in 1981, perhaps to augment the short, dry spring season from April 1st to May 15th. [192] By 1985, the season had expanded once again, going into the first part of June. [193] The *Albany Times Union* reported that there were daily water releases until the end of May, continuing on through the first three weekends in June, with limited releases in September and October.

Despite the best efforts to make river running safe for guests and participants, there has always been an element of risk involved. From the log driving days, there were many who craved the adventure of taking the risk and living to tell about it. When Fran Monthony's boat mate decided to run the Narrows while on a log drive, the risk was part of the motivation. [194] This, of course, was the major attraction for those who went commercial rafting in the early days and, to some degree, it remains so. Like any sport or activity, rafting has had its share of injuries and near-misses. Statistically speaking, though, rafting is one of the safest recreational activities, with an injury rate equal to sports such as golf. One is more likely to get hurt playing basketball or football than when rafting. [195]

On the Hudson, several near-misses were reported in the *HCN*. In May of 1984, Lohr McKinstry reported a man who fell out of a raft and struck his head on a rock in the Indian River. The incident happened about 10:30 a.m. about .7 miles up from the confluence of the Indian River and the Hudson, which puts it in the Gooley Step Rapid. The man was evacuated and taken to the hospital in Glens Falls and later released. [196] Less than a month later, the *HCN* reported that a couple from Los Angeles tried to raft the Hudson River, starting out on the Indian River using a "cheap rubber raft". They were found about 10 p.m. on May 24, 1984, after walking out of the woods near North Creek wearing shorts and a cotton T-shirts. They had not returned to the Adirondack Trails Motel in Indian Lake and were reported missing at 7:30 p.m., coming out exhausted but not hurt. [197]

Dick Carlson reported on some other near-misses, as river runners tried to learn the river. In one instance, Carlson remembers a Wilderness Tours raft that went into the hole on river right halfway down Carter's - known by some as Big Nasty. The company was using Riken Shoshone rafts that day, with the level running from seven to eight feet and up. Carlson's group had eddied out at the end of Carter's, where they saw "all these paddles, people, and bail buckets come down the river" with "people strung out all over the river." The raft went into the hole, was met by the tremendous back current, and ejected the occupants. Carlson recalled that the boat stayed in the hole for forty-five minutes before it came out by itself. [198]

In another instance when Carlson was working for Adirondack Wild Waters, he watched a raft go into the same hole, with predictable results. Wild Waters was using Udesco boats at the time, which Carlson described as "cheap knock-offs of the Avon Pro rafts." On a big water day, Carlson was leading a trip of several rafts, which included himself, Sonny Wooley, and "Carla," who was a short, small-sized woman, as guides. As Carlson described it, the lead boats had just run Carter's and eddied out on river right. Dick was playing up the run with the guests when he saw Carla in one of the boats in the eddy. Realizing that Carla should have been with her boat, Carlson addressed her:

> And I go "Carla, where's *your* raft?" and she goes (almost crying) "I don't know" and I go "Oh my!" as the last anyone knew they had lost a shit-load of people in the Big Nasty hole, recirculated, nearly drowned, *nearly drowned.* The last anyone saw the boat there were three people in it, two paddling…and one going the other way! We never found the boat until below Givney's.

When the trip was able to regroup, several of the guests in Carla's raft did not want to go back with her. The trip did continue. [199]

One of the more memorable near-misses etched in the collective memories of those involved, and has taken on legendary qualities with those who were involved, was the incident that became known as "Black Sunday". Because several of the participants have offered their stories of the incident and because it makes a good guide story, a full account is found in the next chapter and was taken directly from the participants themselves.

Pre trip preparation and safety talk
Left: Northern Whitewater, *Lorraine Moore photo;*
Right: Wilderness Tours Jerry Marquis gives a
safety talk before departure, *Jim Briggs photo.*

Rafts were transported by car and trailer.
Left is Adirondack Wildwater raft transport to the Sacandaga
River, *Bill Crome photo;* **Right** is Northern Whitewater
raft transport to the Hudson, *Lorraine Moore photo.*

<u>Hudson River Raft Company Metzler raft just above Alarm Clock.</u>
Jim Briggs photo

<u>Northern Whitewater raft in the Narrows,</u>
Rick Thompson guide.
Northern Outdoors photo

<u>Wilderness Tours rest stop just above OK Slip Falls rapid;</u>
Gaye Clarke on the far right, Jerry Marquis on the left with the
cap, and budding raft guide Pete Burns in the yellow PFD.
Gaye Clarke photo

Black Sunday: A Great Guide Story

One of the great guide stories from the early days of rafting on the Hudson with legendary qualities is the incident known as "Black Sunday." The short version is that a raft flipped in the Narrows at a very high water level with two of the rafters becoming unaccounted for. The missing rafters made it to shore, tried to walk out of the gorge, and were found alive the next morning after an agonizing all-night search. The event still burns in the collective memories of many of the participants, and as such, vivid recollections and accounts of the event still remain almost thirty years later, making for a fascinating story. In piecing the story together, several sources of information were used, but the bulk of the narrative is taken directly from conversations with Black Sunday participants. While they have been edited for smoothness of flow and understanding, the quotes tell the story better than any secondary source. And so, without further ado, "So there they were!"

To begin with, several of the individuals involved recalled the day and the events but not the exact date. The *Glens Falls Post Star* reported on the lost rafters being found in the Tuesday, April 20, 1982, edition on page thirteen, which fixed the date of Black Sunday as April 18, 1982. The article reported that the rafters were found about 2:30 a.m. Monday morning in the Blue Ledges area after trying to walk out to where the rafts were launched. They were in good condition and required no hospitalization. The incident happened in the Narrows about 11 a.m. Sunday as part of a five raft trip; the two were in a raft with seven others. Rescue efforts led by state forest rangers began after being contacted at 2 p.m. Sunday afternoon. The two rafters wore wetsuits and life jackets, which helped to keep them from becoming hypothermic, as temperatures dropped to 29 degrees that night.[1]

To help set the scene, the North Creek USGS river gauge archives for 1982 showed the Hudson River level starting out on the weekend of April 3rd being around 4,000 to 4,500 cfs, which translates into approximately a six foot plus level. From then, the level dropped over the course of the week, reaching a point of 2,000 cfs (4.3 ft.) on the next weekend of April 10th and bottoming out at about 1,500 cfs (3.9 ft.) by midweek. Then the river started to spike, climbing back to 4,000 cfs by Saturday the 17th and peaking out at 17,000 cfs by late Sunday to early Monday. Thus, the level went from a low water point on Wednesday the 14th to an extreme high water on Sunday the 18th. [2]

Several recollections of the level were around 30,000 cfs, but USGS records indicated the level topped out at only 17,000 cfs, lower than 30,000 but significantly large nonetheless. However, Jay Schurman [3] reported the river level to be eleven feet and rising on the 18th, with Dick Purdue [4] also recalling the level to have been around twelve feet. Recent record amounts of water on the Hudson in 2011 posted a high level of 13.65 ft., which translated into nearly 40,000 cfs, [5] making the 30,000 cfs figure a more accurate reading and putting the level around twelve feet. John Vorhees mentioned that the North Creek USGS gauge station that weekend was washed out due to the water level, which could account for the discrepancies in the exact number. [6] The important point, though, is that the river level was larger than anyone had seen or could remember at that time. Bill Cromie reported going down the Hudson in 1979 the April 21st weekend when the level was recorded at 20,000 cfs. [7] April 18, 1982, would have had much more water.

Both Wayne Hockmeyer and John Vorhees commented on where that water came from. Hockmeyer [8] said that many of the side creeks in the days leading up to Black Sunday were jammed with ice, essentially acting as dams, holding the water back much as the crib dams had done during the logging days. When these jams let go, they released a flood of water down these tributaries and into the Hudson, raising the water level exponentially. Vorhees described it:

> It was a late winter and there was still a lot of snow in the woods. It had started to get patchy but there were still huge areas where there was 2-3 feet of snow, so there was still a lot of moisture upstream. We went down the first day of the season and got to the confluence of the Indian and Hudson and looked upstream and the whole river was ice wall-to-wall. It looked like you could have walked across it with no problem. [9]

Vorhees also recalled after the trip the day before, he went home to relax, thinking about the day and the lines he had done on the river, when it started to rain. "And man, it just poured. It was like the sky opened up and the water just came down. It was solid water coming down and it rained like that all night long". [10] Joe Kowalski also recalled the rain that weekend:

> I was in Indian Lake and drove home to Canada on the Friday night [16th, JTD]. It was raining hard when I left, thinking they would have an exciting day on Saturday. [11]

The rain helped melt the snow and loosen up the ice, sending all that water downstream at once, transforming the river from a friendly adventure ride into a raging torrent exploding from hell. The potential for huge water levels was noted in the April 19th edition of the *Post Star,* reporting on page nine that a flood warning had been issued for the Hudson River north of Glens Falls. [12]

Suzie Hockmeyer remembered waking the morning of April 18th at the Lone Birch Motel in Indian Lake to hear one of the Northern staff, Nelson Coles, "coming down the stairs of the Chalet the first thing in the morning saying 'I dreamt that we were going to drown." Some of the Wilderness Tours staff stopped by the Lone Birch to see what Northern was going to do that day (a common practice even today), as, by then, the river level had started to rise dramatically. When they were informed of Northern's intent to run the gorge that day, the Wilderness Tours staff blessed them, saying, "We're proud of you; go with God!" [13]

Suzie Hockmeyer remarked on the uncertainty of the outfitters as to whether or not to run the gorge that day. Because rafting on the Hudson River was still in its beginning stages, no one had run the river at that level. [14] As such there was no measure with which to determine what it meant to run the Hudson at twelve feet, so no one knew for sure the conditions they would find. As Alan Haley put it, "It was all experimentation." [15] Vorhees agreed saying that rafters at that time "didn't know what the safe limits of the river were. It's a different river at every kind of level." [16] Because outfitters were still learning the river, it should not be surprising that there was a degree of uncertainty.

Suzie also commented how most everyone else that day ran the lower part of the river from North River to the Glen, [17] with Wayne Hockmeyer saying that everyone else cancelled their gorge trip that day. [18] Joe Kowalski remembered getting a call from his river manager, Gaye Clarke, on Saturday, relaying how fast the river was already rising and concurring that they would run the lower part on Sunday. [19] Jay Schurman of Unicorn ran his trip on the lower river, too, and even though the river runs much wider in this section - creating less turbulence than in the gorge - Jay related that the water was still big enough that one of his rafts flipped. No one got hurt and he was able to pick up the pieces and finish the day. Schurman later helped in the search efforts, going into the Boreas on the D&H railroad tracks, where he reported seeing a Northern raft float by. [20]

So with conditions such as these and no one knowing for certain what would be going on in the gorge, why would anyone want to raft the gorge or even offer the opportunity to go? Suzie Hockmeyer shed light on this question:

> Back then, rafting was considered an extreme sport,
> especially those brave enough to challenge the river
> in spring when it was guaranteed to be freezing cold,
> but worth it for the high adventure of running big

spring runoff water. Wayne himself was no exception – nothing thrilled him more than pushing the envelope right to the edge, which was spring rafting's MO at the time.

She continued on, explaining how the legal environment wasn't as charged back then either:

> ...there wasn't government regulation, and insurance companies and lawyers weren't so busy hitting us with lawsuits. Possibly because the profile of our guests were more type A and willing to take risks – we weren't running mainstream America yet since rafting was considered an extreme sport. [21]

Suzie also described how Wayne tried to explain the situation to the Northern guests who were contemplating running the gorge that morning:

> Wayne was renowned for giving a harsh safety lecture when we were running big water, and that day, he put the fear of God into our guests. He offered anyone the chance to run the lower section - North Creek to The Glen, get their money back if they did not want to go at all, or go with him to challenge the river at levels we had never seen before. He warned them of the extreme danger and the fact that rescue attempts would be just as risky and difficult, if not impossible, if anyone fell out, or God forbid, the raft capsized. Frankly, I was surprised that anyone dared to go! [22]

From several accounts then, the group of five Northern rafts had as guides Alan Haley / Suzie Hockmeyer, Carl Otley / John Vorhees, Wayne Hockmeyer, Billy McDonald, John Prescott, George Foster, and probably Nelson Coles along with one other guide. They, along with their guests, left the Indian River put-in for an unforgettable adventure of unknown proportions.

Suzie Hockmeyer:

> Everyone doubled up, with Alan Haley and myself in the same raft, Carl Otley and John Vorhees in another. I had never seen Alan so freaked out, as he is a calm person. The Indian River was like the "Alley Way" on the Kennebec River at high water and running it made us realize that we were screwed, but there was no turning around by then. [23]

John Vorhees:

> Wayne had put two guides in a boat because he knew it was going to be big water. Wayne had gotten a reading from the gauge station, but what he didn't realize when he got the reading was that the river was going up one foot per hour. When we went down to the put-in the water looked like it was going over the top of the Lake Abanakee dam by about three feet; you didn't need a release! The Indian River was like Mile Long (Carter's) would be on a good day; the Indian River was just ass kicking!

> When we got down to the confluence, all the ice was out from upstream and was floating next to us in huge chunks. There were trees, there were outhouses, there were all kinds of stuff coming down the river because everything had flooded. We didn't know how fast the water was rising. To give you an idea, when we got to Elephant Rock (Jump Rock) you couldn't even tell were it was; there wasn't even a riffle of water on top of it. I kept looking for it and it was not there! The river

was going so fast you felt like the camera was sped up and everything was going at high speed. [24]

Wayne Hockmeyer:

> That day I doubled up John Vorhees with Carl Otley, who was one of my guides from Maine. I was confident that we could safely run the river. We had big rafts and experienced guides. We had a thrilling ride down the Indian River. However, when we reached the Hudson, I was taken back by what I saw. What were previously one foot waves had turned into 6 foot waves. The water was running at over 30,000 cubic feet per second. The river was full of trees and ice - the only thing that was missing was dead pigs and cattle! We stopped at the Blue Ledges [probably river right just below the beach, JTD] and I went downriver to scout the rapid below [the Narrows, JTD]. It was terrifying, and I came back and instructed all my guides to dodge the rapid and stay river right next to the trees [the river was in the woods]. Carl did not listen to me and went river left so he could give the guests a "thrilling ride." He never got past the first wave [probably Widow Maker, JTD] which ate them up and instead everyone got "a swim they will never forget." People were all over the river and some had swims of up to a mile long." [25]

Suzie Hockmeyer:

> Carl flipped in the Narrows. We saw him flip. I remember seeing that raft go up; it looked like a leaf. These were big twelve person, 20 ft. long bucket boats and the wave turned the raft over like a leaf. And then the fun was on. I remember pulling several people into our raft. I remember Alan going into holes with him screaming to everyone to hold on. [26]

John Vorhees:

So we got into the Narrows. Unfortunately we took on some water at the beginning and about halfway through, despite our best efforts, the boat flipped. It flipped so fast. I was experienced enough to have a certain reaction time in my mind when something like that happens, but this happened so fast that I was underwater thinking that I'm gasping for air - so shocked that the boat is flipped over - that in fact I'm sucking in water. I don't even know I'm underwater, I'm underwater so fast. So for the rest of the Narrows I'm like a bug in a vacuum cleaner hose and so was everybody else in the boat.

There is absolutely no way to control yourself; you're completely at the mercy of the elements in that situation. You're used to a certain kind of river where there is a scale between the top of the river and the bottom, and that scale was just blown totally out of proportion; it was like three times as high as you have ever seen it. You have no idea how you're going to get out of that. Everything went white, I saw the white lady; I didn't think that I was in this world anymore, it was that simple. Then all of the sudden, just as fast as I was under, I was out of the water again.

So eventually everybody who was underwater came up out of the water and most of the guys got picked up by other boats that were coming along. But when I finally come out of the water, I see the trail boat going down the river, they're pointing me to the shore to try to orient me because I had literally drowned out there.

So I look over and I see where the nearest shore is and at this point we are just past the Blue Ledges, you know how it starts to bank there and all those cedars go up [here John refers to the actual sloping eastern end of the Blue Ledges, not the rapid, as it becomes part of the bank that forms the slope on river right in the Narrows, JTD]. Well, I tried to move up toward those cedars, except that I have only about two seconds for this to happen and then I'm in the next wave. But at least I'm on top of the river. So I'm in and out, in and out. I'm eventually able to work my way over there and just as I'm getting over there I see there's another guy in the river with me, so I help him get out of the river just past the Narrows.

Actually, what we did was just get over near the trees and the river was going by so fast that we had to reach out and grab a tree and hold on while the river was trying to rip us off - it was going by so fast. We were way up on the trunk of the tree, not just at the base. We were way up in the woods trying to hold on and trying to get to the rest of the way to shore. So we went from tree to tree and got to shore and finally got on ground and got out there and thanked God that we were alive! [27]

Meanwhile, the rest of the boats continued down the river, trying to pick up the pieces of a flipped raft while having to go through several other major rapids, dealing with large waves, dangerous holes, and shocked river runners all at the same time in an effort not to create another situation. Suzie Hockmeyer picked up the narrative:

Finally we pulled over at OK Slip the first time we could pull over. We did a head count to see if we were all there. We had two rafts that couldn't pull over so they kept going - one of which was John Prescott of Schenectady. People were so cold, so cold, it was kind of spitting snow, raw, and so wet. Alan built a fire using matches from the patch kit. I remember trying to hold people back because they were burning their wetsuits in the fire because they didn't care, they were so cold, they were trying to warm up. It was not a bright sunny day.

Doing the head count, we knew that we were missing two boats, Billy McDonald and John Prescott, as they couldn't stop. So they sent me and George Foster, who was on his first day of guiding, as he had the best crew, saying to us "You guys got to get help." We had to go alone, making it to the top of Harris Rift. We decided to scout it and even that was hard, with the water going into the trees. We were just looking at it saying "We're screwed," hugging each other saying "We hope we can just make it." We ran river right and at the bottom we found our other two boats. [28]

On the river shore, past the Narrows, John Vorhees continued:

So we're sitting there and I'm remembering everything that they told me: "Wait where you come out of the river and somebody will come back around and get you." Everything inside of me is saying nobody is ever going to come back around in this stuff. I talked it over with this guy and said that protocol says that they'll come around for us again, but I don't believe it, do you? And he said no. So I say to this guy, "I think I can find our way out of here. We'll go up this hill, then we'll walk south and I think that we can get to the highway." So we decided to walk out together.

We got out to where we would have made it out to a road, but I got turned around just before I made it to the critical point. It started to get dark and we ended up spending the night in the woods, and I had to convince this guy to spend the night in the woods because he was freaking out about his family, he had to get home, and he was going to keep going, but it was getting dark and I know we're not near the highway. I knew that if we kept going in the dark that there is a pretty good chance we're going to freeze, as the temperatures were dropping. It got way down below freezing that night. We're in wetsuits but the hats and gloves were gone.

So I had to just about clonk this guy on the head to get him to stop because he was just at that freak-out point. There we made a shelter. We started snapping off branches of balsam trees and I made a haystack out of balsam branches that we crawled underneath, snuggled up, and kept ourselves warm. [29]

Back on the river, after Suzie met up with the other two rafts:

John Prescott, I'll never forget, he was so scared, and he knew he was going into Harris Rift and his people had given up paddling. He tried to tell them to get up and paddle because he knows where they are. Finally he says, "If you don't get up and paddle, we're all going to die!" He said, "Paddle or die; you better paddle or you're gonna die!" All of the sudden they lift their heads up and one by one they start to paddle.

So we make it and get down to the little store in North River [ARO's current base, JTD] and we were a mess in our wetsuits. We go up to Papa Rose [Hank Rose's father] saying "We need help," and when we started to tell him the story, he goes crazy calling everybody. All I remember was going over to the cooler saying, "I really could use a beer right now," and I remember looking at George and saying, "Maybe we should just buy beer for everybody." At that point, the others had started to come down off the river so we went back up to the Lone Birch.

One of our drivers, Dick DuPrey, had it in his head that we needed molt wine with lunch and do you think that any of us are even considering lunch? Half the food and cups were gone because they were in Carl's raft and Dick is worried about the molt wine! We have two people missing and we think they're dead and he's worried about molt wine!

We go through that and our heads are spinning think- ing that we need a one-way trip to South America - it's over, this is it. We were all worried to death. Carl Otley is a wreck, he's crying, frying his brain because he thinks that he killed two people. Guides were out looking, along with Wayne. The rangers were great. John was smart enough to hunker down. It was a good ending, but scared the crap out of us. [30]

Lorraine Moore described the scene at the Lone Birch when the bus returned:

When Suzie got back, she told me about the missing rafters. So Mike and Dan (two of Lorraine's sons) took snowmobiles down through the Gooley Club, then Northern Frontier. It was an all-night thing. I remem- ber there was this lady who didn't go on the trip; she stayed. Then I got to thinking "Well I've got to feed these people," so I got these big pots and we made spa- ghetti and spaghetti sauce; I think I bought out Grand Union. We served the guests, and anyone else that came in, we fed. Anyone who came in to rest from the search we had coffee and spaghetti and whatever else we could put together. So we fed everybody up through the middle of the night. Guests from different trips, some of whom had friends out on the trip, mingled at the motel, with the motel hosting people even if they weren't registered there. People were moving about, talking about it, but nobody knew what was going on. I remember saying to Wayne "Don't do that to me again!" After that day, they decided to not run the river over 10 ft. Very lucky that no one died because they might have shut rafting down entirely. [31]

With forest rangers contacted, teams from the town of Minerva and the town of Indian Lake searched their respective sides of the river. John Monthony, of early rafting fame, became involved with the search, opening up a Northern Frontier camp building he took care of. Monthony said that with a base camp:

> ...the searchers could get warmed. Before long, it was warmed up and I had some coffee and cocoa going. All but two of the fellows in the raft had been found by then. At 7:30 p.m., area ranger Jerry Husson came in with his search party. He had found tracks of two men upstream of Blue Ledges near Carter's Pond. He was calling off the search for the night, as his searchers were all played out from wallowing in snow up to their knees for about six hours. [32]

With tracks found on the Indian Lake side, the Minerva Rescue Squad was soon pulled, with the search concentrating on the Indian Lake side. [33]

Back at the Monthony camp, with the search winding down for the night, Monthony became concerned, as he personally knew Vorhees:

> It was dark and in the mid-teens temperature—wise, and I was concerned as there was still a lot of snow and these men had been soaked in the river. The conditions were perfect for hypothermia. I told Jerry Husson that

I wanted to go out and find them. Roger Freeburn was there and since he knew the area better than I did, I asked him if he'd go with me and he agreed. [34]

The two of them, along with forest rangers Bruce Coon and Vic Sasse, took snowshoes and flashlights and headed back out. Monthony picked up the narrative:

> The lost men went to bare patches of ground as much as possible, so we would have to leave a man at the last visible tracks, and the rest would fan out until a new track was found. Continuing in this manner, time went by until about 2:00 a.m. we heard a shout in the distance and found them. John Vorhees, who had been the guide on the raft trip, had enough sense to gather a large pile of evergreen boughs before dark had set in. He put them in a depression in the ground and he and the other man crawled in and huddled together to stay warm.
>
> Both men were in pretty good shape except for their hands and feet, which, luckily, were only just very cold. The other man with John commented that he wouldn't go near the water again – even a bathtube – for at least two weeks. The whole group was pretty tired when we finally got out of the woods about 7:00 a.m. [35]

John Vorhees:

> About 4-4:30 [2-2:30 am according to Monthony and the *Post Star* paper, JTD] in the morning, good old John Monthony came through the woods. John was one who would never give up, he had that kind of reputation on a search, and he knew me, anyway. He figured that we had walked up out of the river, that we hadn't drowned, because the presumption was that we had.

It turns out that Wayne had come around in a boat again to look for us [probably referring to the Town of Moriah search effort as they did launch a boat, JTD], God bless him, I never thought he would do it, but he did. If we had stayed by the river, we would have saved everybody a lot of aggravation. [36]

Wayne Hockmeyer:

All of our safety procedures dictated that they stay at the river's edge, walk back up the side of the river until they saw another raft, or stay put. I now feared they were both dead. I spent the whole night searching the side of the river for them and concluded they had drowned, and gave up at daylight. When I finally reached the put-in on the river, I was met by my wife Suzie, who told me that snowmobilers had found them just before first light and while very cold, they were alive. [37]

Wayne gave some more details of his search:

We would always walk back up the side of the river in the event we were missing people. I took a guide with me just after dusk and we walked from the Indian Lake Dam (Lake Abanakee) all the way to the Hudson, and then walked a very long way down the side of the river. There was a few feet of snow on the river and this made it very difficult to walk, as we would break through the crust. I had a lot of matches with me and flashlights. I did not know if they had drowned or were trying to walk back up to the put in. It was a very cold night and I feared they might freeze to death. I had hoped that we would cut their tracks, but we never did. I finally realized that we were not going to find them and decided to turn around and walk back to the dam. It was the longest night of my life. I realized that I would be responsible for two men's death as well as the destruction of my company, and no way to take care of my family.

We arrived back at the dam just after daylight. Suzie was there waiting. I walked toward her, not knowing what to say, but before I had a chance to reach her, she yelled, "They found them, they are ok." It was the greatest message I will ever hear. I had spent all night imagining every possible picture of what the rest of my life would be if the two men had died. [38]

DEC Forest Ranger Vic Sasse commented on the search effort in the *Post Star*, calling it "the most grueling one I've ever been on." Part of the challenge was that there was snow on the ground up to depths of two and a half feet, which made tracking the two rafters difficult. Sasse said that if the two had stayed near the river and not tried to walk out, they would have had a better chance of being found quickly, as they could have been spotted by the helicopter that was called in from Plattsburgh Air Force Base. [39] In retrospect, Vorhees, too, realized this, apologizing and giving thanks to the search teams in a letter in the *Hamilton County News* ten days later. [40]

The extreme mental state on the part of those involved with the search effort was draining on all. Suzie Hockmeyer described it:

Suffering through that night while waiting to see if the two missing rafters – the guest and the guide – were rescued, was agonizing. Nobody slept. Carl Otley, the guide on that boat, was an emotional wreck, and nobody could make him feel better, and the rest of us just waited and waited. We all agreed afterwards that we never wanted to go through a night like that again. [41]

In retrospect, Wayne Hockmeyer:

> What I learned on Black Sunday, I never will forget. If you do things that require precision or perfection and the price of failing to achieve precision or perfection could well be death, then you should never involve other people in the undertaking unless they clearly understand the risk involved. If Carl had listened to me and run the rapid hard right, I am quite sure we would have run the river without a hitch; however, the risk was too high to assume that there would be no mistakes. To err is human, and the most talented among us will eventually screw up. The standard I set after that day was, if a mistake is made, everyone will most likely survive. If one has any doubt about the likelihood of survival when things go wrong, then the activity should not be done. The Hudson River on Black Sunday was much too dangerous to depend on everything going right. People who come up to take a raft trip understand there is danger involved, but they really don't believe they might die. They are correct in this belief.
>
> Whitewater rafting is a reasonably safe sport...unless, of course, you went down the Hudson River Gorge on Black Sunday! [42]

Alan Haley [43] remembered that Otley was so traumatized that he never worked as a guide again. Alan also offered his perspective on the reason for the anxiety many felt during the time of the incident and its aftermath. Northern had done big water trips before on the river, "scary" trips, as he put it. Alan had even done a single raft trip on the Hudson at high water. But despite the conditions of those trips and what went on, the guides and trip leaders had always remained in control of the situation and the welfare of the guests. Black Sunday

180

was memorable for those who were involved because "we lost control." Fortunately for all, Black Sunday turned into White Monday when the two were found. A different outcome involving a serious injury, or worse, would have had lasting consequences for, not only the people involved with the incident, but also a young and growing industry on the Hudson River.

Commercial Rafting:
The Gorge Runneth Over

One of the biggest issues facing all involved with rafting on the Hudson in the early 1980s was that of the increasing numbers of guests and how this increase affected both the land and the guests' experience. While the commercial outfitters and the Town of Indian Lake welcomed the business rafting brought, it became a double-edged paddle, presenting management problems for which the solutions created a degree of ill feeling, particularly amongst the outfitters. The short end was that there were a limited number of commercial raft guests that were allowed access to the river on any given day in an effort not to detract from the experience or the river. The conflict revolved around who got those limited spots, how they were given out, and how many spots there were. In the end, the solution did not please everyone and provided another reason for some of the outfitters to abandon the Hudson.

Alice Gilborn summed up the issue of overuse of the Hudson in her article in *Adirondack Life*.[1] In the context of a river trip in the spring of 1981, she not only described her experience on the river but also looked at rafting as a new phenomenon and how it might affect the river and the town. In the subtitle, she asked the question of "How many is too many," in reference to the numbers issue. The article also described the business dilemma of the outfitters: they had a product in demand and wanted to market it to the maximum number of guests. As business people, though, they also realized that too many guests could have an affect on that experience, leading to reduced demand.

Gilborn quoted both Jay Schurman and Wayne Hockmeyer on this double-sided paddle the outfitters faced. Schurman said that with regards to the type of experience the outfitters were trying to market: "Part of the package we sell is wilderness." On the flip side, though, Hockmeyer said, "Wall-to-wall rafts detract from the experience," and mentioned that the outfitters hoped they could manage the issue without outside regulation.

Like many things on the Hudson, this issue was a microcosm of rafting in general. Many other commercial runs faced similar overuse issues, with many of the concerns being over access.[2] Suzie Hockmeyer commented on similar use problems on rivers in Maine, West Virginia, and Pennsylvania.[3] On the Colorado River in the Grand Canyon National Park, numbers grew to a point that, like the Hudson, both the resource and the experience were compromised.[4] Some of the problems Nash listed included 500 people a day at the put-in, a high number of motorized rafts, congested rapids, and busy river shores. The National Park Service eventually stepped in to regulate the river by setting limits on use and banning motors on rafts. With what may sound like a familiar tune, Nash described the intense competition for the permits the Park Service issued as the means to control numbers amongst commercial and private users.

In New York, Briggs summed up well the feelings of the outfitters regarding government regulation of commercial rafting:

> It is this kind of regulation from above that the rafters want to avoid. This dilutes the wilderness experience. Currently, the biggest problem is the sheer number of rafts that want to gain access to the river. This is especially evident later in the season when there is a short release period. Each outfitter has agreed to take no more than 80 people per day. But there is no way to enforce this and no real way to control the number of outfitters unless the state steps in.[5]

183

Nowhere did these use pressures and the increased numbers play out more than at the put-in on the Indian River. For the first three years, very few reliable records exist that document, with any accuracy, the numbers of raft guests per day, with early figures coming mainly from recollections. An early estimate of numbers gave a figure of 10,000 total people over a two-year period that came to the Indian Lake area, presumably to go rafting on the Hudson.[6] In 1982, Wayne Hockmeyer estimated the numbers on the Hudson to be in the range of 4,000 to 5,000 per year and growing.[7] Jim Swedberg also remembered large numbers, saying that on some Saturdays, "we would send 1,100 (plus) down the Hudson. The following Sundays would have 400-500 guests." [8] In a letter dated February 23, 1982, from Delos Mallette to Dick Cipperly, number summaries are given from the sign-in box at the raft access, with 1,625 listed for rafting, although that number included private rafters.[9]

In 1982, DEC river ranger Ben Woodard [10] provided the first picture of daily numbers and, though incomplete, his record of the two weekends helped verify remembrances and recollections:

May 1-2: 351, 399

May 3: 78

May 7: 109

May 8-9: 409, 350-400

Keep in mind that these 1982 numbers are amongst only eight outfitters, a number that almost tripled by 1985.

More complete records exist for 1983 [11] and show similar trends:

April 9-10: 469, 206

April 15, 16, 17: 9, 734, 512

April 22, 23, 24: 113, 709, 383

April 30, May 1: 693, 151

May 7, 8: 493, 190

The math works out for some pretty busy and congested weekends at the put-in, particularly when a few points are considered. First are the physical limitations that the access point had at the time. The only practical, legal access was down the narrow Chain Lakes Road and down an equally narrow access ramp to the river, which was located on state land surrounded by private, undeveloped land. Both Tim Spring [12] and Dick Cipperly [13] recalled that the put-in ramp at that time was no wider than a fisherman's path. The state land the ramp was located on could not be developed due to the "Forever Wild" amendment. As such it couldn't be widened and parking areas couldn't be developed.

Likewise, the neighboring private land could not be developed.

Factor in a short release time from the Lake Abanakee dam and the equation read hundreds of people a day, along with equipment and vehicles, in a congested area, all trying to access the river down a narrow ramp before the dam was closed on a given weekend day. Needless to say, there was opportunity for conflict to arise or, at the very least, the "wilderness" experience would be compromised.

A DEC legal memo dated April 11, 1984, on the legality of Town authority at the put-in talked of "overzealous competition among outfitters for entry into the river at the most advantageous time," with "instances of altercations among rafters" at the put-in. [14] While there may not have been any full-blown, out-of-control incidents, the situation was recognized as having a potential impact on the user experience. This explained the concern of the Town Board at the February, 1981, meeting when the outfitters again asked for scheduled releases for the coming season. The board approved the releases, but on the condition that the put-in situation was more controlled. [15]

Complications arising from these numbers also had the potential for negative user experiences on the river as well, with congested rapids, competition for lunch spots, and the mixing of trips posing problems. [16] Dick Cipperly commented on how these numbers affected other users of the gorge, too, recalling the concerns of hikers who came to the Blue Ledges area seeking a less crowded experience and discovering several hundred rafters running the river, with some outfitters cooking lunch there. [17] All three parties - the outfitters, the Town, and the DEC - realized the need to do something to better manage the growing usage so that the overall experience was not affected.

DEC involvement in the management of the Hudson River Gorge predates commercial rafting, going back to 1971 when the first Unit Management Plan (UMP) was put forth.[18] UMPs are guiding documents that spell out the way individual units of state-owned land in the Adirondacks and Catskills are to be managed. Every unit of state land is generally classified for a particular use, such as Wild Forest, Wilderness, and Primitive, with the UMP of each unit listing the specific regulations, policies, and procedures that apply in order to carry out the general directive of the land classification. Since its formation in the early 1970s the DEC tried to formulate a management plan for the Hudson River Gorge, starting the process as early as 1971. That process has continued since then for the Hudson Gorge, with no final plan completed.[19]

As with many other UMPs, the 1971 DEC document lists the resources present in the area, as well as possible recreational activities, along with goals and potential management regulations. An interesting section looked at recreational activities in the gorge. While there were a variety of outdoor activities listed that could take place in the area, "it is the whitewater canoeing and rafting on the Hudson River that makes the area unique." The plan also talked about managing the area "in a near natural state," in anticipation of future acquisitions in the area so that it might become a Wilderness area with the wild character of the river to be maintained. [20] The very next year, of course, saw passage of the NYS Wild, Scenic, and Recreational Rivers Act, which helped to assure this goal of a "natural state".

In an interesting bit of prophecy, the plan said that usage pressures should be anticipated and that user limits would probably come into being. The "ultimate" method of controlling usage, the

DEC felt, must include both the regulation of entrances to the area and the issuing of day-use permits. The plan anticipated not needing the permits "for at least another decade" and, when they did become necessary, would be made available through local forest rangers. [21]

It is quite possible that these permits where the "licenses" that several outfitters speak of having to get in the early days of rafting.[22] In an effort to control the day use, according to the UMP, fifty permits were to be made available, with the limit increased only to accommodate canoeing or rafting parties during the peak season. Thus, as early as 1971, the DEC recognized overuse of the river as a potential problem, with user and access limits proposed as a management solution. [23]

The Indian Lake Chamber of Commerce was also involved early on with concern for the success of rafting, with Bob Geandreau helping to lay the groundwork for rafting within the town in preparation for the important February, 1980, Town Board meeting. In a letter to the eight outfitters of that time dated March 12, 1981, Geandreau, in his role as president of the Indian Lake Chamber of Commerce, set up a meeting with the outfitters on April 14th to discuss these management problems.

The letter outlined eight issues that would be on the agenda, several of which dealt with the need for the outfitters to organize and suggested specific steps that could be taken. Issue #3 recommended that "the outfitters collectively ELECT a single member of all their groups to be the SOLE spokesman for all the outfitters with the Town Board." Issue #4 "strongly suggests" that the outfitters "collectively develop the necessary rules and regulations" for an orderly put in and assign lunch spots on the river and for the "avoidance of conflicts between operating outfitters."

In Issue #5, the Town insisted that outfitters, under no circumstances, "limit or attempt to limit competition by controlling who may run the river." This is an interesting statement in light of the Town's own resolution two years later that attempted to limit some outfitters' access to the river. The last issue in the letter made specific suggestions as to ways for the outfitters to better organize the put-in. The letter concludes with the threat of the Town withdrawing their support for rafting, which would have meant the end of releases from Lake Abanakee. [24]

Gilborn recorded April 14, 1981, - the same meeting date listed in the Geandreau letter - as the birthday of the Hudson River Professional Outfitters Association (the Association). She also listed the Town Board and DEC representatives as being in attendance, with the formation of the Association being the result of the meeting.[25] Wayne Hockmeyer recalled the back room of the dinning area at the Oak Barrel as the place of the first meeting of the Association.[26] A nine-page document containing the by-laws of the Association came forth that outlined the purpose of the organization, membership application procedures, and the amount of members' annual dues. The document also listed the organizational structure, grievance procedures, and a general order for business meetings. Article Six gave specific guidance on how the put-in order and lunch spot locations were to be determined. [27]

In keeping with the concern for overuse, Article Seven set a limit of eighty guests for each outfitter per day and supported this limit as "necessary to maintain a professional reliable commercial operation." In Article Eight, the Association spelled out concern for the carrying capacity of the river and stated that if each member reached the limit on a given day, the maximum number would be reached. Any amount over that limit would possibly have an impact on the resource of the river.

One of the purposes of the Association, as stated in Article One, Section 2, Number 7, was to keep and maintain records of use, to monitor use, and to "act in a manner to avoid potential over use" if the carrying capacity was "reaching its limits". Numbers 8 and 9 directed the keeping of records of growth and the sharing of these records, along with recommendations to "existing or potential regulating authorities". [28] Although ambiguous as to consequences for overuse, this might explain some of the less-than-cordial greetings some of the new outfitters experienced when they came to run the Hudson commercially.

Wayne Hockmeyer explained the need for an orderly put-in, as the outfitters faced the reality of:

> ...how many companies could launch in the time required to run a decent trip. There couldn't be random launch times without total chaos. We would have had companies arriving before daylight to put their rafts in at the head of the line and force their customers to be there at daylight and have them waiting for hours. Establishing a predetermined time for each company was essential to running a professional trip with happy customers. I argued that each company who had established their business on the Hudson River would be given their launch position according to the date of their first commercial trip. Since we all had the ability to launch our trip at a reasonable time, the vast majority of companies agreed this was the fairest (and most sane) arrangement possible. [29]

Hockmeyer also proposed the limit of eighty guests per company per day as a means to control the numbers. According to Gary Staab of ARO, the number eighty was chosen for the practical reason that it would equate to the number of guests that could fit into two raft buses. [30] Regardless, most of the outfitters supported this number, with only one outfitter opposed.

The paper entitled "A Proposal Affecting the Future of Our Township", written by the Indian Lake Chamber of Commerce and dated January, 1982, also showed concern for the potential impact of increased number of river runners on both the river and the Town. [31] It spelled out many of the issues in establishing and keeping rafting on the Hudson a viable industry for Indian Lake and encouraged the Town, as a whole, to follow through.

The section titled "The Advantages" gave 10,000 as the number of rafters on the Hudson at the end of the 1981 season and saw the possibility of this number doubling or tripling in the near future.

This section also highlighted some of the ways the Town would benefit from this increase. The very next section, "The Disadvantages," demonstrated an awareness of the potential negative impacts the number would have, such as rafter's attitudes, traffic problems, Lake Abanakee water level and fishing problems, costs for the Town, and increased state regulation.

The paper made specific suggestions for managing these numbers, including limiting access, the time and amounts of releases from Lake Abanakee, start times for outfitters, and the acquisition of adjoining property to the launch area to help accommodate the influx of traffic. The paper also mapped out specific steps for the Town to take and the rationale for doing so, such as developing the put-in area to accommodate the influx of traffic.

In 1982, the Town Board began to assess a $2-per-person fee to the outfitters, as indicated in the Town Board minutes. [32] The first contracts between the Town Board and the individual outfitters occurred in 1982 as well, in an attempt by the board to control access to the river through the issuing of slots to outfitters. The contracts also eliminated the yearly need by the outfitters to ask the Town Board for releases. The *HCN* also reported that the board was disappointed at the failure of some raft outfitters to pay the $2 head fee in a timely manner. [33] This corroborated what Wayne Hockmeyer said, that when it came to helping finance the releases, some outfitters essentially objected to the idea of paying for the releases and the water. [34] Most outfitters, though, paid the assessment, as they realized it made good business sense.

In 1982, the Town Board took another step to address the usage issue, asking that the DEC include rafting considerations when drafting the Unit Management Plan for the Hudson River Gorge area which would spell out specific land management policies. [35] At the April 12, 1982, Town Board meeting, a resolution was passed that recommended "inclusion of rafting as a prominent feature in the Hudson Gorge Unit Management Plan" and that the board "expresses its desire to actively participate in the consideration of the plan by the advisory committee to be formed in connection with said plan." [36]

One of the major concerns of the Town Board was the day-to-day management of the put-in from the overcrowding numbers. [37] On a given day, numbers ranged from several hundred up to 1,000, all of whom had to get on the river in a limited time frame. The Town Board saw the need to regulate and manage the access point for the good of rafting, asking the DEC for the power to do so. [38] In 1982, the DEC issued a Temporary Revocable Permit (TRP) that granted the Town the authority for day-to-day management. [39] The TRP was used by the Town in both 1982 and 1983, before the legality of its use for this purpose was called into play.

For the 1983 season, the Town Board also approved the appointment of Barry Hutchins as Rafting Attendant, whose job it was to count the number of rafters and help maintain order at the put-in. [40] These steps seemed to have helped, as Swedberg noted there seemed to be no major problems or conflicts at the put-in when he first started on the river that year. [41] Hutchins was also the person who kept more accurate records as to the annual total and the numbers per day and per outfitter.

Further complication of the put-in issue began in 1983 with the arrival of the "New Kids on the River," as more outfitters with large market areas looked to run the Hudson. When Eastern River Expeditions, who rafted on rivers from Maine to West Virginia, arrived at the Hudson, manager Joe Fabin recalled a less-than-cordial greeting. [42] Originally setting up in Indian Lake at a house across from the present day Stewarts' Shop before moving to Marty's, Fabin recalled instances of not being allowed on the road to the put-in and threats to deny access by the Town Board, spurred on by the Association. Fabin went to the extent of retaining a lawyer and filing litigation against the Town, as well as traveling to Albany for a New York State Certificate of Business.

Although she did not list specific instances, Janet Perrin of Rapid Adventures, a division of WILD/WATERS, wrote of exclusion and pettiness on the part of the Association in a letter to the DEC. [43] Schmale reported a similar exclusionary experience when Whitewater Challengers, with access to a large metropolitan market, came to the Hudson and Association membership was denied. [44]

As the "New Kids" began to arrive, the Town Board attempted to limit their access to the river at a special meeting of the board on April 4, 1983. Joe Fabin was at the meeting, seeking approval for Eastern River Expeditions to access the river. The board approved the access for 1983 with the following resolution:

> The Town reserves the right to exclude from use of water releases, or to place at the end of such releases, outfitters who unnecessarily delay or obstruct put-in. The Town's determination in this respect shall be absolute and will be promptly and completely complied with by the Association and its members.

> The Town further reserves the right to permit put-in by Eastern River Expeditions after Association members and private boaters have put-in, provided that Eastern River Expeditions pay the Town $2.00 per rafting customer and provided, further, that said outfitter present no interference with the operations of Association members and obtain no vested interest in future use of water releases by the town.[45]

The legal authority that the Town felt it had for this regulation at the put-in was through the TRP. The Association, too, felt that its by-laws and desire for protection of the product provided the basis for this action.

While the "New Kids" were seemingly excluded membership in the Association, it is interesting to note that the original by-laws and organizational papers of the Association are ambiguous about excluding outfitters from membership. Article Two, Section 1, stated that active membership of the Association "shall consist of all legitimate commercial outfitters who promote and run scheduled trips" on the Hudson. Thus, the original intent, as written, seemed to not place any restraints or qualifications on membership, with the only part open to interpretation being what was meant by "all legitimate commercial outfitters." No other part of the paper indicated any other qualifications for membership in the Association. [46]

Article One, Section 2, Number 7 did allow the Association to "act in a manner to avoid potential overuse of the resource if said use appears to be reaching its limits," but this, too, seemed broad in scope. The only guideline given as to when the limit was being reached was the self-imposed limit of eighty per outfitter per day in Article 8, but even that section ended by saying that if this number was reached, "that it is possible that the carrying capacity would be being approached or reached." What the by-laws did not specify where what actions should be taken when this limit was reached, only that the Association can "act in a manner." [47] Thus, with no specific guidelines to govern the Association or its members concerning what to do, there was room for interpretation as to what to do when the "New Kids" came to raft the Hudson and sought membership in the Association.

Keep in mind that membership was important, since it was the basis for the Town of Indian Lake to issue contracts which in turn, allowed quicker access to the river. Exclusion from the Association meant relegation of large numbers of rafters to the back of an already crowded line at the put-in, as per the Town resolution from the April, 1983, meeting. While the Association and the Town saw this as a legitimate use of their authority to regulate access, the "New Kids" saw this exclusion as an illegal restraint of trade.

The legal authority for the Town's actions, or so they thought, was the Temporary Revocable Permit requested from the DEC, which had been used for the past two years by the Town in an effort to better manage the ever-growing put-in numbers. But there were some legal concerns as to whether the permit gave the Town the power to prohibit public access from a spot located on public land.

In a letter to the DEC dated November 2, 1984, Dave Johnson, legal counsel for the Association, argued that a restraint of trade regulation was legal if the restraint was reasonable, not injurous to the public, or violated public interest. Johnson further argued that there was no injury or violation, as it was reasonable to set limits on numbers of rafters and outfitters and there had been no attempt by other outfitters to fix prices or eliminate competition. Both the Town and the DEC noted the investment in the raft businesses by outfitters who had acted "in a spirit of cooperation and encouragement to new companies." Johnson concluded that these outfitters, who largely created the raft business on the Hudson, should be allowed to continue. [48]

The DEC legal memo from D. Luciano dated April 11, 1984, presented a different view, that the means of regulating the raft program by the Town had serious legal concerns. [49] The memo began by saying that the TRP used by the Town to regulate rafting on the Hudson, including the April, 1983, resolution, was "an inappropriate vehicle" for implementation of regulation. The memo continued on with a summation of the situation, including the Town's attempts to control numbers, as well as a discussion of the legal issues.

The legal discussion started out by saying that rafting was a legitimate use of state land and that the focus should have been on how the program was being regulated. Several legal problems with this regulation were identified, beginning with the program not having gone through a State Environmental Quality Review. The discussion then continued to say that the TRP did not give the Town the authority to exclude outfitters from accessing the river. An important point is Issue #3, the antitrust implications, with the memo stating quickly that "standing alone, the Town's program smacks of restraint of trade" and that if such restriction continued, there could be grounds for legal challenges from those excluded. In order for the exclusion to hold legal merit, it would have to be proven that the original legislative intent for the TRP was to exclude "the kind of activity complained of." [50] Thus, the Town had to prove that the state legislature specifically contemplated limiting raft numbers when enacting the legislation for the creation of the TRP.

The memo continued on, saying that even if the restraints were accepted by the courts, it could still strike down regulatory programs found to be "blatantly unfair". The fourth and fifth issues addressed the legality of commercial trips on state land and the charging of fees for access to state land. The final aspect looked at the legal authority for the Town to regulate, concluding that such authority existed but that it must be given through the proper means. In conclusion, these concerns made the use of the TRP "legally insufficient" to regulate rafting. There was legal authority for the State to delegate to the Town regulatory authority, but it had to be done on firmer legal grounds.[51]

While helping to clarify the aspect of Town regulation, the issue of who got access and who didn't remained. The established outfitters, following what the Association had originally come up with, felt that the user limit had been reached and, as such, no more outfitters should get access. The "New Kids" felt differently, in that there was still room for expansion. Both sides felt a need for limits on usage, but each had different ideas on when that limit had or would be reached. The major difference seemed to be which standard of limits to use - the 800 originally put forth by the Association or the 1,000–1,100 number that had evolved by then. Which standard used would, in turn, determine who got to raft on the Hudson.

This issue came to a climax at two meetings in the fall of 1984 in Indian Lake. A DEC memo dated October, 1984, contained the minutes of the first meeting between the Town, the DEC, and the outfitters.[52] Highlighting the importance of the meeting, the second page listed the attendees, with thirty-nine people listed specifically - the town hall meeting room was fairly packed!

Town Board representatives, including Dick Purdue, were there, as well as several DEC personnel and Bill Starling of the North Creek Chamber of Commerce. The overwhelming majority in attendance were rafters, representing the range of outfitters and the attorney for the Association, Dave Johnson of Tupper Lake. Dick Cipperly of the DEC was listed as the moderator. The document listed the purpose of the meeting to be "an opportunity for any interested parties to suggest ways of regulating traffic and/or operators on the Indian River-Hudson River system". But Cipperly [53] described it as essentially a gripe session for raft people to express views and make suggestions on the main topic of everyone's agenda: river access.

The minutes listed the only hard rule for the release being the maximum two-hour length, as the Town had to maintain a certain water level in Lake Abanakee. [54] Two alternatives were given for usage regulation, including the option for no action and the other being an allocation system. Such a system recognized the already established presence of outfitters on the river while making room for expansion for both them and the "New Kids". Town Supervisor Purdue voiced this very desire on the part of the Town to have a system that recognized both established outfitters and newer ones.

Ron Smith of ARO, as president of the Association, outlined that organization's position, stating that the overall interest of the Association was "protecting the quality of the raft experience and the quality of the environment." Association members desired to have a set put-in time, multiple-year contracts from the Town, a set limit on numbers per day, and a preference to "original businesses" on the Hudson River. Smith concluded by saying the Association recommended a permit–use system similar to that used by the United States Forest Service. [55]

Jay Schurman, Wayne Hockmeyer, and Dick Cipperly commented on how the busy and not-so-busy times broke up the season, with Jay saying that the season needing regulation was the April to May busy season. Cipperly said that there were really three seasons that needed to be looked at. Wayne thought that since Maine outfitters were there for the early part of the season, there was opportunity for newer outfitters after that time, with slots reallocated then. Ken Kellers of New England River said that in order for him to make it, he would need allocations for the whole season, not just part; [56] Mike Whiting of Whitecap expressed similar feelings later in his letter to the DEC.

Schurman also felt that use limits would "force some outfitters out" and that any limits should be placed at the 1983 level. Ken Powley had concerns with where and how the limits were drawn and felt that any lines should not be tied to Association membership. Dick Purdue said that the Town had tried to draw lines, but had not limited it to Association members. Bill Cromie of Adirondack Wildwaters cited an Army Corps of Engineers study managing rafting and commented that cooperation from all parties had made the 1,000-person limit workable. He also felt that allocation deferences should be given to those on the river and that the allocation system might leave some outfitters short in late, low-water situations. [57]

Wayne Failing of Middle Earth and John Monthony of Indian Lake thought that some consideration should be given to in-state outfitters. Monthony also suggested looking at the release schedule and coordinating the Indian Lake Dam that replenished Lake Abanakee. Several people also spoke on safety concerns. The meeting closed with commentary dealing with a timetable on the resolution of the use issue and possible future meetings. [58]

While the final decision did not come for another month, Marko Schmale commented on the feeling of some at the meeting, remarking that it was a:

> very tense meeting with lots and lots of jockeying...

> After the meeting Ken [Powley, JTD] was pretty certain that Whitewater Challengers would have a space on the river. The legal grounds for the exclusion were sketchy. After the meeting, there were a lot of people that were disappointed, obviously the eight as they wanted it to be just them and nobody else. Dick Cipperly felt that if he said "You can't raft," then there would have been lawsuits, particularly after he consulted DEC attorneys.[59]

In the time between the October meeting and the coming one in November, Dick Cipperly, who was the main DEC person to set the use regulation, sought input from the outfitters and several responded, sharing their thoughts on the matter. In a letter to Cipperly, Joey Fabin of Eastern River Expeditions felt the proposal for using a lottery system would be unfair to all outfitters. Fabin did express support for a limitation on users and an allocation system that was "fair and non-punitive". He also stated that safety standards, along with the quality of guides and river trips, should be factored in, with the number of rafters, when determining what the access limits would be. Fabin also expressed concern that some outfitters were running over the limit on certain days, padding their count to keep their slot numbers up. He did not support the suggestion that rafts be counted, instead of people, feeling that this would lead to rafts being overloaded. Fabin concluded with support for better safety standards and a desire to see the environment protected. [60]

Janet Perrin, director of Rapid Adventures Raft Company, which at the time was a division of WILD/WATERS, also wrote to Cipperly. The content of her letter pointed out the financial investment made by the new outfitters who had run the Hudson, feeling it was not fair to exclude them. Perrin was in favor of freezing user limits at the 1,190 limit set at the October, 1984, meeting and adjusting the amount of the release toward higher use times and days; a little more on big days, a little less on lower days. Perrin also felt that membership in the Association should have been open to all outfitters in order to help self-regulate the industry. A good portion of the letter dealt with river safety issues and concluded with an attached copy of the Eastern Professional River Outfitters safety standards. [61]

Michael Whiting of Whitecap Rafting pointed out that his company was small and limited in number of rivers they could run and had invested in equipment, marketing, and insurance. He needed the Hudson River to be more than just a six-week run in order to make a go of it. He saw any preferential access for out-of-state outfitters during the four week high-water time as limiting his ability to make the business work, pointing out that other states that had rafting did not allow out-of-state outfitters.

Whiting mentioned that "a couple of Maine outfitters" believed that because they were at the start of rafting on the Hudson, they had a right to the river, which he believed was "absurd." He also suggested freezing access numbers at the present levels and also suggested longer releases on busy weekends. Whiting also proposed rotating launch times at the put-in so that each outfitter had a chance to start in a timely manner - a proposal that he felt the "rafting association will disagree with." Raft guide trainees were to be counted with other raft guests and be included with that company's head count. He concluded by asking about the possibility of utilizing the Cedar River for access. [62]

Two other views of the access issue were presented by Wayne Hockmeyer of Northern and Ken Powley of Whitewater Challengers. Powley made the run from Newcomb to North River in 1974 and came back to the area in the fall of 1983 to set up a more permanent base of operations in North River from which to run the Hudson. Powley began his letter by agreeing with the Association that seniority should be "the single most important factor" in determining who got slots and what the launch order was. It was a process that was "sensible and justifiable," as it was unfair to take away slots from an early outfitter to accommodate latecomers, as there were other ways to do this without "robbing spaces" from outfitters operating within the 1,000-person limit.

Powley also commended the Association for wanting to protect its members by applying the seniority standard, but felt it was illogical not to apply the same standard to outfitters not in the Association. If this standard was not used, then the DEC might consider the whitewater standards used in Maine, specifically the one concerning how the presence of an outfitter on a river was "serving the interests of the state." [63]

With regards to the Hudson River, Powley felt that the interests of the state were best served by outfitters would commit to "a full-time, complete season basis." [64] Powley expressed disappointment with outfitters who "disregard" the world-class nature of the Hudson River by abandoning the river "in mid-season." While he had no problem with an outfitter abandoning the Hudson, Powley did not agree that these same outfitters should be allowed to do this while "monopolizing indefinitely quotas or allocations which they have no intention of utilizing over a significant portion of the season." Slots should be allocated with the expectation they be used for the full season, not just part of it. It is interesting to note that Powley saw the Hudson as a multi-season run, while Hockmeyer saw it as "at best, a six week run." [65] Powley concluded by supporting the position of Ron Smith for the outfitters to fill 85% of their slots but that this rate should be applied for the full season and not to those outfitters who abandoned the Hudson prematurely. [66]

Wayne Hockmeyer, on the other hand, felt that the user limit had been reached by the outfitters already operating on the Hudson.

Wayne started his commentary by stating that the Hudson River raft business was created by a few outfitters who put time, effort, thought, and money into developing it. Realizing that there were limits to river use, these outfitters set a limit of rafters per day in order to reduce the potential for serious problems related to usage. The outfitters also agreed to specific launch times and specific lunch areas.

Hockmeyer felt that demand for the trip had exceeded available space, creating a market for new outfitters to offer Hudson trips for which there was no room. The Town and the DEC had to decide "whose 800 people are going down the river" and when that limit was reached, no more should be allowed access. In deciding, Hockmeyer hoped that the Town and the DEC would not try to please everyone and "seriously harm" the outfitters who started Hudson River rafting. He also questioned the validity of guide tests and proposed each outfitter be responsible for cleaning their assigned lunch spot. [67]

The November 9th meeting that year revealed how the DEC would resolve this issue, proving the validity of Schmale's feeling after the October meeting. As the DEC document stated, the meeting was again in Indian Lake and again had several DEC and raft personnel attending, but not in the amounts of the previous month.[68] The main issue, of course, was the resolution of the use and access issues so hotly contested the month before. Who received slots and how many would be available was on everyone's mind.

Dick Cipperly began the meeting by commenting on how the river flows that year were above average. He also reported that the "Abanakee Dam was generally opened 2.5 hours this spring, instead of the 2 hours we have been assuming. We will work with the 2.5 hour period for 1985 and accommodate no more than 1,200 customer slots." The long-term goal was to bring the number down to 1,000, still a far cry from the number the Association proposed in 1981 and continued to advocate for. For slot allocations, the outfitters known to have run "in previous springs" and those who operated in the fall of 1984 or made it known that they intended to run in 1985 would be given slots, with no new applications accepted. Companies who had consistently posted larger numbers were given eighty slots, with smaller companies given forty slots and newer companies given twenty. [69]

Several standards for the slots were also given, one being that a company could be sold to another but "parts of slots cannot be sold." Further, as slots became available and the total number fell below 1,000, slots would be available to other companies. Each company was required to "fill at least 80% of their slots on their four or five best days." In order to protect water levels, the Town did not guarantee a release in low-water periods. Contracts with the outfitters were for a four-year period and the Town would also develop a set of safety standards. In the last part of the minutes of the meeting, the DEC said it would designate the put-in as a "Waterway Access Site" and develop a "memorandum of understanding" with the Town for maintenance and operation of the access site, putting access regulation by the Town on firm legal grounds. [70]

While the "New Kids" were happy with this decision, other people were not. At the March 17, 1985, Town Board meeting, Gary Flanagan and Tammy Blanchard from Eastern Slopes Specialty Sports were on hand to voice their feeling that the directive to maintain the 80% of their forty slots on their five best days in the first year of their contract was unfair. [71] They wanted to "grow" into their forty slots gradually, or they might have to cut to twenty slots. While also not happy with the new deal, some of the original eight outfitters worked with it. Others saw it as one more way of tilting the playing field for local outfitters. [72]

Like the soma drug from *Brave New World,* the testosterone eventually died down as the 1980s progressed and rafting began to lose a certain allure. Numbers of guests on the Hudson leveled off after hitting a high mark in 1985. The dynamics of the industry began to change, too, in the late 1980s and into the early 1990s. The passing of the 1985 season proved to be one of transition for commercial rafting on the Hudson, with the industry working its way through these growing pains.

By this time, the extra effort needed to bring its raft operation to Indian Lake had begun to wear on the Northern business. It was quite an investment of time and resources to pack up and make the trip from Maine, run the business in Indian Lake, and then return to Maine - all for a month and a half of rafting, at the most. Likewise, Gaye Clarke and Joe Kowalski of Wilderness Tours told of continued problems crossing the border on the way down from the Ottawa. [73] By the mid 1980s, the Kennebec operation had begun to grow for Northern and did not require the migration of personnel and equipment to the Hudson. [74]

Likewise, the Ottawa operation grew for Wilderness Tours. Neither operation required guides to travel ten hours one way to take a licensing exam or require a commitment of time and resource above an acceptable level of profitability and desire. Thus, for Hockmeyer and the Northern crew, and Clarke and Kowalski of Wilderness Tours, while they fully enjoyed their time in Indian Lake running the Hudson, there was no real reason for them to stay. The 1985 season was the last year for both Northern and Wilderness Tours to run the Hudson River, with Northern selling their slots to Whitewater Challengers and Wilderness Tours selling to Whitewater World. Other non-local outfitters soon followed, and for much the same reasons.

A busy put-in.
Jim Briggs photo

Commercial Rafting: A Maturing Industry

As commercial rafting on the Hudson grew out of its infancy and into a mature industry in the 1990s, both the Indian Lake Town Board and the outfitters were confronted with several new issues. Foremost was the exodus of outfitters based in Indian Lake, coupled with the economic viability of rafting in the face of a changing economic and demographic picture. As the 1980s waned, rafting as a whole began to lose some of its early luster and Hudson numbers leveled off and dropped. Some provision was needed to redirect these numbers in order to make rafting on the Hudson a viable economic business venture and not just a wet adrenaline rush. As other northeast rivers were rafted during the summer months, the Hudson, too, found itself being considered for summer rafting. After going full time in 1997, summer rafting on the Hudson took off and never looked back, drawing numbers that continue to climb and provide the much needed economic redirection. Thus, thirty plus years later, rafting on the Hudson continues to be an important part of local life, even attracting the first sitting governor of New York to run the river in 2010.

Even with the access issue gaining some closure and total numbers beginning to level off, there still remained some rather busy days on the river. DEC attendance records for 1986 [1] and 1987 [2] show several weekends of 1000 plus rafters:

1986	**1987**
April 5:	**April 4:**
401	692
April 12-13:	**April 11-12:**
943, 469	1121, 450
April 19-20:	**April 18:**
1120, 724	621
April 26-27:	**April 24-26:**
1219, 1041	374, 1033, 702
May 3:	**May 2-3:**
955	1081, 462
May 10:	**May 9-10:**
766	751, 124

These busy days were reflected on-river as well. As part of the on-going information-gathering process for the Blue Mountain Wild Forest Unit Management Plan (UMP, or Blue Mountain UMP), DEC Forester Rick Fenton gave an excellent snapshot of river activity at that time period. [3] Hiking into Blue Ledges in the spring of 1994, Fenton described the scene as the rafters passed by. The first raft was spotted at 11:20 a.m., with the last one passing by at 2:00 p.m. Fenton recorded that he saw 129 rafts, forty-two kayakers, and one private raft. Most of the rafts were sixteen-foot, eight-person rafts, with several holding nine or ten people. There were also a few fourteen-foot, six-person rafts that went by, mostly in groups of 6-10 rafts by company. The clientele consisted mostly of men, with about 30% being women and numerous female guides. Fenton also noted that despite massive use of the Blue Ledges area for lunch stops by rafters, time spent there was short in duration, with "little impact" to the land. Extended lunch stops with cookout meals of the early 1980s had become a thing of the past.

With numbers such as these, the put-in ramp remained a very busy and congested place as described by users at that time period. A letter from Roger Reinicker, a kayaker from Glens Falls dated January 14, 1985, to John English of the DEC, expressed concern over several issues, including the improvement of the put-in. [4] A letter from Wayne Failing, as president of the Association, dated January 20, 1992, to Dick Cipperly listed specific suggestions for the improvement of the put-in. [5] Failing commented on how the Association discussed with the Town the widening of the Chain Lakes Road to the fullest extent (fifty feet) of the Town's right of way. Failing also suggested a cooperative effort between the Town and the DEC to clear a staging area opposite the ramp.

Ramp congestion and other raft issues became part of the DEC's UMP process as well. Initially, raft issues were to be addressed jointly in both the Hudson River Gorge UMP and the Blue Mountain UMP because of the "geographical proximity" of the units. [6] But the Hudson UMP was delayed in its completion, as other planning efforts and changing staff assignments slowed progress over the years. Eventually, "different land classifications and variety of public uses in each" area required separate UMPs. [7] Work on the Hudson River Gorge UMP has continued through 2013. Put-in issues, though, could be covered in the Blue Mountain UMP, as the ramp is located in that unit.

Work on the Blue Mountain UMP was less complicated and began with the appointment of a Citizens Advisory Committee in 1986. The committee was comprised of thirteen people representing a wide variety of interests and included Ron Smith of ARO, Bob Gates of the Indian Lake Town Board, and Jim Briggs of the Cornell Cooperative Extension, who had written several articles promoting rafting for the *Hamilton County News* (*HCN*). Over the course of the next several years, the committee met to discuss the issues, evaluate information, and elicit commentary from the public. A draft proposal was released in the winter of 1993/1994, with UMP approval coming in 1994.

The Blue Mountain UMP described the put-in congestion from the limited turn out spaces, which were often used by private boaters. "On busy weekends as many as 50 vehicles have been parked along Chain Lakes Road at one time. The availability of safe parking was limited and did not accommodate use levels". [8] This was the reasoning for the Town to manage the congestion by stopping and unloading passenger buses at the Lake Abanakee dam and having the guests walk the quarter mile to the waiting rafts and the ramp. Dean Molton of the Town Water Department recalled outfitters having to stack rafts on top of each other at the ramp in order to conserve space. [9] Keep in mind that development of parking areas was restricted by the state land the ramp was located on and by the private land next to the ramp.

In the fall of 1984, the DEC designated the put-in ramp as a "waterway access site" to help establish firmer legal grounds for the management of the site by the Town. [10] A waterway access site designation allowed for access to waterways "with attendant parking facilities which does not contain a ramp for or otherwise permit launching of trailered boats". [11] According to the Blue Mountain UMP, the designation also confirmed that there were no other reasonable and safe access points for rafters and that even with use levels of up to 1,000 per day, there had been "no observable adverse impacts" to the river or surrounding land. The UMP also states that use of the area for rafting "will not impair the wilderness quality of the area" or the user experience. The designation concluded with the allowance of basic maintenance of the ramp, a prohibition of motor use, and that there should be no unmitigated impact on the surrounding land or waterway.[12] The designation allowed for better management, regulation, and development of the access.

Part of the Town's response to the space issue at the ramp was first put forth in the 1982 Chamber of Commerce "Proposal" paper.[13] Here was an early recognition of the need to expand and develop the access area to accommodate commercial raft use, with the paper urging the Town to acquire the private parcel surrounding the access ramp, owned by Rocco Denino of Glens Falls. Although the Chamber of Commerce put a high priority on the Denino property acquisition, not all seemed to share this desire. Ten years later at a Town Board meeting on October 14, 1991, a list of land acquisitions was examined. [14] The draft of the Indian Lake Land Acquisition Advisory Committee November 29, 1991, rated the priority of the Rocco Denino property as "moderate". [15]

Less than a year later, though, the board took a more serious look at the property. At the Town Board meeting on February 27, 1992, the property was discussed, with Supervisor Purdue reporting that the property had been used for years by private boaters and rafters as a staging area and that the Town was comfortable with this situation. Perhaps this was the basis for the low priority on acquisition since 1982.

At the February meeting, the Town was also informed of a proposal by Pat Cunningham to buy the Denino property and lease its use to other rafters and boaters, which was of grave concern to other commercial users. There was also discussion on widening the road and getting a permit to do so. Purdue mentioned financing options to acquire the Denino tract, including the use of federal funds from the Forest Legacy Program. [16] At the May 5, 1992, meeting, the Town Board passed a resolution on the Denino property expressing the support of the board to work out an acquisition proposal for the property and recognition of the value of the property to the town for public ownership. [17]

The DEC provided support, contacting the Denino family in March about selling. [18] By July, the Town Board minutes report that Purdue and Councilman John Monthony had met with the DEC and the Forest Legacy representative to discuss acquiring the Denino property. Originally, the Town was looking only at eighteen acres for "recreational purposes," but now they were looking at acquisition of the whole parcel, with recreational rights to the eighteen acres and shared ownership of the rest. The DEC appraised the various aspects of ownership of the property in order to give the Town a figure on the cost of acquisition. Initial figures indicated a value of $6,000 to $8,000. The board felt that acquisition of the property "will be a great asset to the Town for recreational purposes." [19]

The acquisition process began to enter the final stages, but by November of 1992, momentum slowed somewhat with ownership and property values still needing to be sorted out. At the December meeting, the board looked at a proposal to acquire the Denino property, outlining meetings with the DEC and the Forest Legacy Program personnel. The holdup to the deal was on the value of certain rights such as mineral, timber, and development, along with the question of who would own the rights.

Ownership of the whole parcel would be a cooperative venture, with part of the rights being retained by the federal government and outright fee title being held on twenty acres by the Town, with a figure of $15,000 for the Town's contribution. [20] The board approved the management plan for the property the next month, agreeing to improve parking areas, allow primitive camping with sanitary facilities on the eighteen acres, and maintain a trail to Bullhead Pond on the other 141 acres. [21]

Finalization of the deal happened over the next year, with the board authorizing Supervisor Purdue to sign the Stewardship Plan for the Denino tract as previously approved by the board at the March 8, 1993. [22] In August, the board passed the resolution to make the Denino property purchase at $16,567, [23] with final authorization to execute the contract coming at the April 8, 1994, meeting. [24] Final acquisition occurred with funding help from the Federal Forest Legacy Program, with the federal government picking up a right of way and a conservation easement on 141 acres and the Town acquiring eighteen acres "to be used for parking, camping, and picnicking in addition to a staging area for whitewater users". [25]

While there continued to be some large number days, acquisition and development of the property helped free up the log jam at the put-in. Town Highway Supervisor Tim Spring reported at the February 13, 1995, Town Board meeting on the development of the Denino property, saying that he would flag the area, along with some minor clearing, grading, and filling in of the foundation. [26] Spring reported on the completion of the improvement project at the August 29, 1996, meeting. [27]

An important issue that commercial rafting on the Hudson faced during the 1980s was that of safety, with several instances of near-misses taking place on river trips. The "Black Sunday" incident comes to mind, as well. Concern for river safety, though, predates commercial rafting, going all the way back to logging days. When Jack Donohue took over as foreman for the log drives for Finch, Pryne, he gave standing orders that no one was to run the rapids in the jam boats. [28] During the 1970s, as recreational river running in the Hudson Gorge increased, so did the number of serious mishaps, with resulting rescues prompting the DEC to formulate rescue plans.[29] When commercial rafting took hold, it also had its share of mishaps and incidents, as outlined in an earlier chapter. Several outfitters voiced their concern on the topic, listing specific incidents during the early years and describing safety management policies that they did or felt should be followed.

Janet Perrin of WILD/WATERS, writing to the DEC on the overuse problem, gave insight into safety concerns and management policies of the time. [30] Perrin expressed the concern that although "there have been only limited incidents and accidents" with no serious injuries or fatalities, she felt "that this is due, in many ways, to luck." She then listed specific instances of unsafe practices that took place, such as raft trips without support boats, one or two person rafts with inexperienced people in them left to fend for themselves, no safety lines around the outside of the raft, unqualified guides, and intoxicated guests.

Perrin also listed specific safety management policies of WILD/WATERS, such as helmets for guests, guides at least being eighteen years old with previous whitewater experience, and minimum level of first aid and CPR, with many guides having advanced medical training. Each raft had a throw bag and carabiners, with the sweep raft having an extensive medical kit. Perrin also said that her company would offer the use of backboards placed along the river at strategic locations. Each raft was accompanied by a safety boater and had two guides in it during high water days. Perrin also offered to host river rescue workshops for any interested guides. She concluded the letter by attaching a sheet listing the safety standards of the Eastern Professional River Outfitters. [31]

Joey Fabin of Eastern River Expeditions also wrote of safety concerns in his letter to Dick Cipperly dated November 2, 1984. Like

WILD/WATERS, Eastern had a helmet policy for guests and required a minimum of first aid and CPR training for their guides, as well as "numerous training runs" on the river. Several of the guides had advanced medical training. Fabin mentioned the concern of overloading of rafts and inexperienced guides on the part of some outfitters, pointing out the danger of these practices in an emergency situation. Fabin also wrote of an instance where a raft from another company "blasted right through" an Eastern trip while trying to catch up to theirs. [32] Thus, despite the nature of rafting during the 1980s, there was a realization of the risk posed by rafting and an intentional effort on the part of several outfitters to manage the risk and provide a safer experience. Many of these policies were incorporated into the guide licensing requirements when the DEC revamped the program in 1986.

Raft safety again came to the fore in the 1990s as some of the incidents went beyond a serious injury. Four fatalities on the Hudson from commercial rafting took place during this period. This book is not the forum to go into details of the incidents; for the curious, they are well documented elsewhere. As historical events, though, they need to be mentioned and the aftermath examined. All four fatalities happened in the early 1990s, with the first occurring in 1990 and the last one in 1996. Each one happened at different spots on the river and under different circumstances, with three occurring in spring and the fourth in early summer.

In the aftermath of the first commercial rafting fatality in 1990, both the Town Board and the outfitters responded in an effort to manage the safety of the guests who came. At the Town Board meeting in December 10, 1990, Paul Fogal, manager of the outfitter involved with the fatality, was on hand to discuss safety issues. [33] An article by Ellen Craig in the Hamilton Count News (*HCN*) gave details of the meeting and what was said on the safety issue. Much of what Fogal spoke about to the Town Board and the suggestions he made must be seen in the light of how the incident unfolded, as guide qualifications, protection of body parts, and incident response time were called into question. In general, Fogal felt that "there is no single glaring thing that needs to be done to make rafting safer," as "safety is already a primary focus but efforts can be intensified". Referring to all involved parties, Fogal said, "We have pretty much the same concerns."[34]

Specifically, Fogal said that a more in-depth training program for guides, including the sandwiching of experienced guides around those with less experience, was important. Although Fogal wasn't convinced of the safety value of helmets for guests, his company would make them available. With hypothermia always a present danger, an "additional emphasis" would be placed on awareness by the guides. A more thorough pre-trip safety briefing on the dangers of rafting would be paired with signed liability forms. When asked about intoxicated guests by Councilman Fasset, Fogal said that all guests were screened for drugs and alcohol before the trip and any who were suspected to be under the influence were not allowed to go. An EMT was on each trip, along with a first aid kit, and guides would have familiarity with emergency evacuation procedures. Comments on the use of radios from the board prompted Fogal to point out the spotty communications on the river, with the board saying that a new tower would help and suggesting the establishment of emergency communications with Warren County as well.[35]

With regards to emergency procedures, Fogal said that each situation would be evaluated as to the seriousness and, if evacuation was needed, the person would either be taken to Blue Ledges or paddled directly to the take-out. With this location determined, the two fastest boats would be sent ahead to summon more emergency help. Fogal concluded by saying that the great unknown factor in such a situation was the availability of an evacuation helicopter and where it could land [a specific issue in the first incident, JTD]. Supervisor Purdue said that the DEC could be involved with that determination. Councilman Fasset added that the DEC should pre-determine appropriate landing spots and that these spots should become common knowledge amongst the outfitters and guides.[36]

Several months later, Craig wrote in the *HCN* that Wayne Failing reported to the Town Board on safety management by the outfitters. Failing said that the "ratio of rafters to guides is down, backboards are now stored at eight locations along the river, guides have maps of the six escape routes along the course, and more companies are carrying equipment to deal with hypothermia." Failing also stated that outfitters were continually working with the DEC to improve safety.[37]

One of the issues in the first fatality was the length of time between the incident and the connection with more advanced medical treatment. This time element seemed to have been reduced when the second fatality occurred in 1993. McKinstry reported that a raft flipped in the Narrows and, after the victim was recovered, CPR was administered. When the person became unresponsive, they were transported directly to the take-out in North River. The same article also noted that after the 1990 fatality, both the guide and the outfitter were fined $250 each.[38]

The very next year, safety was on the front page of the May 2nd *HCN* again, with Craig reporting on both the third fatality and a near-miss. In the near-miss, a person fell out of a raft and became unresponsive after being recovered by another outfitter. A passing boat was asked to paddle ahead to summon an ambulance, CPR was successfully administered, and the person recovered. As for the fatality, after falling out of a raft, the person was able to swim to the raft and get back in, at which point the person became unresponsive. CPR was administered and the person was rafted to the take-out but did not recover.

Craig also noted that, in both instances, the raft guests were wearing neoprene, PFDs, helmets, and received a pre-trip safety briefing. While the water level was reported as a possible factor in both incidents, it was noted that there was no agreement amongst guides and outfitters as to when the level was too high, leaving it up to the individual outfitters to determine. One veteran guide commented that the water level was not as much of a factor as guests "saying that they are in good physical condition when they are not". Craig also noted that Supervisor Purdue thought the raft program could be in jeopardy unless there was better pre-trip screening of rafters done by the outfitters. Purdue also felt that, while the Town had no expertise in setting safety standards and left it instead to the outfitters, that perhaps the DEC could take the lead in setting some safety standards.[39]

The Town Board minutes also recorded the resolve of the board with regards to safety issues several days later. At the May 4th meeting, discussion of the raft fatalities included a suggestion to limit the access of outfitters who had fatalities or when their guests sustained certain types of injuries, adding these provisions to the next contract. [40]

Craig, writing in the May 10th *HCN,* gave more details, saying that Supervisor Purdue had spoken to the outfitter who had the fatality about the incidents and that, overall, outfitters were trying to work together to make the run safe. Purdue also commented that, in terms of regulation, the Town Board "does not have the expertise to set rafting regulations" and by doing so, the Town would "share in the liability for any accidents with the outfitters." "Our hands are kind of tied," Purdue continued, but he thought the Town could warn the outfitters to tighten safety regulations and policies and possibly bar outfitters from the river who had fatalities or did not observe safety standards. He also thought that perhaps there could be "automatic penalties" for both fatalities and accidents. Purdue also wrote the DEC, asking them to take more control over rafting on New York rivers. [41] The Town Board minutes of May 9, 1994, also recorded a proposal by John Monthony to develop the Pete Gay Eddy state trail to be used for assisting with river access for on-river rescues. [42]

Ellen Craig, in the May 17th *HCN,* also reported on the Town Board meeting, saying that the board discussed the possibility of renovating old trails into the Hudson River Gorge to better facilitate rescue and evacuation of raft injuries. Councilman Tom Potter also suggested developing a place along the river where a helicopter could land to evacuate an accident victim. Superintendent Purdue stated he would write the DEC to look at the possibility of opening trails into the gorge. [43] Craig also reported on the December, 1995, Town Board meeting when Purdue recommended the board include in the next contract a requirement that all outfitters adhere to the safety policies the Association had set. In the past, the board had not set safety polices due to liability of the Town. The board agreed to have the town attorney comment on the proposal. [44]

In June of 1996, the fourth fatality occurred when the victim stood up in a rapid after he fell out of the raft, with his foot becoming wedged under a rock. Rescue efforts took over two hours to complete, with outfitters afterward adding increased emphasis in explaining the need of never standing up in moving current to guests. [45] The *Glens Falls Post Star* also reported that guides attempted to use rafts and swimmers in the rescue attempts. [46]

Some of the more interesting and unique Hudson River trips of the 1990s were those offered by the Sagamore Institute of the Raquette Lake area that used wooden drift boats similar to those used on the Colorado River. A Sagamore flier described these trips, but gave no date or author. An early 1990s date was most likely, as another Sagamore brochure confirmed that these trips began in 1993.

According to the brochure, Sagamore would offer six river trips in the spring and fall, emphasizing a variety of topics such as fly fishing, photography, geology, and plant ecology. Trips were two days and one overnight, with some trips leaving from Newcomb and numbers limited to eight guests per trip with two guests per boat. The trip featured wooden McKenzie River driftboats developed in the northwest and similar to the Colorado River dory boats. These boats would "mark the first return to upper Hudson of open wooden boats" since the log driving days. [47]

As rafting on the Hudson grew out of its infancy and into a mature industry, there also came a realization that there were certain costs involved with providing releases for rafting. Town of Indian Lake budgets [48] reflected this expense, with appropriations for personal services for rafting, equipment, and contractual expenses with total appropriations for several years listed below:

Total Raft Expenses

1984..........$2,525

1985..........$8,100

1986..........$6,000

These figures help to document that there was a cost of time, personnel, and equipment for the Town to provide releases.

By the mid-1980s, the Town Board began to show a concern for the economics of providing releases for rafting. At the July 14, 1986 Town Board meeting, several outfitters were on hand to ask about fall releases. The Town voted not to have fall releases due to the "small benefit and large liability". [49] At a special meeting on the releases two weeks later, Dick Purdue explained to raft outfitters, local businesses, and local residents that "there was no change in the concern of the Town Board as to the level of business generated in the Town by fall rafting" and as such, the board did not support fall rafting. Responding to questions raised by the public, Purdue further said that "the business generated and the money received do not compensate" the Town for the liability of a possible fatality. Purdue also suggested outfitters and businesses document rafting revenue. [50]

Two years later, the Lake Abanakee dam was in need of repairs. At a meeting on August 8, 1988, the board carried a motion to suspend the fall raft season in order to fix it. The suspension of the season would begin when the contractor started work and the Town would try to notify outfitters. [51] An indication of the expense and extent of these repairs was given at the December 23, 1988, Town Board meeting, when $13,000 was authorized for the rollers and gate rehabilitation. [52] Clearly, there were expenses in providing dam releases for rafting on the part of the Town beyond normal operating costs, with both the Town Board and Indian Lake businesses looking for some kind of return for the extra expense. One of the tools that the Town used to try to balance this equation was the contract negotiations between the Town and the outfitters.

Legally binding contracts between outfitters and the Town have not always been the norm and have evolved since the first full season of rafting in 1980, when outfitters went before the Town Board to ask for releases from Lake Abanakee. The result was the Town Board passed a resolution approving a schedule of releases. [53] This arrangement took place for the next season, when outfitters again went before the board in February of 1981 to ask for releases, with a resulting resolution. [54] At the March meeting, Wayne Hockmeyer suggested that "a fee should be assessed to each outfitter" and paid to the town for the releases, the first time on record that the basic idea of slot fees came up. [55] This was put into the agreement for 1982, when the board approved a $2-per-rafter fee to the outfitters, the next step toward a full-fledged contractual agreement. [56]

At the July 12th board meeting, the results of the fee were reported. The Town collected $10,494 from the outfitters as per the agreement, with the revenues added to the town's General Fund. [57] Fees were again collected in 1983, with the November 22nd *HCN* reporting the Town Board approved a contract for "regulating Indian River rafting" for the 1984 season, with a limit of 900 per day at a $5-per-person fee, representing the first contract between the town and outfitters.[58] Contract renewals afterward continued to be a seemingly straight-forward process and all seemed well with rafting in Indian Lake. But as the economics of rafting began to morph in the late 1980s, the relationship between the Town and the raft outfitters became a little more complicated. An undercurrent of discontent with the raft program amongst some local businesses began to swell and reveal itself as the dynamics of the maturing industry unfolded in the early 1990's.

In the beginning of commercial rafting, many of the Hudson River outfitters based their temporary mobile operations in Indian Lake, with Northern staying at the Lone Birch Motel, Wilderness Tours at Adirondack Trails Motel and the American Legion, Eastern at Marty's, ARO had operations across from the Indian Lake Theater, Adirondack Wildwaters at the Lake Abanakee parking area and the Wilderness Lodge, etc.

As some of these outfitters left Hudson rafting, several of the "New Kids" came in and settled outside of Indian Lake, such as Whitewater Challengers in North River, Whitecap Rafting at Friends Lake Inn, and Whitewater World relocating to North Creek. With this flow of outfitters downriver from Indian Lake also came the relocation of the revenue that they generated by their immediate presence. This move, of course, raised alarms with Indian Lake businesses and provided the basis of the undercurrents of discontent.

Negotiations for the 1990 contract began at the May 8, 1989, Town Board meeting, with Councilman Ed Meade moving that contracts with raft companies be for three years, charge $70 per position (compared to $2 in 1984), charge outfitters any cost the Town incurred for any DEC-required fishery studies on Lake Abanakee, and that none of the contracts be in effect until all contracts were executed with the motion passing. [59]

At the August 21, 1989, meeting, the board approved the terms for the contract, settling on a $60 fee for outfitters who ran a full season, $40 for those who ran April only. The board also set the release schedule for the 1990 season, as well as holding harmless the Town for any required DEC fishery studies and "1991 fees to be reduced if significant rafting business moves to Indian Lake during 1990." [60]

Negotiations continued at the September 18th meeting, with some of the previous contract resolutions being rescinded while accepting slot fees for each season and the length of season an outfitter was on the river. Also included were provisions that companies could not use the river for commercial customers until the season started, but could use it for training trips. The Town would also not incur the expense of DEC fish surveys. The sale of a raft business was permitted, but the sale of slots separately was prohibited. These terms were acceptable, with the board approving a motion for Supervisor Purdue to execute the contract with the outfitters. [61] The undercurrent, though, remained.

Three years later, in 1992, when it came time to negotiate the next contract, this undercurrent became a raging rapid when the Town upped the effort to keep outfitters in Indian Lake, and negotiations proved to be a little more heated. At a Town Board meeting on March 9, 1992, some of the opening salvos were fired as the question was put forth as to what the Town was doing to bring more rafting to Indian Lake. Supervisor Purdue spoke to the town's attorney about ideas on "controlling the location of the rafting outfitters" and had not heard back. The board was "very disappointed with the loss of business from outfitters that have moved to North River," with one of the suggested ways to return this business being an increased fee for non-Indian Lake outfitters. With contract negotiations looming, Purdue asked the board "how hard nosed they were willing to get?"

Purdue also said that several options would be reviewed. He continued by mentioning that outfitters in North River liked their guests to be able to change to dry clothes when they got off the river instead of having to endure a bus trip back to a base in Indian Lake. He also expressed the frustration on the part of the Town of Indian Lake in that "the Town of Indian Lake assumes the liability, has the resource, it's our fishery that is being impacted," and that the North Creek area was gaining the benefit of rafting "without any risk or expense." [62]

The raging rapid continued to escalate at the next Town Board meeting on April 13, 1992, when there was a public commentary period on how to keep rafting in Indian Lake. [63] Tom Scully spoke on behalf of the Indian Lake Chamber of Commerce and concerned citizens, saying that after the last contract negotiations, "outfitters promised to help local businesses in Indian Lake and to send people to accommodations in Indian Lake" and to promote the area. "This did not happen". The Chamber appreciated those outfitters who had stayed in Indian Lake and stood ready to help accommodate those seeking to return. Several other local business people spoke on the lack of business from rafting.

Supervisor Purdue spoke to these concerns, stating that the board had been aware of this problem for some time and had tried several solutions, such as requiring all outfitters to report to Town Hall to record their numbers. This only added to the travel time the outfitters had to make it to the river, giving the Town an undesirable image amongst raft guests and did not accomplish what was intended.

Purdue continued, saying that there wasn't much the Town could legally do to force outfitters to relocate to Indian Lake, and that one way to approach this was to tell the outfitters that they needed to provide proof of business within the town before negotiations could begin. Jim Jackier proposed building a base camp for the outfitters, located in Indian Lake, but the board had thought of this idea years ago, rejecting it out of concern for the Town to pay off the debt it incurred. Wayne Failing, president of the Association, spoke about getting together to find solutions to benefit all parties. The outfitters were concerned with fairness, he said, and the Association also suggested building a "base center". [64]

Ellen Craig, in the April 21st edition of the *HCN,* provided another ringside view on this meeting. She reported that the Town Board felt "besieged" by outfitters, local businesses, Lake Abanakee residents, and fishing people, a "four front battle" - all of whom were at odds as to the future of commercial rafting on the Hudson. Craig reiterated on how Oak Barrel owner Tom Scully felt rafters had not promoted Indian Lake businesses as they said they would when rafting began in the 1980s. At that time, there were twenty outfitters based in Indian Lake and "making a significant contribution to the local economy". Of the remaining eleven outfitters that currently ran the Hudson, only four remained in Indian Lake, with local businesses receiving "only 10-15 percent of revenues" generated by rafters looking for services. As a result of this change, Scully said that the board should not "renew the contracts of any raft companies based outside Indian Lake." The Indian Lake Chamber of Commerce offered its support to any outfitter willing to relocate to Indian Lake. Perhaps recalling the access issue of 1984, Supervisor Purdue said that while the board was aware of the situation, the Town couldn't legally offer contracts only to locally based outfitters while excluding others. [65]

On the rafting side, Bruce McGinn of Pocono Whitewater World summed up the outfitters' position. Responding to Scully, McGinn said that his business "was forced to leave Indian Lake when it outgrew the facilities available locally," as he needed space for 270 people per day to park and change into wetsuits. McGinn explained the basis for the need: "The market has changed in the past twelve years. People today are demanding more amenities – they want heated changing rooms, hot food, and paved parking. We're willing to move if anyone can guarantee the space." [66]

Wayne Failing of Middle Earth Expeditions, and president of the Association, highlighted the successful arrangement he had with Jim Jackier of the Adirondack Trail Complex in Indian Lake. Failing outlined that his guests often ate and stayed in Indian Lake and that outfitters recognized the changing dynamics and wanted to help. Failing supported the idea that the town construct a "large common base facility" in Indian Lake from which all outfitters would operate. Failing concurred with McGinn, concluding that the majority of outfitters would move back to Indian Lake if there were facilities large enough to accommodate rafters, which were now often up to 1,000 per day. Failing also added that the outfitters might be more willing to cooperate if the dam release schedule ran into July and August. [67]

Supervisor Purdue responded, saying that the economic climate at the time forbid the risk to the Town in constructing such a building to entice outfitters to locate in Indian Lake. He also added that outfitters always seemed to ask for something from the Town without the Town getting much in return. Purdue felt that the outfitters needed to "step forward and tell us what you can do for us", referring to the town in general. Local fishing people and Lake Abanakee residents were also on hand at the meeting to express their concern on the effect of releases from the lake on local fishing. [68]

With regards to the Town and the outfitters, here were two sides of an issue, both trying to cope with the changing dynamics and economic realities of a maturing industry.

A few weeks later, on April 27th after an executive session in which the raft contract was considered, the board passed a motion to consider stopping rafting. [69] The motion stated that since the beginning of rafting, one of the aims was to "provide a significant stimulus to the local economy," but that expansion had occurred over the course of a few short years before outfitters moved to Warren County. While there were financial benefits to the town for rafting, they did not offset the expense or risk the Town took on to provide for rafting. As such, the board would not undertake contract negotiations until "reasonably assured" that rafting would provide an economic stimulus.

The Indian Lake Chamber of Commerce provided guidance on the types of proof needed to assure the board. Craig reported in the August 18th issue of the *HCN* that the board decided at the July 10th meeting not to have "prolonged negotiations" with the rafters, and that the board would "present a contract the rafters will be free to accept or reject as written". [70] With such a charged atmosphere, it was vital that both sides open a dialogue and work out the differences in order for commercial rafting on the Hudson to continue.

At the August 8, 1992, meeting, the Board had another open comment period on rafting issues, which seemed to indicate that such talks had begun .[71] The minutes of the meeting state that the Town Board, the Chamber of Commerce, and the rafters would work together to promote Indian Lake during raft season and would contribute toward this; the Board would keep slot fees the same. As such, the Town had directed the Chamber of Commerce to coordinate talks with the outfitters and advise what types of proofs would be needed to document efforts by the outfitters to steer business to Indian Lake.

Craig, reporting on the August 8th Town Board meeting, noted that Chamber president Eris Thompson gave a preliminary report on the July talks with the outfitters. [72] Thompson said that several Indian Lake businesses were willing to expand or improve their facilities in order to accommodate rafters. In spite of this, no outfitters had indicated a desire to relocate to Indian Lake, to which Thompson said that the Chamber was "very disappointed," feeling that some of the outfitters didn't have facilities any better than Indian Lake could offer. "The rafters are not willing to move" she said, and that even with a willingness on the part of the town businesses, outfitters "are not willing to do much." She said that the Chamber had hoped to form a partnership with the outfitters but that it "hasn't worked out that way."

Thompson also noted that the Town went to great lengths to accommodate rafters by providing releases even on low number days. Thompson concluded with some preliminary recommendations from the Chamber, the first of which was to provide financial incentives through slot fees for relocation to Indian Lake. She also thought that any unused slots could revert back to the Town with no refund and then be redistributed to Indian Lake-based outfitters. Finally, Thompson thought that a percentage of the head fees could be diverted to cooperative advertising.

Supervisor Purdue responded to the idea of selective slot fees by saying that the town attorney thought that the Town couldn't legally discriminate between local and non-local outfitters. He added that perhaps there could be a provision in the contract that could specify that all outfitters pick up guests at a parking area located in Indian Lake.[73]

Whitewater Challengers manager Marko Schmale replied that, due to the economic situation, raft companies were having a hard time, that economics were driving the situation: "We are just getting by," he said. Schmale continued by pointing out that the Town already got $60,000 annually from fees charged to the outfitters. Rafting also generated local business and produced sales tax for the Town and Hamilton County, as well as providing employment. In the Whitewater Challengers brochure, accommodations for both Indian Lake and North Creek were listed. Faced with the threat of discontinuing rafting on the Hudson, Schmale pointed out that more than just the outfitters would be affected unfairly. [74]

The coming month would prove more productive for both the outfitters and the Town, but there were still differences. Craig reports in the *HCN* that at the September 14th Board meeting, Thompson made the Chamber report official and hinted at some progress in the negotiations, saying that "We don't agree on everything, but we can talk and we've come a long way". Much of what was presented were the proposals from the draft presented the month before such as discounted fees, five year-term contracts, and cooperative advertising with the Town. [75]

Ken Powley from Whitewater Challengers was on hand to state the financial situation of the outfitters, saying that most outfitters were operating" near the edge" and could not relocate back to Indian Lake. If such a discount to local outfitters was made policy, two or more outfitters could go out of business. Powley also explained that it cost each outfitter around $3,500 per raft to operate, in addition to wetsuit and safety equipment costs, transportation of raft guests, and guide training. Having the five-year contract would give outfitters more time to recoup these expenses and focus on improving the raft program. Powley concluded by saying that the outfitters needed to show that spring rafting could benefit the Town before getting into the issue of extending the season into June, as some had proposed. Outfitters were also open to the proposal for cooperative advertising with the Town, as he said, "The Chamber of Commerce, the Town Board, and the outfitters have a unique opportunity to do something positive. Cross-marketing, mutual programming, and support could enhance the economic life of Indian Lake." [76]

Town Board Minutes also recorded that Thompson noted that several outfitters were members of the Chamber and presented several proposals for the upcoming contract.

1. Economic incentives for outfitters locating in Indian Lake.
2. Five-year contract period to provide more stability for outfitters to plan their business.
3. Length of season to run from April to first weekend of June for spring and fall season to be on weekends from Labor Day in September to Columbus Day in October.
4. Reallocation of slots will make slots open for new companies and that unused slots would revert back to the Town for reassignment.
5. Cooperative advertising of rafting between the Town, Chamber of Commerce, and the Association.
6. Administration of unused slots would involve the Chamber of Commerce.
7. Financing of this administration would be from money collected from head fees.
8. Better Town supervision of Lake Abanakee water levels. [77]

Supervisor Purdue stated that the town attorney felt that #1 was illegal, while Chamber of Commerce attorney felt that it was legal and that Dean Moulton would be consulted with regards to the water level issue.

Thompson also stated that the outfitters did not agree with all of these proposals and then asked that Ken Powley, representing the Association, be allowed to speak, to which Powley read a letter into record. Powley began by stating that many of the Chamber proposals, while being significant, were endorsed by the outfitters who were Chamber members with the underlying intention to be the economic health and well-being of Indian Lake. Some of the underlying aspects of these proposals needed to be worked out, along with improved communication and cooperation between all three parties in order to take advantage of the opportunity to shape the future of rafting.

Powley also stated that the Association supported efforts to increase Indian Lake tourism through cooperative marketing and improved communication between the three parties. The Association also supported efforts to consider the needs of the Lake Abanakee homeowners and sportsmen. Powley concluded that there were mutual goals that should be vigorously pursued. [78]

Several comments were given during a public comment period, including concerns for keeping better track of raft money, Lake Abanakee water levels, the cost of releases, the condition of the Lake Abanakee dam, tourism opportunities, and using environmental issues as the sole entity for decision making. Powley also stated the need for rafters to look at advertising targeted for families coming to the area. Purdue concluded this aspect of the Town meeting by saying that no action would be taken without DEC commentary and stated the need for further discussion. [79]

At the October 26th Board meeting, raft contracts were discussed, as well as two proposed draft amendments. The first one proposed a 10% fee increase for water releases if the Chamber could not report on the positive efforts of raft companies to generate business in Indian Lake. The second was a right for the Town to terminate contracts if the Town's liability insurance was withdrawn. After discussion, the Board dropped the first proposal and adopted the second. It was also suggested to recommend that outfitters offer their customers coupons from local business to encourage spending time and money in Indian Lake. The Board also agreed to mandate membership of the outfitters in the Chamber of Commerce. [80] The contract was reviewed and approved at the Board meeting on November 30th, with outfitters returning the signed deal soon after. [81]

Even with the contract in place, sentiment and ill feelings remained amongst some of the parties for some time after. Marko Schmale talked about the 1992 negotiations:

By the contract renegotiations in 1992, there were some issues with the Town of Indian Lake, as a number of outfitters had already moved out of Indian Lake and that's when they were threatening to stop the program. That was the worst contract negotiations the Town or the outfitters ever experienced. The Indian Lake Chamber of Commerce and others floated the idea that the Town would build a big huge building on Chain Lakes Road in Indian Lake and all the outfitters would be there similar to what is done on the Youghiogheny. There was also a proposition to say that you would not get a contract if you were not based in Indian Lake, period. The term that the outfitters came up with that kind of resounded legally was "restraint of trade". You cannot legally force someone to relocate their business because you want them to. It's essentially blackmail.

That first negotiation was pretty intense. Wayne Failing and I went to meetings, spent days on the phone talking to Dick Purdue, Dick Cipperly, Eris Thompson, Tom and Cathy Scully. The process disenchanted any hangers-on, like Unicorn. Jay Schurman thought that this was crazy, that the Town of Indian Lake wanted to blackmail the outfitters was off the charts. [82]

Efforts to encourage outfitters to locate in Indian Lake continued early in 1993, as several new outfitters expressed interest in running the Hudson. At the February meeting, the Board discussed offering extra raft slots for one year to some new outfitters, such as John Duncan of Syd & Dusty's, Dave Braglia of Northern Pathfinders, and a few other locals. The Board approved a motion to allocate 100 extra slots for one year with the expectation that those outfitters would locate in Indian Lake. [83] Braglia was on hand

at the March 8th meeting to document his efforts to bring customers to Indian Lake. The package that he offered included lodging at
Lone Birch, breakfast at Wilderness Lodge, and a post-trip visit to
Oak Barrel. [84] Such favoring measures did not escape other outfitters not located in Indian Lake, as Marko Schmale of Whitewater
Challengers wrote the Board in April concerning the special consideration given the one-year slot contract for Northern Pathfinders. [85]

Town Board records also showed a continued attempt to persuade
new outfitters to locate in Indian Lake. At the October, 1995, meeting, the Board sold slots to Professional River Outfitters (PRO) from
Maine on the condition that they located in Indian Lake. [86] PRO did so,
locating in downtown Indian Lake right next to the Oak Barrel. The
very next month, Adirondack Raft Company (ARC) from Lake Placid
also requested slots from the Board. The Board carried a motion to
approve the slot request on condition that ARC show proof of their
intent to locate in Indian Lake, which they did, reaching agreement
with Wilderness Lodge in Indian Lake to locate there. [87] ARC eventually relocated near the Adirondack Trails Motel in Indian Lake
where Wilderness Tours had done so ten years earlier.

One of the outcomes of the 1992 negotiations was the forging of
a closer working relationship between the Town of Indian Lake and
the rafters. As Wayne Failing said, "We all have a mutual goal of
working together in out best interests." A good example of this was
the Town-sponsored Whitewater Festival in May of 1993. Failing
was highly complimentary of Mark Sherwin, who was the president
of the Indian Lake Chamber of Commerce, saying how Sherwin was
"doing a fantastic job" in putting the Festival together. [88]

The Festival was to be held at Byron Park in Indian Lake on
Saturday, May 15, 1993. Robert Engel, the assistant curator at the
Adirondack Museum at the time, was the coordinator of the Festival.
Earley reports how Engel described the event, saying it was time for
"whitewater sports to become more well-known to people seeking recreational outlets. The Festival – which will encompass historical and
contemporary photographic exhibits, storytellers, licensed guides,
two musical acts, food, equipment and trip raffles, river trips, and
more – is a real celebration of the river." [89]

The *Glens Falls Post Star* also reports on a unique part of the Festival with some of the outfitters offering short, one mile raft trips on the Indian River. "These short trips emphasize safety and paddling skills and are intended to introduce the sport to newcomers. The trips will begin at 1:30 p.m. and attendance is limited. Participants should wear light, non-cotton clothing and bring an extra pair of sneakers..." [90]

Earley also reported in the *Glens Falls Business Journal* on some of the other changes in Hudson River rafting that took place during this time period. [91] In the article Marko Schmale commented on how rafting had peaked during the late 1980s, with the market eventually stabilizing. Previously, rafting had grown exponentially since 1982, as it was the "in" thing to do. But as rafting began to lose some its luster, that growth began to level off. Town of Indian Lake attendance records show this trend, with a steady increase from a base number of 4,748 in 1983, when records became more reliable.

After hitting the high mark in 1986, the numbers begin to level out and decline going from 10171 in 1987 down to 9516 in 1991. The numbers gain again in 1992 with 10512, up to 12042 in 1994, before dropping to 9065 in 1995 with spring season rising to 11168 in 1994 before diving to 8018 the very next year. Thus, even as some of the "New Kids" gained numbers, market access, and influence, rafting on the Hudson had begun to lose some its appeal and the total numbers cited above show this. [93]

In the Earley article, Schmale described how the peak season had shifted and now extended into late June with May becoming the middle of the season "instead of the end". Earley writes on with what Marko told her:

> In 1992, one half of Whitewater Challengers' business occurred in April, with the balance in May and June. Previously, 60 percent was in April, and only 40 percent in May and June. Part of the reason for the shift is the changing clientele. In the early years of rafting, Marko observed that the typical customers were all male groups. Now, customers are more typically

couples and groups who work together; these people are less likely to want to brave the colder April water temperatures, he observed. [94]

Bruce McGinn, who managed the Pennsylvania-based Whitewater World, concurred, observing how the Hudson River runner of the 1990's "is a much less gung-ho type of rafter" from the 1980's requiring a different marketing approach and making it a much "harder sale." McGinn also said that river runners of the '90s "are older clientele than the past." With the change in clientele, McGinn said the company had to spend more advertising dollars per guest to get the same amount of business. [95]

Profitability, then, would become *the* issue that outfitters faced as the 1990's progressed, as both numbers and clientele changed from the 1980s. Town Board records give insight into this issue, as at the January 1996 meeting, the board received copies of a letter written by Marko Schmale on behalf of the Association asking for a reduction in the slot fees. [96] Schmale listed several reasons for the request, among them "weaker demand, static trip prices, and ever increasing costs for capital equipment, liability insurance, payroll and other costs" which had "squeezed profits of most outfitters." The letter also stated the feeling of the outfitters that slot fees had not kept pace with the realities of a low-growth market and, as a result, some outfitters faced the prospect of abandoning the Hudson commercially. Thus, for the Hudson River to remain a viable commercial run, the downward trend of profitability needed to be redirected for both the Town and the outfitters, which helped plow fertile ground for the idea of summer rafting.

Although the actual negotiations on summer rafting took place in 1995-96, the idea of summer rafting on the Hudson River had been around for a while, dating back to 1982. Summer river running on the Hudson, too, had been going on for some time, dating back as far as Charles Farnum's 1880 run, through the recreational runners of the 1960-70s - such as Ed Hixon and Clyde Smith - and continuing on with private kayakers during the 1980s and 1990s.

In a proposal prepared by the Indian Lake Chamber of Commerce on commercial rafting dated January, 1982, the potential of the Hudson run was noted. In the document, the Chamber envisioned numbers for Hudson rafting rising up to 20,000, "possibly growing to 27,000–30,000" per year. [97] By comparison, the 2009 season had over 25,000 total for all three seasons. [98] These potential numbers that Geandreau cited in the proposal were based on the notion that they would include both summer and fall raft seasons. Later in the proposal, it was noted that the impact that such numbers might have on the Town and the river could be spread out over a six-month season. Anticipating that summer and fall releases might pose a concern for the Lake Abanakee water levels, the proposal had two specific recommendations. One was that a "late spring and summer release should not exceed one half to three quarters of an hour" to minimize the effect of the drawdown. Second was that such releases "should not occur more than four days a week." [99]

The idea of summer rafting appears in other places, with the Warren County tourism brochure of 1981 describing raft trips in the area, the outfitters who offered them, and specific fee and contact information. [100] The brochure noted in the Hudson section that, depending on water levels, "trips are also run in July and August," this despite no agreement with the Town for releases during these months. A trip on the Sacandaga River in Lake Luzurene was also described, with the season there starting in April and the best whitewater from late May through early September. Outfitters listed as offering the Sacandaga trip include ARO, Adirondack Wildwaters, and Hudson River Rafting, who also promoted a trip on the East and West Branch of the Sacandaga in Wells. The *Hamilton County News* also reports on HRRC looking to set up a base in Tupper Lake to raft the Oswegatchie River. [101]

Outfitters themselves had begun to think about summer releases no later than 1993, as noted in the Blue Mountain UMP, and probably even earlier. [102] At a Town Board meeting in March of 1992, Wayne Failing offered' to trade some spring dates for extended summer dates as a "pilot program for possible permanent status". [103]

An actual summer season of sorts did take place on the Hudson in 1987. The dam on Indian Lake was in need of repairs, so the water level on the lake was lowered, with the Lake Abanakee dam responding by being open as well, providing a continual flow of water down the Indian River. Indian Lake was drawn down twenty-three feet, giving a good flow of water down the Indian River from August 15th through to September 15th, allowing outfitters to offer raft trips on the Hudson in summer conditions. [104]

Marko Schmale remembered that the drawdown happened gradually, over a month's time, so as not to flood out docks and buildings. Many of the outfitters did not run during the 1987 summer season, as "most of us were doing other things" and, as such, there wasn't much commercial activity during the drawdown. Some of the outfitters weren't sure the drawdown would take place, either, so they did not schedule trips. "Pat Cunningham had some customers and some others paddled the gorge but that was mainly it." [105]

Town Board records indicate that only Cunningham and John Starling of Adventure Sports came before the Town Board for permission to offer raft trips during this period. [106] Pat Cunningham was quoted as saying, "Summer rafting on the Hudson in 1987 is going to be remembered for a long time," [107] ten years, to be exact, when summer rafting became permanent. Schmale felt this summer season helped lay the foundation for a permanent summer season, proving how well it could happen. [108]

Although the Indian Lake Chamber of Commerce may have thought that summer rafting would be part of the whole rafting equation, initially, there wasn't much support for it on the Town Board or at the DEC. The Town Board records show that the spring season had attained a level of acceptance and, to a certain degree, the fall season, but summer releases were not supported. [109] That being said, in 1983, the board did approve releases into July 4th. [110] Town Board minutes of the January, 1996, meeting also record that the outfitters asked for a five-year contract to give them "a measure of financial stability and operating safety." A longer summer season, though, was not supported, as there was consensus on the board not to add days to a summer raft season. [111]

The DEC did not support summer releases either, with much of the concern centering on the effect of releases on Lake Abanakee levels. As stated in the 1995 Blue Mountain Wild Forest UMP, DEC regional fisheries staff opposed the expansion of the raft season into June and July out of concern releases from Lake Abanakee would have on spawning and hatching fish. The fear was that low summertime water levels would not allow sufficient time to refill the lake and thus affect the Abanakee water level. [112] A key element for a wider acceptance of summer rafting would be the coordinated releases of water from Indian Lake into Lake Abanakee to help refill Abanakee after a release.[113]

At the April meeting, the Town Board and the DEC began to seriously consider summer releases. At a special meeting that was held in Indian Lake on April 11, 1996, attended by the Board and Dick Cipperly, several things were considered. Cipperly started the meeting by saying how the Town had been involved with the rafting program, that fees were a concern for the outfitters, that business had moved to Warren County, and noted a drop in Sunday and weekday numbers, concluding by stressing the role that local business could play. [114]

Outfitters also discussed the possibility of fishing trips in the gorge as a way to boost numbers, along with looking at a longer season, such as beginning in April and going through to October. Dick Cipperly responded by saying that releases from the Indian Lake dam could be coordinated to minimize the potential impact on the Lake Abanakee water level. The parties agreed that the outfitters should look into the feasibility of summer releases and make a proposal to the Town of release days and estimated numbers. Safety and slot issues were also looked at, with the Town and outfitters agreeing to reconsider slot fees. [115]

The outfitters would meet with Councilman Brian Farrel at the end of the meeting to discuss rafting. The result of this meeting was the presentation at the May, 1996, meeting of the Town Board for a limited summer raft program. [116] The proposal was presented to the board in the form of a letter by Marko Schmale, acting as president of the Raft Association. Releases would happen on Wednesday,

Thursday, Saturday, and Sunday during June; Wednesday and Saturday during the last two weeks of July and the first two weeks of August; and Wednesday, Saturday, and Sunday during the last two weeks of August. The Association also asked to keep the current schedule of spring and fall releases. Councilman John Monthony, who had played a part in the early history of Hudson rafting, moved that the board approve the schedule of releases for the summer of 1996, limiting draw downs to within 3 inches of the tops of the splash-boards on top of the dam. Councilman Farrel seconded the motion and it was approved.

In the letter that was sent to the board, Schmale stated the belief that summer rafting would have a large appeal and that, with approval from the DEC and the Town, along with the likelihood of coordinated releases with the Indian Lake dam, "a limited schedule of summertime rafting on the Hudson appears to be quite feasible." [117] At the August 12, 1996, meeting, the board records indicated the willingness to reconsider summer rafting under a heading referred to as "Town Recreation Plan." In that plan, the raft section stated that up to that point, rafting had been confined to spring and fall seasons and that "the Board is currently experimenting with summer rafting... If small, managed releases of water result in enhanced use of the rivers by rafters and other boaters, the summer activity will be proposed for permanent DEC approval, water availability permitting".[118]

Lake Abanakee residents predictably raised concerns about the proposed summer season. As the winds of summer rafting were beginning to filter through town, the presence of Jerry Rosenthal and LeRoy Spring was made known at the January, 1996, Board meeting. [119] They were there to express their concern about the water level of Abanakee during raft season and the effect of releases on the environment.

Spring was also at the April 11, 1996, board meeting, where he said that he would like to see the Abanakee water level maintained at a reasonable level. He also restated his belief that releases from the dam for rafting were affecting pike spawning in the lake, this despite the 1992 DEC study that found no such effect. Spring also wanted the board to "consider fishermen in their waders in the summer, during the proposed summer dam releases." [120] When the Town contract with the DEC was considered at the request of the Lake Abanakee Association, the DEC included wording that stated that the Abanakee dam would have "a maximum four-inch drawdown" at a time and that this limit would be in effect even at high water times. [121]

A limited schedule of releases took place during the summer months of 1996, with several outfitters taking advantage of them. Pat Cunningham reported on his numbers to the board at the December 9, 1996, meeting, saying that between 1,200 and 1,500 people went summer rafting. [122] Marko Schmale reported that Whitewater Challengers had 167.[123] The experiment worked well enough for a full season of summer rafting to be considered for the 1997 season. [124]

The Town Board did have concerns about the cost of releases for a full summer season, for at the February 10, 1997, meeting, the board directed Supervisor Purdue to write the outfitters to inform them that the board would "pro-rate personnel costs and charge participating outfitters our costs according to the number of people each outfitter takes down the river." [125] Marko Schmale responded at the May 12, 1997, meeting with a request for a full season of summer rafting. Contained in the request was an agreement by the outfitters to pay for "any direct labor costs and benefits" related to summer rafting. [126] With this assurance, the board prepared a draft for consideration by the board for all outfitters who would be participating in summer rafting.

At the June 23, 1997, meeting the board considered and approved this proposal for a full season of summer rafting:

> The Town of Indian Lake agrees to provide releases from Lake Abanakee Dam during the summer of 1997 in support of commercial rafting. The undersigned outfitters agree to pay the Town of Indian Lake, through the Hudson River Professional Outfitters Association by September 20, 1997, their share of the cost to release water. Any unpaid bills will be paid by the HRPOA and it will be the Association's responsibility to collect the money from the individual outfitters. [127]

DEC attendance figures document the success of the experiment. If Cunningham is accurate in the 1,200 to 1,500 number for the 1996 summer season, then that total number for summer rafting went to 2,389 in 1997, [128] with a continual rise ever since:

Spring/Summer	Total
1997	
7319, 2389	9708
1998	
9102, 4067	13169
2000	
9040, 6936	15976
2002	
7718, 8555	16263
2004	
7308, 9781	17089
2006	
7516, 10827	18343
2009	
8192, 15000	23192

Attendance figures also show the total number of rafters going up since 1996, from 9,895 to 20,227 in 2006 and a record-setting 25,455 in 2009, with the rise in summer rafting accounting for this increase. [129] In her report to the DEC for the year 2000, Pam Howard of the Town of Indian Lake highlights the success of the summer raft program, saying how it "seems to be the thing to do." [130] Rafting on the Hudson had reached the potential that Bob Geandreu had envisioned many years before and become a full fledged, important part of the social and economic fabric of the Indian Lake–North Creek area!

The upper Hudson River and the gorge continued to evolve and make history. In August of 2010, Governor David Patterson became the first sitting governor of New York to run the Hudson. Although he had done the run before, this was the first time Patterson or any-one else had done so while governor of New York. Arriving at the put-in with a small group of friends on the weekend of August 21st, the group loaded up three Beaver Brook Outfitters rafts with people and gear and made their way down to the campsite on river left after Cedar Ledges and above Jump/Elephant Rock. There they stayed for an overnight before continuing down to North River the next day. Pete and Diana Burns had the honor of guiding Patterson's raft on both days.[131] This author's personal remembrances of these two days are of a general welcome put forth by many at the put-in and pointing the "Gov" out to raft guests and saying hello.

The very next year, the Hudson River again made history by achieving the highest recorded river level on the North Creek USGS gauge, at 13.65 feet on April 28, 2011, which translates to almost 40,000 cfs. [132] Levels such as this had not been seen since 1982, the year of the "Black Sunday" incident, when the level was up to 30,000 cfs or 12 ft. Similar circumstances led to these conditions in 2011 as well, with 1 to 2 feet of snow hanging around and several inches of rain falling on top of the snow. Levels rose in North River to overflow the rock and stone-reinforced banks spilling onto State Rt. 28 with several inches of river water flooding the lanes of the highway. State Transportation officials had to close the road that Thursday until the water receded, which left maintenance crews to repair washouts and remove wood and stick debris caught in the guide rails. No one ran the gorge, though, until Sunday, when the level had dropped to 8 ft.

Note: At this time there is a pending legal matter concerning an outfitter who had a commercial fatality in September of 2012. It has never been the purpose of this work to report the details of these fatalities, only to report that they happened and look at the aftermath and how it affected the industry. As that aspect is still unknown, this work will only report the fatality.

Rafters enjoying a plunge into the Hudson at Jump/Elephant Rock,
Marko Schmale directing traffic.
Jeff Dickinson photo

Gov. David Patterson running the Narrows,
Pete and Dianna Burns guiding.
Jim Swedberg photo

Whitewater Challengers take out on Rt 28, April 27, 2011,
with the ramp already underwater. The next day the river reached
the other side of State Rt. 28, flooding and closing the road.
Jeff Dickinson photo

Footnotes

Introduction

1. Twain, M. (1986). *The Adventures of Huckleberry Finn*. Penguin Books: New York, p. 128.

2. Wallack, J. (1996). *What the River Says: Whitewater Journeys Along the Inner Frontier*. Blue Heron Publishing: Hillsboro, OR, p. 25

3. Amos, W. (1972). *The Infinite River: A Biologist's Vision of the World of Water*. Ballantine Books: New York, p. xi.

4. Harris, E. (1989). *Mississippi Solo: A River Quest*. Harper & Row: New York, p. 1.

5. Krakel II, D. (1987). *Downriver: A Yellowstone Journey*. Sierra Club Books: San Francisco, p. vx.

6. Leydet, F. (1968). *Time and the River Flowing: Grand Canyon*. Sierra Club–Ballantine Books: New York, p. 52.

7. Wheat, D. (1983). *Floater's Guide to Colorado*. Falcon Press: Billings, p. 7.

8. Krakel II, D. (1987). *Downriver,* p. xvii.

9. Jamison, P. (1986). *Adirondack Pilgrimage.* Adirondack Mountain Club: Glens Falls, p. 181.

10. Dickerman, P. (1991). *Adventure Travel North America.* Adventure Guides Inc.: New York, p. 145.

11. Armstead, L. (1994). *Whitewater Rafting In North America.* The Globe Pequot Press: Old Seybrook, p. xi, 3.

12. Wallack, J. (1996). *What the River Says,* p. 20, 21.

13. Ibid, p. xi-xii, 4.

14. Harper, J. (2008). "Woman Guides Live Their Dreams," *Adirondack Explorer*: March/April 2008, p. 57.

14. Goodspeed, S. (1997). From "Mountain Views" in *Yesterday's River,* North Creek News-Enterprise, Sawyer Press: North Creek, p. 2.

15. Tillich, P. (1957). *Dynamics of Faith,* Harper Colophon Books, New York, p. 9, 13.

16. Van Zandt, R. (1992). *Chronicles of the Hudson.* Black Dome Press: Hensonville, p. 261-5.

17. Ibid, p. 252.

18. Ibid, p. 252.

Adirondacks in General

1. DiNunzio, M. (1984). *Adirondack Wildguide: A Natural History of the Adirondack Park.* Brodoack Press: Utica, p. 89.

2. Ibid., p. 19.

3. Ibid., p. 95.

4. Barnett, L. (1974). *The Ancient Adirondacks*. Time Life Books: New York, p. 44.

5. Brown, P. (1999). *The Longstreet Highroad Guide to the New York Adirondacks*. Longstreet: Atlanta, p. 11.

6. Department of State, New York State (2012). New York State Constitution, Article XIV, Conservation, Forest Preserve to be forever kept wild.
www.dos.ny.gov/info/constitution.htm.

7. Adirondack Park Agency (2003). State Land Classification Definitions. www.apa.ny.gov/stateland/definitions.htm.

8. White, W. (1983). *Adirondack Country*. Alfred A. Knoff: New York, p. 9.

9. Dawson, C. (2009). "Recreation and Tourism in the Adirondacks" in *The Great Experiment in Conservation: Voices From the Adirondacks,* Porter, W., Erickson, J., and Whaley, R., ed., Syracuse University Press: Syracuse, p. 134.

10. Terrie, P. (2009). "Cultural History of the Adirondack Park" in *The Great Experiment in Conservation*, p. 209.

11. Keller, J. (1980). *Adirondack Wilderness: A Story of Man and Nature*. Syracuse University Press: Syracuse, p. 114.

12. Terrie, P. (1973). "Introduction" in *Peaks and People of the Adirondacks,* Carson. R., Adirondack Mountain Club: Glens Falls, p. xxxv.

13. Sulavick, S. (2007). *Adirondacks: Of Indian and Mountains*. Purple Mountain Press: Fleischmanns, p. 13-14.

14. Ibid.

15. Terrie, P. (1973). "Introduction" in *Peaks and People*, p. xxxv.

16. Sulavick, S. (2007). *Adirondacks,* p.36.

17. Sylvester, N. (1973). *Historical Sketches of Northern New York and the Adirondack Wilderness.* Harbor Hill Books: Harrison, p. 39.

18. Sulavick, S. (2007). *Adirondacks,* p.71.

19. Ibid., p. 17.

20. White, W. (1983). *Adirondack,* p. 50.

21. Wallace, E.R. (1894). *Descriptive Guide to the Adirondacks.* Watson Gill: Syracuse, p. xi.

22. White, W. (1983). *Adirondack,* p. 50.

23. Isachsen, Y. (1992). Still Rising After All These Years, <u>Natural History</u>. May 1992, p. 31-3.

24. Ibid.

25. DiNunzio, M. (1984). *Adirondack,* p. 19.

26. McLelland, J. & Selleck, B. (2009). "Geology of the Adirondacks" in *The Great Experiment in Conservation,* p. 20.

27. Sulavick, S. (2007). *Adirondacks,* p. 69-70.

28. Isachsen, Y. (1992). "Still Rising", *Natural History,* p. 31-3.

29. DiNunzio, M. (1984). *Adirondack,* p. 23.

30. Ibid., p. 25-7.

31. Adirondack Ecological Center (2012). Adirondack Ecological Communities. www.esf.edu/aec/adks/forestcomm.htm

32. Ketchledge, E. (1996). *Forests and Trees of the Adirondack High Peaks Region.* Adirondack Mountain Club: Lake George, p.20.

33. DiNunzio, M. (1984). *Adirondack*, p. 49-51.

34. Ibid., p. 103.

35. Keller, J. (1980). *Adirondack*, p.63.

36. Ketchledge, E. (1996). *Forests*, p. 20.

37. McMartin, B. (1990). *Discover the Northwestern Adirondacks.* Backcountry Publications: Woodstock, p. 11.

38. Ketchledge, E. (1996). *Forests*, p. 20-31.

39. Keller, J. (1980). *Adirondack*, p. 65.

40. DiNunzio, M. (1984). *Adirondack,* p. 113.

41. Ketchledge, E. (1996). *Forests*, p. 22.

42. Weber, S. (2001). *Mt. Marcy: The High Point of New York.* Purple Mountain Press: Fleischmanns, p. 17.

43. Aber, T. & King, S. (1965). *The History of Hamilton County.* Willard Press: Boonville, p. 5.

44. White, W. (1983). *Adirondack,* p. 3.

45. Ibid., p. 3-4.

46. Jamieson, P. (1994). *The Adirondack Reader.* Adirondack Mountain Club: Lake George, p. 12.

47. Keller, J. (1980). *Adirondack,* p. 17.

48. White, W. (1983). *Adirondack,* p. 48-9.

49. Ibid., p. 65.

50. Graham, F. (1984). *The Adirondack Park: A Political History.* Syracuse University Press: Syracuse, p. 6.

Upper Hudson River Itself

1. Dunwell, F. (2007). *The Hudson: America's River.* Columbia University Press: NY, p. 208.

2. Brown, P. (1999). *The Longstreet Highroad Guide to the New York Adirondacks.* Longstreet: Atlanta, p. 79.

3. Lorrie, P. (1995). *River of Mountains: A Canoe Journey Down the Hudson.* Syracuse University Press: Syracuse, p. 7.

4. Sulavick, S. (2007). *Adirondacks: Of Indian and Mountains.* Purple Mountain Press: Fleischmanns, p. 142-172.

5. Vandrei, C. (2009). "Explorateur: Samuel Champlain, Intrepid Explorer", *The Conservationist,* 64:1, p. 13.

6. Adirondack Museum Archive, (2012). Maps of the Adirondack Region, Adirondack Museum, Blue Mountain Lake, NY.

7. Ibid.

8. Sylvester, N. (1973). *Historical Sketches of Northern New York and the Adirondack Wilderness.* Harbor Hill Books: Harrison, p. 93.

9. Ibid, p. 93.

10. Lossing, B. (1972). *The Hudson From Wilderness to the Sea.* New Hampshire Publishing Company: Somersworth, p. 3.

11. Boyle, R. (1969). *The Hudson River: A Natural and Unnatural History.* W.W. Norton: New York, p. 21.

12. Dunwell, F. (2007). *The Hudson,* p. 3.

13. Fenton, R. (1992). Draft of Hudson River Gorge Unit Management Plan dated February 1992, p. 10, archived at DEC office in Northville, NY.

14. McMartin, B. (1992). *Discover the Central Adirondacks.* Backcountry Publications: Woodstock, p. 77.

15. Ibid.

16. Fenton, R. (1992). Draft of Hudson River Gorge UMP, p. 10.

17. Miller, B. (1985). *The Adirondacks: High Peaks Region,* series of combined USGS maps. Plinth, Quoin, & Cornice: Keene Valley, NY.

18. Donaldson, A. (2002). *A History of the Adirondacks, v.I.* Purple Mountain Press: Fleischmanns, p. 138.

19. New York State Archives (2013). Map of *Ground Plan of Beds and Veins of Magnetic Oxide of Iron.* Digital Collection, NYS Archives, NYSA B1405-96 310. www.iarchives.nysed.gov.

20. Carson, R. (1973). *Peaks and People of the Adirondacks.* Adirondack Mountain Club: Glens Falls, p. 38.

21. Stoddard, S. (1983). *The Adirondacks Illustrated.* Excelsior Printing: North Adams, p. 117-18.

22. Smith, H. (1885). *The History of Essex County.* D. Mason & Co.: Syracuse, p. 642.

23. Headley, J. (1982). *The Adirondack, or Life In the Woods.* Harbor Hill Books: Harrison, p. 49.

24. Schaefer, P. (1989). *Defending the Wilderness: The Adirondack Writings of Paul Schaefer.* Syracuse University Press: Syracuse, p. 133-5.

25. Weber, S. (2001). *Mt. Marcy: The High Point of New York.* Purple Mountain Press: Fleischmanns, p. 14.

26. Healy, B. (1999). *The High Peaks of Essex: The Adirondack Mountains of Orson Schofield Phelps.* Purple Mountain Press: Fleischmanns, p. 26-7.

27. Weber, S. (2001). *Mt. Marcy*, p. 92.

28. Donaldson, A. (2002). *A History*, p. 43.

29. Carson, R. (1973). *Peaks*, p. 110.

30. Healy, B. (1999). *The High Peaks*, p. 66.

31. Sylvester, N. (1973). *Historical Sketches*, p. 53.

32. Donaldson, A. (2002). *A History*, p. 162

33. Weber, S. (2001). *Mt. Marcy*, p. 93, 162.

34. Wallace, E.R. (1894). *Descriptive Guide to the Adirondacks.* Watson Gill: Syracuse, p. 310.

35. Proskine, A. (1984). *Adirondack Canoe Waters: South and West Flow.* Adirondack Mountain Club: Lake George, p. 31.

36. Miller, B. (1984). *The Adirondack maps.*

37. Wallace, E.R. (1894). *Descriptive Guide,* p. 377-8.

38. USGS, (2013). Topographical map archives, 1898 Newcomb, NY, quadrangle, www.usgs.gov.

39. Ibid.

40. Adirondack Ecological Center (no date). *Hudson River Log Driving System,* replica of 1929 Finch, Pruyn Company map.

41. Adirondack Museum web site, (2013). *Olive Gooley, 1859-1946.* www.adirondackhistory.org/new guides/olive.

42. Ibid.

43. Kaufman, J. (1994). "The Upper Hudson" in *The Adirondack Reader.* Adirondack Mountain Club: Lake George, p. 441.

44. Clarke, G. (2011). Personal interview on the *Early Days of Commercial Rafting on the Hudson River,* Beachburg, Ontario.

45. Kaufman, J. (1994). *The Upper Hudson,* p. 442.

46. Swedberg, J. (2009). *A Few Remembrances,* email dated March 15, 2009.

47. USGS, (2013). Topographical map archives, 1898 Newcomb, NY, quadrangle, www.usgs.gov.

48. Ibid.

49. Ibid.

50. Proskine, A. (1984). *Adirondack,* p. 34.

51. Carlson, D. (1986). *Official Map of River Names: Hudson River Gorge.*

52. Wilson, L. (1986). *The Northwoods Club 1886 –1986.,* Leila Wilson: NY, archived at DEC office Northville, NY.

53. Fosburgh, H. (1955). *The Sound of Whitewater.* Charles Scribbner: NY, p. 17-18.

54. Proskine, A. (1984). *Adirondack,* p. 34.

55. Miller, B. (1984). *The Adirondacks: Central Mountains,* series of combined USGS maps. Plinth, Quoin, & Cornice: Keene Valley, NY.

56. Proskine, A. (1984). *Adirondack,* p. 34.

57. Burns, P. (2011). Personal conversation on the *Origins of the Virgin Falls Story,* Indian Lake, NY, July 24, 2011.

58. Clarke, G. (2011). Personal interview on the *Early Days of Commercial Rafting on the Hudson River,* Beachburg, Ontario.

59. Adirondack Ecological Center (no date). *Hudson River Log Driving System,* replica of 1929 Finch, Pruyn Company map.

60. Hall, R. (1967). "The Unsullied Hudson – It Sings, It Skips, It Dances." *New York Times,* July 16, 1967, p. 296.

61. Miller, B. (1984). *The Adirondacks* maps.

62. Trudell, D. (1980). "Hudson River Trip Report" in *Bow & Stern, June 1980,* at www.vtpaddlers.net/talk/bowstern/archive.

63. Carlson, D. (2008). "A Whitewater Tale" in *Winter Guide to the Gore Mountain & Lake George Area.* No publisher given, p. 12.

64. Carlson, D. (1986). *Official Map of River Names: Hudson River Gorge.*

65. Proskine, A. (1984). *Adirondack,* p. 34.

66. Carlson, D. (1986). *Official Map.*

67. Miller, I. (1985). History of Hudson River Gorge, handwritten notes from Greg George.

68. Fenton, R. (1992). Draft of Hudson River Gorge UMP, p. 6.

69. Carlson, D. (1986). *Official Map.*

70. Buck, R. (1972). "The Hudson Continued". *Adirondack Life* 3:2, p. 24-7.

71. Miller, B. (1984). *The Adirondacks: Central Mountains,* series of combined USGS maps, Plinth, Quoin, & Cornice: Keene Valley, NY.

72. Ibid.

73. Ibid.

74. Proskine, A. (1984). *Adirondack,* p. 35.

75. Miller, B. (1984). *The Adirondacks: Central Mountains,* maps.

76. Fox, W. (1976). *History of the Lumber Industry in the State of New York.* Harbor Hill Books: Harrison, p. 74.

77. Adirondack Museum Archive, (2011). *Articles of Agreement for Driving Logs on the Hudson River and its Tributaries.* Blue Mountain Lake, NY.

78. Carlson, D. (1986). *Official Map.*

79. Proskine, A. (1984). *Adirondack,* p. 35.

80. Kohl, M. (2011). *Personal conversation on river names.* North River, NY.

81. Schaefer, P. (1989). *Defending the Wilderness: The Adirondack Writings of Paul Schaefer.* Syracuse University Press: Syracuse, p.129.

82. Miller, B. (1984). *The Adirondacks: Central* maps.

83. Adirondack Daily Enterprise (1983). Article on *Rafting the Hudson,* May 20, 1983, p. 10, archived at DEC office in Northville, NY.

84. Burns, M. (2013). Personal interview with Milda Burns, daughter of Jack Donahue: *River Driving on the Hudson River.*

85. Adirondack Museum photo archives, (2013). www.adirondackhistory.org, Adirondack Museum, Blue Mountain Lake, NY.

86. Proskine, A. (1984). *Adirondack*, p. 39.

87. Van Zandt, R. (1992). *Chronicles of the Hudson.* Black Dome Press: Hensonville, p. 258.

88. Wallace, E.R. (1894). *Descriptive Guide to the Adirondacks,* Watson Gill: Syracuse, p. 390.

Early Hudson Explorers

1. Kaufman, J. (1994). "The Upper Hudson" in *The Adirondack Reader.* Adirondack Mountain Club: Lake George, p. 443.

2. Adams, A. (1996). *The Hudson Through the Years.* Fordam University Press: NY, p. 1.

3. Boyle, R. (1969). *The Hudson River: A Natural and Unnatural History.* W.W. Norton: New York, p. 29-30.

4. Buckell, B. (1999). *Boldly into the Wilderness: Travelers in Upstate New York 1010- 1646.* Buckle Press: Queensbury, p. 13.

5. Boyle, R. (1969). *The Hudson River,* p. 29.

6. Adams, A. (1996). *The Hudson,* p. 5.

7. Ibid.

8. Buckell, B. (1999). *Boldly into the Wilderness,* p. 115.

9. Boyle, R. (1969). *The Hudson River,* p. 29-30.

10. Sylvester, N. (1973). *Historical Sketches of Northern New York and the Adirondack Wilderness.* Harbor Hill Books: Harrison, p. 36-8.

11. Carmer, C. (1974). *The Hudson.* Holt, Rinehart, and Winston: New York, p. 16-25.

12. Ibid, p. 17.

13. Ibid., p. 16-25.

14. Sylvester, N. (1973). *Historical Sketches,* p. 36-8.

15. White, W. (1983). *Adirondack Country.* Alfred A. Knoff: New York, p. 46.

16. Keller, J. (1980). *Adirondack Wilderness: A Story of Man and Nature.* Syracuse University Press: Syracuse, p. 16.

17. White, W. (1983). *Adirondack,* p. 47-8.

18. Beetle, D. (1984). *Up Old Forge Way.* Utica Observer Dispatch: Utica, p. 15.

19. White, W. (1983). *Adirondack*, p. 47-8.

20. Sulavick, S. (2007). *Adirondacks: Of Indian and Mountains.* Purple Mountain Press: Fleischmanns, p. 86.

21. Aber, T. & King, S. (1965). *The History of Hamilton County.* Willard Press: Boonville, p. 5.

22. Carson, R. (1973). *Peaks and People of the Adirondacks.* Adirondack Mountain Club: Glens Falls, p. 36.

23. Weber, S. (2001). *Mt. Marcy: The High Point of New York.* Purple Mountain Press: Fleischmanns, p. 17.

24. Masten, A. (1968). *The Story of Adirondac.* Syracuse University Press: Syracuse, p. xxxvii-xxxviii .

25. Weber, S. (2001). *Mt. Marcy*, p. 18-19.

26. Adirondack Museum Staff (2010). Lecture on mining and logging in the Adirondacks entitled *Working For the Man,* Fall 2010, North Creek, NY.

27. Weber, S. (2001). *Mt. Marcy*, p. 21.

28. Masten, A. (1968). *Adirondac*, p. 21-3.

29. Shaunghnessy, J. (1997). *Delaware & Hudson.* Syracuse University Press: Syracuse, p. 115.

30. Masten, A. (1968). *Adirondac*, p. 33-4.

31. Manchester, L. (2010). *Tales From the Deserted Village.* www. cefles.org/version 1.03.

32. Wessels, W. (1961). *Adirondack Profiles.* Adirondack Resorts Press: Lake George, p. 64.

33. Masten, A. (1968). *Adirondac,* p. 59-63.

34. Ibid., p. 36.

35. Carson, R. (1973). *Peaks,* p. 38-9.

36. Ibid., p. 39-40.

37. Ibid., p. 42.

38. Shaunghnessy, J. (1997). *Delaware,* p. 115-6.

39. Masten, A. (1968). *Adirondac,* p. 58.

40. Wallace, E.R. (1894). *Descriptive Guide to the Adirondacks.* Watson Gill: Syracuse, p. 350.

41. Shaunghnessy, J. (1997). *Delaware,* p. 89, 115.

42. Ibid., p. 115-6.

43. Ibid., p. 116-29.

44. Ibid., p. 353.

45. Kudish, M. (1996). *Railroads of the Adirondacks: A History.* Purple Mountain Press: Fleishmanns, p. 137.

46. Weber, S. (2001). *Mt. Marcy,* p. 28.

47. Donaldson, A. (2002). *A History of the Adirondacks, vol.1.* Purple Mountain Press: Fleischmanns, p. 152-5.

48. Carson, R. (1973). *Peaks*, p. 53-5.

49. Ibid., p. 53-5.

50. Ibid., p. 53-5.

51. Terrie, P. (1973). "Introduction" in *Peaks and People of the Adirondacks*. Adirondack Mountain Club: Glens Falls, p. xliii.

52. Weber, S. (2001). *Mt. Marcy*, p. 29.

53. Ibid., p. 31.

54. Marshall, G. (1973). "Preface" in *Peaks and People of the Adirondacks*. Adirondack Mountain Club: Glens Falls, p. xix.

55. McMartin, B. (1996). *Discover the Adirondack High Peaks*. Lake View Press: Canada Lake, p. 118.

56. Weber, S. (2001). *Mt. Marcy*, p. 31-2.

57. Nash, R. (1982). *Wilderness and the American Mind, 3rd ed.* Yale University Press: New Haven, p. 61.

58. Hoffman, C. (1970). *Wild Scenes In the Forest and Plain, vol 1*. Literature House: Upper Saddle River, NJ, p. 5, 8.

59. Ibid., p. 79-80.

60. Ibid., p. 77.

61. Headley, J. (1982). *The Adirondack or Life In the Woods*. Harbor Hill Books: Harrison, p. 50.

62. Ibid., p. 46.

63. Ibid., p. 52, 57-8.

64. Street, A. (1993). *The Indian Pass: Source of the Hudson.* Purple Mountain Press: Fleishmanns, p. 4.

65. Ibid., p. 28-9.

66. Ibid., p. 54-5.

67.Ibid., p. 67.

68. Lossing, B. (1972). *The Hudson From Wilderness to the Sea.* New Hampshire Publishing Company: Somersworth, p. 4.

69. Ibid., p. 4-15.

70. Ibid., p. 15-20.

71. Ibid., p. 22.

72. Ibid., p. 22-50.

73. Ibid., p.44.

74. Ibid., p. 27-8.

75. Carson, R. (1973). *Peaks,* p. 67.

76. Weber, S. (2001). *Mt. Marcy,* p. 62-5.

77. Ibid., p. 62-5.

78. Ibid., 63-4.

79. White, W. (1983). *Adirondack,* p. 201.

80. Colvin, V. (1994). "The Discovery of Lake Tear" in *The Adirondack Reader*. Adirondack Mountain Club: Lake George, p. 268-9.

81. Weber, S. (2001). *Mt. Marcy*, p. 91-2.

82. Bond, H. (1995). *Boats and Boating in the Adirondacks,* Syracuse University Press: Syracuse, p. 119.

83. Farnum, C. (1992). Excerpt from *Chronicles of the Hudson,* Roland Van Zandt, Black Dome Press: Hensonville, p. 253-67.

84. Ibid., p. 119, 253.

85. Ibid., p. 255-6.

86. Ibid., p. 257.

87. Ibid., p. 261-5.

Loggers and Log Drives

1. Graham, F. (1984). *The Adirondack Park: A Political History.* Syracuse University Press: Syracuse, p. 10.

2. Porter, W. (2009). "Forestry in the Adirondacks" in *The Great Experiment in Conservation: Voices From the Adirondacks,* Porter, W., Erickson, J., and Whaley, R., ed., Syracuse University Press: Syracuse, p. 102.

3. Aber, T. & King, S. (1965). *The History of Hamilton County.* Willard Press: Boonville, p. 143.

4. Porter, W. (2009). "Forestry", p. 103-5.

5. Hyde, F. (1985). "Resources for the Taking" in *A Century Wild,* Neal Burdick, ed. The Chauncy Press: Saranac Lake, NY, p. 85.

6. Wessels, W. (1961). *Adirondack Profiles.* Adirondack Resorts Press: Lake George, p. 21.

7. Hyde, F. (1985). "Resources", p. 85.

8. Smith, H. (1885). *The History of Essex County.* D. Mason & Co.: Syracuse, p. 634.

9. Miller, I. (1985). History of Hudson River Gorge, handwritten notes from Greg George, Blue Mountain Lake, NY, p. 1.

10. McMartin, B. (1994). *The Great Forests of the Adirondacks.* North Country Books: Utica, p. 38.

11. Smith, H. (1885). *Essex County*, p. 634.

12. Aber, T. & King, S. (1965). *Hamilton County*, p. 145.

13. Merrill, R. (2007). *Log Marks on the Hudson.* Nicholas Burns: Utica, p. 13.

14. Ibid., p. 17-20.

15. Aber, T. & King, S. (1965). *Hamilton County*, p. 146.

16. Welsh, P. (1995). *Jacks, Jobbers, and Kings: Logging the Adirondacks 1850-1950.* North Country Books: Utica, p. 66-7.

17. Fox, W. (1976). *History of the Lumber Industry in the State of New York.* Harbor Hill Books: Harrison, p. 62-5.

18. Aber, T. & King, S. (1965). *Hamilton County*, p. 146.

19. Fox, W. (1976). *Lumber Industry*, p. 65.

20. Ibid., p. 65.

21. Aber, T. & King, S. (1965). *Hamilton County*, p. 145.

22. Fox, W. (1976). *Lumber Industry*, p. 65.

23. Miller, I. (1985). *Hudson River Gorge*, p. 2.

24. Fox, W. (1976). *Lumber Industry*, p. 66-9.

25. Miller, I. (1985). *Hudson River Gorge*, p. 2.

26. Aber, T. & King, S. (1965). *Hamilton County*, p. 146.

27. Ibid., p. 146.

28. Headley, J. (1982). *The Adirondack, or Life In the Woods*. Harbor Hill Books: Harrison, p. 29-30.

29. Fox, W. (1976). *Lumber Industry*, p. 69.

30. Aber, T. & King, S. (1965). *Hamilton County*, p. 147.

31. Fox, W. (1976). *Lumber Industry*, p. 70.

32. Merrill, R. (2007). *Log Marks*, p. 23-5.

33. Fox, W. (1976). *Lumber Industry*, p. 40.

34. Merrill, R. (2007). *Log Marks*, p. 4.

35. Fox, W. (1976). *Lumber Industry*, p. 36.

36. Ibid., p. 28-31.

37. Ibid., p. 28-31.

38. Ibid., p. 27.

39. Ibid., p. 26.

40. Thompson, H. (1967). *New York State Folktales, Legends, and Ballads,* Dover Publications: NY, p. 278.

41. Donaldson, A. (2002). *A History of the Adirondacks, vol. 1.* Purple Mountain Press: Fleischmanns, p. 52.

42. Fox, W. (1976). *Lumber Industry,* p. 36, 40.

43. Aber, T. & King, S. (1965). *Hamilton County,* p. 143.

44. Hochschild, H. (1993). *Lumberjacks and Rivermen in the Central Adirondacks 1850-1950.* Adirondack Museum: Blue Mountain Lake, p. 2.

45. Miller, I. (1985). *Hudson River Gorge,* p. 1.

46. Adirondack Ecological Center (no date). Hudson River Log Driving System, *Finch, Pruyn 1929 Map.*

47. Fenton, R. (1990). Personal notes from a conversation with Dick Nason, Finch, Pruyn historian, archived at DEC office in Northville, NY.

48. Seaman, F. (1970). "Refinding Hudson Spring", *Adirondac,* 34:5, September–October 1970, p. 34-5.

49. Colvin, V. (1874). *Topographical of the Adirondack Wilderness of New York.* Weed, Parsons and Company: Albany.

50. Seaman, F. (1970). *Refinding Hudson Spring,* p. 34-5.

51. Fox, W. (1976). *Lumber Industry,* p. 70.

52. Donohue, H. & Conroy, D. (1994). "The Hamlet of North River" in *Rivers, Rails, and Ski Trails: The History of the Town of Johnsburg,* Johnsburg Historical Society, ed. Sawyers Press: North Creek, p. 71.

So There We Were: River Running in the Hudson Gorge

53. Fox, W. (1976). _Lumber Industry_, p. 43.

54. Bird, B. (1952). _Calked Shoes: Life In Adirondack Lumber Camps._ Prospect Books: Prospect, p. 114-15.

55. Thompson, H. (1967). _New York State Folktales,_ p. 257.

56. Fox, W. (1976). _Lumber Industry,_ p. 43.

57. Donohue, H. & Conroy, D. (1994). "The Hamlet of North River", p. 70.

58. Fox, W. (1976). _Lumber Industry,_ p. 40.

59. Hochschild, H. (1993). _Lumberjacks,_ p. 13-14.

60. Ibid., p. 13-14.

61. Fox, W. (1976). _Lumber Industry,_ p. 78.

62. Ibid., p. 70.

63. Hochschild, H. (1993). _Lumberjacks,_ p. 14.

64. Bird, B. (1952). _Calked Shoes,_ p. 118-19.

65. Hochschild, H. (1993). _Lumberjacks,_ p. 19.

66. McMartin, B. (1992). _Discover the Central Adirondacks._ Backcountry Publications: Woodstock, p. 154-5.

67. Fenton, R. (1990). Personal notes from a conversation with Dick Nason, Finch, Pruyn historian, archived at DEC office in Northville, NY.

68. USGS, (2013). Topographical map archives, 1898 Newcomb, NY, quadrangle, www.usgs.gov.

69. Fenton, R. (1990). Dick Nason.

70. USGS, (2013). 1898 Newcomb, NY, quadrangle.

71. Miller, I. (1985). Hudson River Gorge, p. 3.

72. Savarie, B. (1997). "River Drives", *North Creek News Enterprise* supplement, <u>Yesterday's River</u>, May 1997, p. 4.

73. Ibid., p. 4.

74. Miller, I. (1985). *Hudson River Gorge,* p. 3.

75. Savarie, B. (1997). *River Drives,* p. 4.

76. Donohue, H. & Conroy, D. (1994). "The Hamlet of North River", p. 71.

77. Savarie, B. (1997). *River Drives,* p. 4.

78. Fosburgh, P. (1947). "Big Boom", *New York Conservationist.* 1:5, p. 16.

79. Ibid., p. 17

80. Ibid., p. 16.

81. Fox, W. (1976). *Lumber Industry,* p. 70-3.

82. Headley, J. (1982). *The Adirondack,* p. 39-40.

83. Ibid., p. 41-2.

84. Aber, T. (1982). *Adirondack Folks.* Prospect Books: Prospect, p. 38.

85. McMartin, B. (1992). *Central Adirondacks,* p. 154.

86. Fosburgh, P. (1947). "Big Boom", p. 17.

87. Ibid., p. 17.

88. Burns, M. (2009). Personal interview with Milda Burns, daughter of Jack Donohue: *River Driving on the Hudson River.*

89. Savarie, B. (1997). *River Drives,* p. 1.

90. Bird, B. (1952). *Calked Shoes,* p. 122-3.

91. Hochschild, H. (1993). *Lumberjacks,* p. 16.

92. LaForest, J. & LaForest, A. (2004). *Along the Cedar River.* Indian Lake Library: Indian Lake, NY, p. 3.

93. Bird, B. (1952). *Calked Shoes,* p. 124-5.

94. Burns, M. (2009). Personal interview

95. Lorrie, P. (1995). *River of Mountains: A Canoe Journey Down the Hudson.* Syracuse University Press: Syracuse, p. 107.

96. Burns, M. (2013). Personal interview with Milda Burns, daughter of Jack Donohue: *River Driving on the Hudson River.*

97. Donohue, R. (2009). Personal interview with Ray Donohue, son of Jack Donohue: *River Driving on the Hudson River.*

98. Lorrie, P. (1995). *River of Mountains,* p. 110.

99. Burns, M. (2009). Personal interview.

100. Ibid.

Recreational River Runners

1. Jensen, C. (1970). *Outdoor Recreation In America*. Burgess Publishing: Minneapolis, p. 195-202.

2. McCall & McCall, (1977). *Outdoor Recreation: Forest, Park and Wilderness,* Benziger, Bruce, & Glencoe: Beverly Hills, p. 55.

3. Wells, G. (1968). *Handbook of Wilderness Travel.* Colorado Outdoor Sports: Denver, p. 3-4.

4. Nash, R. (1982). *Wilderness and the American Mind, 3rd ed.* Yale University Press: New Haven, p. 330-1.

5. Armstead, L. (1994). *Whitewater Rafting In North America.* The Globe Pequot Press: Old Seybrook, p. xv.

6. Jenkinson, M. (1973). *Wild Rivers of North America.* E.P. Dutton & Co.: NY, p. 18.

7. Dickerman, P. (1991). *Adventure Travel North America.* Adventure Guides, Inc: NY, p. 12.

8. Gruspe, A. (2009). "A History of Whitewater Rafting in West Virginia", *West Virginia Historical Society Quarterly,* www.wvculture.org/history/wvhs124.html, p. 1-2.

9. Jensen, C. (1970). *Outdoor Recreation,* p. 159.

10. Hendee, J., Stankey, J., Lucas, R. (1978). *Wilderness Management.* United States Forest Service: Washington, p. 128.

11. Nash, R. (1982). *Wilderness,* p. 236-7.

12. Canham, H. (1981). *Forest Recreation: New York State Forest Resources Assessment Report #10,* DEC: Albany, p. 7.

13. Schaefer, P. (1989). *Defending the Wilderness: The Adirondack Writings of Paul Schaefer.* Syracuse University Press: Syracuse, p. 209-11.

14. Brown, E. (1985). *The Forest Preserve of New York State: A Handbook For Conservationists,* p. 55.

15. Graham, F. (1984). *The Adirondack Park: A Political History.* Syracuse University Press: Syracuse, p. 219.

16. Brown, E. (1985). *The Forest Preserve,* p. 38-40.

17. Graham, F. (1984). *The Adirondack Park,* p. 219

18. Porter, W. & Whaley, R. (2009). "Public and Private Land-use Regulation of the Adirondacks" in *The Great Experiment in Conservation: Voices From the Adirondacks,* Porter, W., Erickson, J., and Whaley, R., ed., Syracuse University Press: Syracuse, p. 227.

19. Graham, F. (1984). *The Adirondack Park,* p. 229.

20. Adirondack Park Agency (2012). *Adirondack Park State Land Master Plan,* www.apa.ny.gov/Documents/Laws_Regulations/SLMP, p. 1, 14.

21. Ibid., p. 25-8.

22. Ingersoll, E. (1905). *Guide To the Hudson River, 13th ed.* Rand McNally: Chicago, p. 217.

23. Wallace, E.R. (1894). *Descriptive Guide to the Adirondacks.* Watson Gill: Syracuse, p. 397.

24. Manchester, L. (2010). *Tales From the Deserted Village.* www.cefles.org/version 1.03.

25. Mills, B. (1955). "Tupper to Tahawus", *Adirondac,* 44:7, May–June 1955, p. 44.

26. Shaw, G & R. (no date).*Tahawus – Newcomb and Long Lake.* Reference in Saranac Free Library, Saranac Lake, NY.

27. Wallace, E.R. (1894). *Descriptive Guide,* p. 377-80.

28. Grinnel, L. (1956). *Canoeable Waterways of New York State.* Pageant Press: NY, p. 9-26, 129-31.

29. Ibid., p. 127.

30. Ibid., p. 131-8.

31. Ibid., p. 130.

32. Ibid., p. 130-1.

33. Duel, A. (1979). "Faltbooting Mit Silulium". *American Whitewater Journal,* July–September 1979, p. 10.

34. Ibid., p. 115.

35. Bond, H. (1995). *Boats and Boating in the Adirondacks.* Syracuse University Press: Syracuse, p. 211.

36. Cunningham, P. (2012). Personal conversation on the *First Inflatable Raft Trips in the Hudson River Gorge,* September, 2012, Blue Mountain Lake.

37. Wilson, L. (1986). *The Northwoods Club 1886–1986,* Leila Wilson: NY, archived at DEC office Northville, NY, p. 24.

38. Bond, H. (1995). *Boats and Boating,* p. 211.

39. Wilke, L. (2010). Local resident, interview on *Early Raft Trips on the Hudson,* North River, NY, February, 19, 2010.

40. Hixon, E. (2010). Personal interview on recreational boating in the Hudson River Gorge, Saranac Lake, NY.

41. Randolph, J. (1961). "Wood, Field, and Stream", *New York Times*, May 2, 1961, p. 47.

42. Prime, W. (1967). "The Kennedy Hudson Hegira", *American Whitewater Journal*, Autumn 1967, p. 15.

43. Clarity, J. (1967). "Kennedy Falls Out of Kayak Shooting Hudson Rapids", *New York Times,* May 7, 1967, p. 70.

44. Prime, W. (1967). "The Kennedy", p. 15.

45. Clarity, J. (1967). "Kennedy Falls", p. 70, 1.

46. Prime, W. (1967). "The Kennedy", p. 16.

47. Ibid., p. 15.

48. Clarity, J. (1967). "Kennedy Falls", p. 70.

49. Harrigan, R. (1968). "Robert Francis Kennedy", *American Whitewater Journal*, 13:1, Spring, 1968, p. 3.

50. Clarity, J. (1967). "Kennedy Falls", p. 70.

51. Binger, D. (1967). "The Log", *American Whitewater Journal*, Autumn 1967, p. 17-18.

52. Clarity, J. (1967). "Kennedy Falls", p. 70.

53. Binger, D. (1967). "The Log", p. 18.

54. Clarity, J. (1967). "Kennedy Falls", p. 70.

55. Binger, D. (1967). "The Log", p. 18.

56. Hawksley, O. (1968). "Conservation Comment", *American Whitewater Journal*, Summer, 1968, p. 23.

57. Butler, T. (1997). "Confessions of a River Rat", *North Creek News Enterprise supplement Yesterday's River*, May, 1997, p. 3.

58. Garand, D. (2009). Personal interview on *Early Rafting in the Hudson River Gorge,* Newcomb, NY.

59. Trautwein, B. (1971). "The Rip Trip", *Cloudsplitter*, Summer, 1971, p. 10-11, 26.

60. Ibid., p. 10.

61. Ibid., p. 10.

62. Ibid., p. 11.

63. Ibid., p. 26.

64. Masters, B. & Smith, C. (1970). "Whitewater Wilderness: Adventure in the Upper Hudson". *Adirondack Life* 1:2, p. 25.

65. Buck, R. (1972). "The Hudson Continued", *Adirondack Life* 3:2, p. 26-7.

66. Smith, C. (1976). *The Adirondacks*. Viking Press: New York, p. 24.

67. Hixon, E. (2010). Personal interview.

68. Smith, C. (1976). *The Adirondacks*, p. 24.

69. Ibid., p. 24.

70. Ibid., p. 29.

71. Ibid., p. 26.

72. Cummins, P. (2009). Local resident of Indian Lake on *Tubing on the Hudson*, Indian Lake, NY, June, 24, 2009.

73. McKenney, R. (2011). Personal interview on *Northern Frontier Camp in the Hudson River Gorge*, Indian Lake, NY.

74. McKenney, K. (2010). Phone conversation on *Northern Frontier Camp in the Hudson River Gorge.*

75. Bayse, J. (2011). Email on *Northern Frontier Camp Staff Use of the Hudson River Gorge*, p. 1.

76. Hennigan, R. (2007). "To be or Not To Be Dammed in New York State". *Clearwaters*, Summer, 2007, p. 22.

77. Phillips, M. (1965). "Hudson Proposed As a Key Source City's Water", *New York Times*, August 12, 1965, p. 1.

78. Colvin, V. (1872). "The Water Question", *The Argus.* Adirondack Museum Archives, Blue Mountain Lake, NY.

79. Mitchell, J. (1994). The Watering Place, *Adirondack Life*, 25:6, p. 59.

80. New York State Water Supply Commission (1907). *New York's Water Supply and Its Conservation, Distribution, and Uses,* archives at Adirondack Museum, Blue Mountain Lake, NY.

81. Fanning, J. (1881). *Report on Water Supply For New York and Other Cities of the Hudson Valley,* archived at Adirondack Museum, Blue Mountain Lake, NY, p. 9-15.

82. Fanning, J. (1884). *Report No. 2 on a Water Supply For New York and Other Cities of the Hudson Valley,* archived at Adirondack Museum, Blue Mountain Lake, NY, p. 18-21.

83. Board of the Hudson River Regulating District, (1923). *Official Plan of the Hudson River Regulating District,* NYS Archives, www. archives.nysed.gov, p. 24.

84. Ibid., p. 25-6.

85. Ibid., p. 27.

86. Ibid., p. 35-53.

87. Ibid., p. 26.

88. Hennigan, R. (2007). "To Be", p. 22.

89. Schanberg, S. (1967). "New Reservoirs Urged For State". *New York Times*, December 20, 1967, p. 57.

90. Temporary Study Commission on the Future of the Adirondacks (1970). *Forest, Minerals, Water and Air, Technical Report 3.* Albany: New York, p. 89.

91. Schaefer, P. (1989). *Defending the Wilderness*, p. 137.

92. Temporary Study Commission on the Future of the Adirondacks (1970). *Forest,* p. 140.

93. Schaefer, P. (1989). *Defending the Wilderness,* p. 38.

94. Hennigan, R. (2007). "To be", p. 22.

95. Schaefer, P. (1989). *Defending the Wilderness,* p. 140.

96. Schenectady Chapter, Adirondack Mountain Club, (1968). "Why Gooley Dam", *Adirondac*, September-October, p. 85-7.

97. New York Times, (1969). "Protect Adirondack Park". *New York Times*, February 24, 1969, p. 36.

98. Schaefer, P. (1989). *Defending the Wilderness,* p. 145.

99. New York Times, (1971). "Danger In the Adirondacks". *New York Times*, March 5, 1971, p. 34.

100. New York Times (1969). "Adirondack Town Fears Extinction in Dam Plan", *New York Times,* July 13, 1969, p. 64.

101. Schaefer, P. (1989). *Defending the Wilderness,* p. 146.

102. Payne, P. (2012). Phone conversation on the *New York State Wild, Scenic, and Recreational Rivers Act of 1972,* January 7, 2012.

103. NYS Environmental Conservation Law, (1982). *Wild, Scenic, and Recreational Rivers System,* Title 27, Article 15. New York State Environmental Conservation Law: Albany, #15-2701, #15-2707.

104. Ibid., appendix A.

105. Schaefer, P. (1989). *Defending the Wilderness,* p. 36-8.

106. Payne, P. (2012). Phone conversation.

107. Hixon, E. (2010). Personal interview.

108. Cooney, D. (1971). "Hydrological Characteristics of the Upper Hudson", *American Whitewater Journal*, Summer, 1971, p. 61.

109. Carman, B. (1979). "Doing It", *Adirondack Life*, May–June, 1979, p. 37.

110. Zwick, D. (1969). "Fast Water Canoeing", *Adirondac*, March – April 1969, p. 30-1.

111. Smith, C. (1976). *The Adirondacks*. Viking Press: New York, p. 25-6.

112. Carpenter, C. (1979). "Rescue in the Hudson River Gorge". <u>*Adirondack Life*</u> 10:2, p. 12-15, 44-7.

113. Hockmeyer, W. (2010). *More on Black Sunday and 1ˢᵗ Day on the Hudson,* email dated July 2, 2010.

In the Beginning

1. Gruspe, A. (2009). "A History of Whitewater Rafting in West Virginia", *West Virginia Historical Society Quarterly,* www.wvculture.org/history/wvhs124.html, p. 1.

2. Schmale, M., Greene, D., Cunningham, P., Thomas, & Heidrich, (1994). "Recreation and Sports" in *Rivers, Rails, and Ski Trails: The History of the Town of Johnsburg,* Johnsburg Historical Society, ed. Sawyers Press: North Creek, p. 128.

3. DEC, (1985). *Raft Attendance Records*, archived at DEC office, Northville, NY.

4. Bennet, J. (1996). *The Complete Whitewater Rafter,* Ragged Mountain Press: Camden, ME, p. 3.

5. Staveley, G. (2009). "A Brief History of Grand Canyon River Running". Gcroa/pages/history.htm., p. 3.

6. Quist, R. (2008). "History of Utah River Running". www.utah.com/raft/history.htm, p. 2.

7. Hatch, D. (2008). "Don Hatch River Expeditions". donhatchriver-trips.com/hatch-
legacy.php, p. 1.

8. Quist, R. (2008). "History", p 2.

9. Staveley, G. (2009). "A Brief History", p. 5.

10. Staveley, G. (2009). *The Caynoneers Story.*
Canyoneers.com/pages/canyoneers.htm#principals, p. 2

11. Gaines, E. (2003). "The Re-signification of Risk in Whitewater: Ritual Initiation and the Mythology pf River Culture" in *Case Studies in Sport Communication*, Greenwood Publishing: Westport, CT, p. 11.

12. Schmale, M. (2010). Personal interview on *Rafting on the Hudson River*, North River, NY.

13. Gruspe, A. (2009). "A History", p1.

14. Wildwater Rafting (2012).
www.wildwaterrafting.com/mediacobackground.

15. Whitewater Challengers (2012).
www.whitewaterchallengers.com/lehigh/lehigh-guides.

16. Northern Outdoors Staff (2000). "Pioneer Rafting Days on Maine's Kennebec River", Northern Outdoors web site, www.north-ernoutdoors.com/blog/whitewater-rafting.

17. Wilderness Tours (2011).
www.wildernesstours.com/the-river/history.

18. Cromie, W. (2011). CD on the *History of Adirondack Wildwaters Rafting.*

19. Hamilton County News (1978). *Hamilton County News(HCN) Hudson River Whitewater Derby* supplement, May, 1978, p. 8.

20. Hamilton County News (1975). *HCN Hudson River Whitewater Derby* supplement, May 1, 1975, p. 8.

21. Denis, M. (1984). "Fishing, Rafting, & Hunting – Still Good in the Adirondacks", *Barkeater*, p. 42, no further reference available.

22. Monthony, K. (2010). Personal interview on *Early Days of Rafting on the Hudson River,* North Creek, NY.

23. Cole, Dane (2011). Personal interview on *Early commercial raft trips on the Hudson River,* Indian Lake, NY.

24. Monthony, J. (2010). Wife of John Monthony, phone conversation on *John Monthony's Rafting on the Hudson,* Indian Lake, NY, March, 5, 2010.

25. Denis, M. (1984). "Fishing", p. 42.

26. Schmale, M. (2010). Personal interview.

27. Ibid.

28. Carlson, R. (2013). Personal interview on *Early Days of Rafting on the Hudson River,* North Creek, NY.

29. Monthony, K. (2010). Personal interview.

30. Hockmeyer, W. (2009). Phone interview on *Early Days of Northern Outdoors Rafting on the Hudson River,* Indian Lake, NY.

31. Ibid.

32. Haley, A. (2010). Personal interview on *Early Days of Northern Outdoors Rafting on the Hudson River,* Schohegan, ME.

33. Indian Lake Town Board (1979). "Bob Geandreau goes before the Board", *Indian Lake Town Board Minutes (ILTBM),* May 7, 1979, p. 245.

34. Indian Lake Town Board (1979). "Bob Geandreau asks board to Approve Raft trips", *ILTBM,* September 4, 1979, p. 256.

35. Wilderness Tours (2011).
www.wildernesstours.com/the-river/history.

36. Cromie, W. (2011). CD on the *History.*

37. Hamilton County News (1988). "Hudson River Rafting Company Celebrates 10th Birthday", *HCN* April 20, 1988, p. 9.

38. Bond, H. (1995). *Boats and Boating in the Adirondacks.* Syracuse University Press: Syracuse, p. 211.

39. Cunningham, P. (2012). Personal conversation on the *First Inflatable Raft Trips in the Hudson River Gorge,* September 2012, Blue Mountain Lake.

40. Virgil, G. (2010). Personal interview on *Rafting on the Hudson River,* Indian Lake, NY.

41. Suchecki, M. (1988). "Rafting Helps North Country Bridge Economic Seasons", *Albany Times – Union,* April 3, 1988, p. E1.

42. Indian Lake Town Board (1979). "Bob Geandreau goes before the Board", *ILTBM,* May 7, 1979, p. 245.

43. Cromie, W. (2011). CD on the *History.*

44. USGS, (2010). United States Geological Service river gauge archives for Hudson River at North Creek for April 14, 1979, www. waterdata.usgs.gov.

45. Hamilton County News (1979). "Huge Snowstorm Hits County", *HCN*, April 11, 1979, p. 1.

46. Glens Falls Post Star (1979). "Weather Forecast", *Glens Falls Post Star*, April 6, 1979, p. 10.

47. Glens Falls Post Star (1979). "Weather Forecast", *Glens Falls Post Star*, April 7, 1979, p. 1, 8, 10.

48. Glens Falls Post Star (1979). "Weather Forecast", *Glens Falls Post Star,* April 14, 1979, p. 1, 6.

49. Kowalski, J. (2011). Email letter dated February 2, 2011 on *Early Commercial Rafting on the Hudson.*

50. Hockmeyer, W. (2009). *First Few Years on the Hudson,* email dated September 28, 2009, p. 1.

51. Kowalski, J. (2011). Email letter dated Feburary 2, 2011, p. 1.

52. USGS, (2010). United States Geological Service river gauge archives for Hudson River at North Creek for April 7, 1979, www. waterdata.usgs.gov.

53. Kowalski, J. (2010). Phone interview on *Early Years on the Hudson.* May, 2010.

54. Hill, M. (2009). Rapid Transit. *Adirondack Life*, 40:3, p. 30.

55. Hockmeyer, W. (2010). *More on Black Sunday and 1ˢᵗ Day on the Hudson,* email dated July 2, 2010, p. 1.

56. Cromie, W. (2011). CD on the *History*.

57. USGS, (2010). United States Geological Service river gauge archives for Hudson River at North Creek for April 14, 1979, www.waterdata.usgs.gov.

58. Cromie, W. (2011). CD on the *History*.

59. Indian Lake Town Board (1979). "Bob Geandreau goes before the Board", *ILTBM*, May 7, 1979, p. 245.

60. Indian Lake Town Board (1979). "Bob Geandreau asks Board to Approve Raft trips", *ILTBM*, September 4, 1979, p. 256.

61. Vorhees, J. (2010). Personal interview on *Early Days of Rafting on the Hudson River,* Indian Lake, NY.

62. Moore, L. (2010). Personal interview on *Early Days of Rafting in Indian Lake,* Indian Lake, NY.

63. Hamilton County News (1979). "Indian Lake Chamber of Commerce ads for Hudson River Whitewater Derby", *HCN* Supplement, May 2, 1979, p. 5-7.

64. Satterlee, S. (1979). "High On Whitewater", *HCN* Supplement, May 2, 1979, p. 6.

65. Satterlee, S. (1979). "River Rafting Facts", *HCN* Supplement, May 2, 1979, p. 7.

66. Hockmeyer, W. (2009). Phone interview on *Early Days*.

67. Aber, T. & King, S. (1965). *The History of Hamilton County.* Willard Press: Boonville, p. 549-50.

68. Fenton, R. (1992). Draft of Hudson River Gorge Unit Management Plan dated February 1992, archived at DEC office in Northville, NY, p. 24, 44.

69. Fenton, R. (1991). Personal notes from an interview with Dick Purdue, Indian Lake Town Supervisor, archived at DEC office in Northville, NY.

70. Ibid.

71. Hamilton County News (1980). "Rafting Down Indian River Ok'd by Indian Lake Board", *HCN*, 32:2, February 13, 1980, p. 12.

72. Indian Lake Town Board (1980). First Agreement Between the Town and Rafters Providing for Releases, *ILTBM*, dated February 2, 1980, p. 275.

73. Ibid., p. 275.

74. Ibid., p. 275-6

75. Hamilton County News (1980). "Rafting Down the Rivers: Indian Lake to North River", *HCN*, 34:9, May 7, 1980, p. 1.

76. Briggs, J. (1982). "Whitewater – Indian Lake Gold", *HCN*, 35:30, May 19, 1982, p. 9.

77. Smith, M. (1985). "Big Water: The Hudson Gorge", *Adirondack Life*, 16:2, p. 22.

78. Houston, M. (1985). *Rapid Transit*, p. 11.

79. Ibid., p. 11.

80. Hockmeyer, W. (2009). Phone interview on *Early Days.*

81. Allen, M. (1978). "Rafting Through Kennebec Gorge on the Silver Bullet", *Yankee Magazine* Archive, May, 1978, <u>archive.yankeemagazine.com/article</u>, p. 37.

82. Haley, A. (2010). Personal interview on *Early Days of Northern Outdoors Rafting on the Hudson River,* Schohegan, ME.

83. Gilborn, A. (1982). "Down the Wild River", *Adirondack Life,* 13:3, p. 33.

84. Silk, S. (1987). "Riding the Wild Whitewater Rafting Down Hudson a Great Thrill of Spring", *Albany Times–Union,* May 23, 1987, p. B3.

85. Clarke, G. (2011). Personal interview on the *Early Days of Commercial Rafting on the Hudson River,* Beachburg, Ontario.

86. Briggs, J. (1982). "Whitewater Fever", *HCN,* 35:30, May 19, 1982, p. 9.

87. Fabin, J. (2010). Personal interview on *Early Days of Rafting on the Hudson River,* Indian Lake, NY.

88. Unicorn, (1982). *Rafting Brochure,* Indian Lake Chamber of Commerce, Indian Lake, NY.

89. Rose, H. (2009). *Personal conversation on Early Days of Rafting,* North River, NY.

90. Unicorn, (1982). *Rafting Brochure.*

91. Whitewater World, (1982). *Rafting Brochure,* Indian Lake Chamber of Commerce, Indian Lake, NY.

92. Wilderness Raft Expeditions, (1982). *Rafting Brochure,* Indian Lake Chamber of Commerce, Indian Lake, NY.

93. Adirondack River Outfitters, (1982). *Rafting Brochure,* Indian Lake Chamber of Commerce, Indian Lake, NY.

94. Benton, L. (2009). *Hudson River Stories,* email dated March 12, 2009, p. 1.

95. Schurman, J. (2010). Phone interview on *Early Days of Rafting on the Hudson River,* Indian Lake, NY.

96. Cipperly, R. (1983). *DEC Raft Questionnaire,* September 29, 1983.

97. Cipperly, R. (1983). *DEC Raft Questionnaire Results.*

98. Failing, W. (2009). Personal interview on *Early Days of Rafting on the Hudson River,* Indian Lake, NY.

99. Staab, G. (2009). Conversation on the *Early Years of Rafting on the Hudson River,* North River, NY. August, 2009.

100. Failing, W. (2009). Personal interview on *Early Days.*

101. Hockmeyer, W. (2009). Phone interview on *Early Days.*

102. Staab, G. (2009). Conversation on the *Early Years.*

103. Canan, K. (2010). Personal conversation on *Effects of Commercial Rafting on the Hudson River for Town of Indian Lake Court,* Indian Lake, NY.

104. Staab, G. (2009). Conversation on the *Early Years.*

105. Hockmeyer, W. (2009). Phone interview on *Early Days.*

106. Gilborn, A. (1982). "Down", p. 31.

107. Briggs, J. (1982). "Whitewater – Indian Lake Gold", *HCN*, 35:29, May 12, 1982, p. 14.

108. Woodard, B. (1982). *Level of Use Record for Hudson River,* attendance report archived at DEC Office in Northville, NY.

109. Indian Lake Town Board (1983). "Appointment of Barry Hutchins as Raft Attendant", *ILTBM*, March, 24, 1983, p. 111-12.

110. Town of Indian Lake (1983). *1983 Raft Attendance Records,* archived at DEC Office, Northville, NY.

111. Town of Indian Lake (1985). *1985 Raft Attendance Records,* archived at DEC Office, Northville, NY.

112. Schurman, J. (2010). Phone interview on *Early Days.*

113. Wallace, W. (1982). "Outdoors: Rafting Emerges in the East", *New York Times* May 17, 1982 p. C9.

114. Knapp, C. (1987). "Summer Times", *HCN* Supplement, May 20, p. 4.

115. Hamilton County News (1982). Ads for Hudson River Raft Company, American Hotel raft packages, night entertainment, Hudson River Derby Supplement, April 23, 1982, p. 3-4.

116. Adirondack Life, (1982). Raft Advertisements, May/June, 1982, p. 36-7.

117. Hamilton County News (1982). Ads for Hudson River Raft Company, American Hotel raft packages, night entertainment, Hudson River Derby Supplement, April 23, 1982, p. 3.

118. Hamilton County News (1980). "Indian Lake", *HCN*, 31:6, March 12, 1980, p. 2.

119. Gilborn, A. (1982). "Down", p. 35.

120. Blanchard, A. (2013). Personal interview on Ernie Blanchard's role in Rafting Releases, Indian Lake, April, 2013.

121. Hutchins, B. (2010). Personal interview on *Early Days of Rafting on the Hudson River,* Indian Lake, NY.

122. Indian Lake Town Board (1987). "Local people express concern over the effects of releases", *ILTBM*, May 11, 1987, p. 276.

123. Jennings, V. (1988). "Drawdowns May Effect Fish", *HCN,* May 25, 1988, p. 9.

124. Craig, E. (1993). "Dwindling Pike Population is Blamed on Short Rations", *HCN*, April 13, 1993, p. 7.

125. LeBrun, F. (2003). "Effect of Rafting", *Albany Times-Union,* July 10, 2003, p. C1.

126. Hill, M. (2009). "Rapid Transit", p. 76-7.

127. Baldigo, B., Mulvihill, C., Ernst, A., Boisvert, B. (2010). *Effects of Recreational Flow Releases on Natural Resources of the Indian and Hudson Rivers in the Central Adirondack Mountain, 2004-2006.* USGS Scientific Investigations Report, 2010-5223, p. 72.

128. McKinstry, L. (1984). "Town Day Raft Tour Set", *HCN,* April 4, 1984, p. 3.

129. Fabin, J. (2010). Personal interview on *Early Days of Rafting on the Hudson River,* Indian Lake, NY.

130. Hamilton County News (1984). "Students Learn Rafting", *HCN*, June 20, 1984, p. 18.

131. Hockmeyer, W. (2009). Phone interview on *Early Days*.

132. Indian Lake Town Board (1981). "Wayne Hockmeyer Goes before the Board to Express Support for Town Involvement in Rafting at the Put-in and to Support Charging Outfitters a Fee", *ILTBM*, March 2, 1981, p. 31.

133. Indian Lake Town Board (1982). "First Slot Fees Approved", *ILTBM*, dated March 8, 1982, p. 70.

134. Gilborn, A. (1982). "Down", p. 35.

135. Proskine, A. (1984). *Adirondack Canoe Waters: South and West Flow*. Adirondack Mountain Club: Lake George, p. 34.

136. Gilborn, A. (1982). "Down", p. 34-5.

137. Cipperly, R. (2011). Personal interview on *Early Days of Commercial rafting on the Hudson River,* Warrensburg, NY.

138. Purdue, R. (2010). Personal interview on *Town of Indian Lake Involvement with Rafting on the Hudson River,* Indian Lake, NY.

139. Hamilton County News, (1986). "Snow Times in the Adirondacks" in *Hamilton County News* Supplement, February, 1986, p. 4.

140. Cannan, K. (2010). Personal conversation on *Effects of Commercial Rafting*.

141. Cipperly, R. (2011). Personal interview on *Early Days*.

142. Benton, L. (2009). *Hudson River Stories,* p. 1.

143. Cole, Doug. (2010). Personal interview on *Rafting on the Hudson River,* Weavertown, NY.

144. Unicorn, (1982). *Whitewater Rafting Brochure.*

145. Briggs, J. (1985). "Whitewater Guide Training to be Offered", *HCN,* 38:16, February 6, 1985, p. 5.

146. Briggs, J. (1986). Whitewater guides training in March, Hamilton County News, February, 1986, p. 5.

147. DEC (1982). Memo dated June 10, 1982 on *Guide Licensing Committee,* archived at DEC office in Northville, NY.

148. Monroe, T. (1982). "Letter to the Editor on Response to Alice Gilborn Rafting Article", Adirondack Life, May 19, 1982, p. 54.

149. Hockmeyer, W. (1982). Letter to DEC's Mark Brown on *Hudson River Professional Outfitters Association position on Guide Licensing Proposals,* May 16, 1982, p. 1-2.

150. Ibid., p. 1-2.

151. Geandreau, R. (1982). Letter from Wayne Hockmeyer to DEC's Mark Brown on "Hudson River Professional Outfitters Association position on Guide Licensing Proposals", May 16, 1982.

152. Geandreau, R. (1982). Letter to Wayne Hockmeyer dated May 24, 1982 on *Hudson River Gorge UMP advisory committees.*

153. Hamilton County News, (1986). *"Snow Times in the Adirondacks"* in *HCN* Supplement, February 1986, p. 4.

154. Hamilton County News (1986). "Guides to be Issued Contingent Licenses", *HCN,* March 26, 1986, p. 5.

155. Hockmeyer, W. (1982). Letter to DEC's Mark Brown, p. 2.

156. Hockmeyer, W. (1984). Letter to Dick Cipperly on *Access to the Hudson River for Rafting,* October 15, 1984, p. 4.

157. Neuman, L. (2009). Personal interview on *Recollections of Rafting on the Hudson,* April 12, 2009, North Creek, NY.

158. Ebert, T. (2009). Email on *Personal Recollections of Rafting on the Hudson River,* March, 4, 2009.

159. Gilborn, A. (1982). "Down", p. 31.

160. Gargan, E. (1985). "In the Adirondacks, River Rafters Get Adventure and Challenge", *New York Times,* April 16, 1985, p. B1.

161. Gilborn, A. (1982). "Down", p. 32-3.

162. LeBlanc, A. (2010). Personal recollections on *Rafting on the Hudson River,* Indian Lake, NY.

163. Fabin, J. (1984). *Hudson River Access Issues,* letter to Dick Cipperly dated November, 2, 1984.

164. Perrin, J. (1984). *Hudson River Access Issues,* letter to Dick Cipperly dated October 29, 1984, p. 2.

165. Hamilton County News, (1984). *HCN,* June 13, 1984, p. 8.

166. Hamilton County News, (1984). "Raft Accident Occurs in Indian Lake", *HCN*, May 9, 1984, p. 1.

167. Gilborn, A. (1982). "Down", p. 30, 32.

168. Houston, M. (1985). "Rapid Transit", p. 11.

169. Smith, M. (1985). "Big Water", p. 26.

170. Wallace, W. (1988). "An Undercurrent of Safety Questions", *New York Times*, March 21, 1988, p. C8.

171. Smith, M. (1985). "Big Water", p. 22.

172. Silk, S. (1987). "Riding the Wild Whitewater Rafting Down Hudson a Great Thrill of Spring", *Albany Times–Union*, May 23, 1987, p. B3.

173. Houston, M. (1985). "Rapid Transit", p. 11.

174. Gilborn, A. (1982). "Down", p. 36-7.

175. Houston, M. (1985). "Rapid Transit", p. 11.

176. Carr, S. (1986). "Q and A", *New York Times*, May 11, 1986, p. XX4.

177. Wolff, B. (2010). Personal conversation on *Early Days of Whitewater Challengers on the Hudson River,* North River, NY.

178. Unicorn, (1982). *Rafting Brochure.*

179. Wilderness Raft Expeditions, (1982). *Rafting Brochure,* Indian Lake Chamber of Commerce, Indian Lake, NY.

180. Adirondack River Outfitters, (1982). *Rafting Brochure.*

181. Pocono Whitewater World, (1982). *Whitewater Rafting Brochure,* Jim Thorpe, PA.

182. Barkley, K. (2010). *Personal Recollections of Running the Hudson River,* June, 2010, The Forks, Maine.

183. Gilborn, A. (1982). "Down", p. 35.

184. Silk, S. (1987). "Finding Outfitters For a Trip in Gorge", *Albany Times-Union*, May 23, 1987, p. B3.

185. Rafferty, R. (2009). *Early Remembrances on the Hudson,* email dated March 10, 2009, p. 2.

186. Hamilton County News (1986). "Snow Times in the Adirondacks" supplement to *HCN*, February 1986, p. 4, 8.

187. Hockmeyer, W. (2009). *First Few Years on the Hudson,* email dated September 28, 2009, p. 1.

188. Schmale, M. (2010). Personal interview.

189. Benton, L. (2009). "Hudson River Stories", p. 1.

190. Indian Lake Town Board (1980). "First Agreement Between the Town and Rafters Providing for Releases", *ILTBM*, dated February 2, 1980, p. 275.

191. Gilborn, A. (1982). "Down", p. 35.

192. Gargan, E. (1985). "In the Adirondacks", p. B1.

193. Silk, S. (1987). "Finding Outfitters", p. B3.

194. Carlson, D. (1989). "A Boatman's Progress", *Adirondack Life*, 20:2, p. 22-3.

195. Myers, T. (2003). "Grand Canyon River Trip Safety", *Grand Canyon River Outfitters Association*, www.gcroa.org/Pages/safety.

196. McKinstry, L. (1984). "Raft Accident Occurs in Indian Lake", *HCN*, May 9, 1984, p. 1.

197. Hamilton County News (1984). "Lost Couple Found on River", *HCN,* June 6, 1984, p. 2.

198. Carlson, R. (2010). Personal interview on *Early Days of Rafting on the Hudson River,* North Creek, NY.

199. Ibid.

Black Sunday

1. Glens Falls Post Star (1982). "Missing Rafters Found", *Glens Falls Post Star*, April 20, 1982, p. 13.

2. USGS, (2010). United States Geological Service river gauge archives for Hudson River at North Creek for April 18, 1982, www. waterdata.usgs.gov.

3. Schurman, J. (2010). Phone interview on *Early Days of Rafting on the Hudson River,* Indian Lake, NY.

4. Purdue, R. (2010). Personal interview on *Town of Indian Lake Involvement with Rafting on the Hudson River,* Indian Lake, NY.

5. USGS, (2012). United States Geological Service river gauge archives for Hudson River at North Creek for April 28, 2011, www. waterdata.usgs.gov.

6. Vorhees, J. (2010). Personal interview on *Early Days of Rafting on the Hudson River,* Indian Lake, NY.

7. Cromie, W. (2011). CD on the *History of Adirondack Wildwaters Rafting.*

8. Hockmeyer, W. (2009). Phone interview on *Early Days of Northern Outdoors Rafting on the Hudson River,* Indian Lake, NY.

9. Vorhees, J. (2010). Personal interview on *Early Days*.

10. Ibid.

11. Kowalski, J. (2011). Email letter dated February 2, 2011, on *Early Commercial Rafting on the Hudson*.

12. Glens Falls Post Star, (1982). "Flood Warning Issued", *Glens Falls Post Star*, April 19, 1982, p. 9.

13. Hockmeyer, S. (2010). Personal interview on *Early Days of Northern Outdoors Rafting on the Hudson River,* The Forks, ME.

14. Ibid.

15. Haley, A. (2010). Personal interview on *Early Days of Northern Outdoors Rafting on the Hudson River,* Schohegan, ME.

16. Vorhees, J. (2010). Personal interview on *Early Days*.

17. Hockmeyer, S. (2010). Personal interview on *Early Days*.

18. Hockmeyer, W. (2009). Phone interview on *Early Days*.

19. Kowalski, J. (2011). Email letter dated February 2, 2011.

20. Schurman, J. (2010). Phone interview on *Early Days of Rafting on the Hudson River,* Indian Lake, NY.

21. Hockmeyer, S. (2010). *A Few More Details on Black Sunday,* email dated June 27, 2010.

22. Ibid.

23. Ibid.

24. Vorhees, J. (2010). Personal interview on *Early Days*.

25. Hockmeyer, W. (2010). *More on Black Sunday and 1ˢᵗ Day on the Hudson,* email dated July 2, 2010.

26. Hockmeyer, S. (2010). Personal interview on *Early Days*.

27. Vorhees, J. (2010). Personal interview on *Early Days*.

28. Hockmeyer, S. (2010). Personal interview on *Early Days*.

29. Vorhees, J. (2010). Personal interview on *Early Days*.

30. Hockmeyer, S. (2010). Personal interview on *Early Days*.

31. Moore, L. (2010). Personal interview on *Early Days of Rafting in Indian Lake,* Indian Lake, NY.

32. Denis, M. (1984). "Shorts", *Barkeater*, p. 42, no further reference available.

33. Glens Falls Post Star (1982). "Raft Capsizes; 2 People Missing", *Glens Falls Post Star*, April 19, 1982, p. 1.

34. Denis, M. (1984). "Shorts", p. 42.

35. Ibid.

36. Vorhees, J. (2010). Personal interview on *Early Days*.

37. Hockmeyer, W. (2010). *More on Black Sunday and 1ˢᵗ Day on the Hudson,* email dated July 2, 2010.

38. Hockmeyer, W. (2011). Email response to *Black Sunday Draft*.

39. Glens Falls Post Star (1982). "Missing Rafters Found", *Glens Falls Post Star*, April 20, 1982, p. 13.

40. Vorhees, J. (1982). "Letter to the Editor", *HCN*, April 28, 1982.

41. Hockmeyer, S. (2010). Personal interview on *Early Days*.

42. Hockmeyer, W. (2011). E-mail response to *Black Sunday Draft*.

43. Haley, A. (2010). Personal interview on *Early Days of Northern Outdoors Rafting on the Hudson River*, Schohegan, ME.

The Gorge Runneth Over

1. Gilborn, A. (1982). "Down the Wild River", *Adirondack Life* 13:3, p. 31, 35-6.

2. Kowalski, J. (2011). Email letter dated February 2, 2011 on *Early Commercial Rafting on the Hudson*.

3. Hockmeyer, S. (2011). Email on *River Access Issues*.

4. Nash, R. (1982). *Wilderness and the American Mind, 3rd ed.* Yale University Press: New Haven, p. 333-7.

5. Briggs, J. (1982). "Rafting the Upper Hudson" in *Clearwater Navigator*, July, 1982, p. 5.

6. Geandreau, R., ed. (1982). *A Proposal Affecting the Future of Our Township,* unpublished paper dated January 1982 prepared by the Indian Lake Chamber of Commerce, p. 3.

7. Briggs, J. (1982). "Whitewater–Indian Lake Gold", *HCN*, 35:29, May 12, 1982, p. 14.

8. Swedberg, J. (2009). *A Few Remembrances,* email dated March 15, 2009.

9. Mallette, D. (1982). Letter on *Usage of the Put-in Area,* February 23, 1982.

10. Woodard, B. (1982). *Level of Use Record for Hudson River,* attendance report archived at DEC Office in Northville, NY.

11. Town of Indian Lake (1983). *1983 Raft Attendance Records,* archived at DEC Office, Northville, NY.

12. Spring, T. (2011). Phone interview on *Early Days of Commercial Rafting in Indian Lake,* Indian lake, NY.

13. Cipperly, R. (2011). Personal interview on *Early Days of Commercial Rafting on the Hudson River,* Warrensburg, NY.

14. Luciano, D. (1984). Legal letter dated April 11, 1984, on *Access to the Hudson River,* archived at DEC office in Northville, NY, p. 1.

15. Hamilton County News (1981). "Indian Lake", *HCN,* February 11, 1981, p. 8.

16. Hockmeyer, S. (2011). Email on *River Access Issues.*

17. Cipperly, R. (2011). Personal interview on *Early Days,* Warrensburg, NY.

18. DEC (1971). *Hudson River Gorge Primitive Area Unit Management Plan Draft,* p. 1, Albany, NY.

19. Fenton, R. (2011). Email dated on *Hudson River Gorge UMP.*

20. DEC (1971). *Hudson River Gorge Primitive Area,* p. 9-12.

21. Ibid., p. 13.

22. Failing, W. (2009). Personal interview on *Early Days of Rafting on the Hudson River,* Indian Lake, NY.

23. DEC (1971). *Hudson River Gorge Primitive Area,* p. 13-14.

24. Geandreau, R. (1981). Letter to outfitters on *Organizing Outfitters,* business letter to Hudson River Outfitters dated March 12, 1981, p. 1.

25. Gilborn, A. (1982). "Down the Wild River", p. 34.

26. Hockmeyer, W. (2009). Phone interview on *Early Days of Northern Outdoors Rafting on the Hudson River,* Indian Lake, NY.

27. Hudson River Professional Outfitters (1981). *Articles and Bylaws of Hudson River Professional Outfitters.*

28. Ibid., p. 8, 1-2.

29. Hockmeyer, W. (2011). Email on *Over Use on the Hudson River,* dated January 28, 2011.

30. Staab, G. (2011). Personal interview on the *Early Years of Commercial Rafting on the Hudson River,* North River, NY.

31. Geandreau, R., ed. (1982). *A Proposal Affecting the Future of Our Township,* unpublished paper dated January 1982 prepared by the Indian Lake Chamber of Commerce.

32. Indian Lake Town Board (1982). "Discussion on Charging Outfitters a Fee", *ILTBM,* March 8, 1982, p. 70.

33. Hamilton County News (1982). "Indian Lake", *HCN,* June 23, 1982, p. 21.

34. Hockmeyer, W. (2009). Phone interview on *Early Days of Northern Outdoors Rafting on the Hudson River,* Indian Lake, NY.

35. Briggs, J. (1982). "Whitewater–Indian Lake Gold", *HCN,* 35:29, May 12, 1982, p. 14.

36. Indian Lake Town Board (1982). "Resolution to Include Rafting in the Hudson River Gorge UMP", *ILTBM,* dated April 12, 1982, p. 72.

37. Gilborn, A. (1982). "Down the Wild River", p. 35.

38. Luciano, D. (1984). Legal letter dated April 11, 1984, on *Access,* p. 1.

39. DEC (1995). *Blue Mountain Wild Forest Unit Management Plan,* Department of Environmental Conservation: Albany, p. 69.

40. Indian Lake Town Board (1983). "Appointment of Barry Hutchins as Raft Attendant", *ILTBM,* March, 24, 1983, p. 111.

41. Swedberg, J. (2011). Personal interview on *Rafting on the Hudson River,* Indian Lake, NY.

42. Fabin, J. (2010). Personal interview on *Early Days of Rafting on the Hudson River,* Indian Lake, NY.

43. Perrin, J. (1984). *Hudson River Access Issues,* letter to Dick Cipperly dated October 29, 1984, p. 2.

44. Schmale, M. (2010). Personal interview on *Rafting on the Hudson River,* North River, NY.

45. Indian Lake Town Board (1983). "Resolution to Limit River Access for Eastern River Expeditions", *ILTBM,* April 4, 1983, p. 112.

46. Hudson River Professional Outfitters (1981). *Articles and Bylaws of Hudson River Professional Outfitters,* p. 2.

47. Ibid., p. 1, 8-9.

48. Johnson, D. (1984). Business letter dated November 2, 1984, on *Hudson River Rafting Legal Issues,* archived at DEC office in Northville, NY, p. 2.

49. Luciano, D. (1984). Legal letter dated April 11, 1984, on *Access,* p. 1.

50. Ibid., p. 3-4.

51. Ibid., p. 5-7.

52. Cipperly, R. (1984). "Minutes of DEC/Town of Indian Lake Meeting with Rafting Companies", DEC document, Northville, NY October, 24, 1984, p. 2-3.

53. Cipperly, R. (2011). Personal interview on *Early Days of Commercial Rafting on the Hudson River,* Warrensburg, NY.

54. Cipperly, R. (1984). *Minutes of DEC,* p. 3.

55. Ibid., p. 3

56. Ibid., p. 3-4.

57. Ibid., p. 4.

58. Ibid., p. 4.

59. Schmale, M. (2010). Personal interview on *Rafting on the Hudson River,* North River, NY.

60. Fabin, J. (1984). *Hudson River Access Issues,* letter to Dick Cipperly dated November, 2, 1984, p. 1-2.

61. Perrin, J. (1984). *Hudson River Access Issues,* letter to Dick Cipperly dated October 29, 1984, p. 1.

62. Whiting, M. (1984). *Hudson River Access Issues,* letter to Dick Cipperly dated October 29, 1984, p. 2.

63. Powley, K. (1984). *Hudson River Access Issue,* letter to Dick Cipperly dated October 29, 1984, p. 1.

64. Ibid., p. 2.

65. Hockmeyer, W. (1984). Letter to Dick Cipperly on *Access to the Hudson River for Rafting,* October 15, 1984, p. 2.

66. Powley, K. (1984). *Hudson River Access Issue,* letter to Dick Cipperly dated October 29, 1984, p. 2-3.

67. Hockmeyer, W. (1984). Letter to Dick Cipperly on *Access to the Hudson River for Rafting,* October 15, 1984, p. 1-2.

68. Cipperly, R. (1984). *Minutes of DEC-Town of Indian Lake Rafting Meeting,* November 9, 1984, p. 1.

69. Ibid., p. 1.

70. Ibid., p. 1-2.

71. Indian Lake Town Board, (1985). "Town Board Meeting", *ILTBM,* March 11, 1985, p.197.

72. Hockmeyer, W. (2011). Email on *Over Use on the Hudson River.*

73. Clarke, G. (2011). Personal interview on the *Early Days of Commercial Rafting on the Hudson River,* Beachburg, Ontario.

74. Hockmeyer, S. (2010). Personal interview on *Early Days of Northern Outdoors Rafting on the Hudson River,* The Forks, ME.

A Maturing Industry

1. Town of Indian Lake (1986). *1986 Raft Attendance Records,* archived at DEC Office, Northville, NY.

2. Town of Indian Lake (1987). *1987 Raft Attendance Records,* archived at DEC Office, Northville, NY.

3. Fenton, R. (1994). Personal notes on *Checking Conditions at Blue Ledges,* archived at DEC office in Northville, NY.

4. Reinicker, R. (1985). Letter to John English of the DEC on the Hudson River Gorge UMP dated January 14, 1985, archived at DEC office in Northville, NY.

5. Failing, W. (1992). Letter dated January 20, 1992, to Dick Cipperly with specific suggestions for the improvement of the put-in, archived at DEC office in Northville, NY.

6. DEC (1995). *Blue Mountain Wild Forest Unit Management Plan,* Department of Environmental Conservation: Albany, p. 70.

7. Kapelewski, T. (1994). Letter to Mike Wilson dated April 14, 1994, on Wilson's concerns for the Hundson River UMP, archived at DEC office in Northville, NY.

8. DEC (1995). *Blue Mountain,* p. 56.

9. Molton, D. (2011). *Personal Conversation on the History of Rafting on the Hudson River,* May 2011, Indian Lake, NY.

10. DEC (1995). *Blue Mountain*, p. 194-5.

11. Adirondack Park Agency (2001). "Wild, Scenic, and Recreational Rivers". www.apa.state.ny.us/documents/laws_regs/slmp PDF 2001. pdf, p. 69.

12. DEC (1995). *Blue Mountain*, p. 194.

13. Geandreau, R., ed. (1982). *A Proposal Affecting the Future of Our Township,* unpublished paper dated January, 1982, prepared by the Indian Lake Chamber of Commerce, p. 10.

14. Indian Lake Town Board, (1991). "Town Board Meeting", *ILTBM,* October 14, 1991, Indian Lake, NY, p. 206.

15. Indian Lake Town Board, (1991). "Town Board Meeting", *ILTBM,* November 29, 1991, Indian Lake, NY, p. 208.

16. Indian Lake Town Board, (1992). "Town Board Meeting", *ILTBM,* February 27, 1992, Indian Lake, NY, p. 236.

17. Indian Lake Town Board, (1992). "Town Board Meeting", *ILTBM,* May 5, 1992, Indian Lake, NY, p. 267.

18. Indian Lake Town Board, (1992). "Town Board Meeting", *ILTBM,* March 30, 1992, Indian Lake, NY, p. 251.

19. Indian Lake Town Board, (1992). "Town Board Meeting", *ILTBM,* July 27, 1992, Indian Lake, NY, p. 5.

20. Indian Lake Town Board, (1992). "Town Board Meeting", *ILTBM,* December 28, 1992, Indian Lake, NY, p. 93.

21. Indian Lake Town Board, (1992). "Town Board Meeting", *ILTBM,* January, 1992, Indian Lake, NY, p. 97.

22. Indian Lake Town Board, (1993). "Town Board Meeting", *ILTBM,* March 8, 1993, Indian Lake, NY, p. 138.

23. Indian Lake Town Board, (1993). "Town Board Meeting", *ILTBM,* August 9, 1993, Indian Lake, NY, p. 232.

24. Indian Lake Town Board, (1994). "Town Board Meeting", *ILTBM,* April 8, 1994, Indian Lake, NY, p. 321.

25. DEC (1995). *Blue Mountain,* p. 38.

26. Indian Lake Town Board, (1995). "Town Board Meeting", *ILTBM,* February 13, 1995, Indian Lake, NY, p. 14.

27. Indian Lake Town Board, (1996). "Town Board Meeting", *ILTBM,* August 29, 1996, Indian Lake, NY, p. 13.

28. Burns, M. (2009). Personal interview with Milda Burns, daughter of Jack Donohue: *River Driving on the Hudson River.*

29. Carpenter, C. (1979). "Rescue in the Hudson River Gorge". *Adirondack Life,* 10:2, p. 12-15, 44-7.

30. Perrin, J., (1984). *Hudson River Access Issues,* letter to Dick Cipperly dated October 29, 1984, p. 2.

31. Ibid., p. 2.

32. Fabin, J. (1984). *Hudson River Access Issues,* letter to Dick Cipperly dated November, 2, 1984. p. 1-2.

33. Indian Lake Town Board, (1990). "Town Board Meeting", *ILTBM,* December 10, 1990, Indian Lake, NY, p. 1.

34. Craig, E. (1990). Whitewater World: Emphasis is on Safety, in *HCN,* December 18, 1990, p. 10.

35. Ibid., p. 10.

36. Ibid., p. 10.

37. Craig, E. (1991). "Indian Lake Town Board Meeting", *HCN*, May 21, 1991, p. 8.

38. McKinstry, L. (1993). "Whitewater Claims a Life", *HCN*, May 4, 1993, p. 1.

39. Craig, E. (1994). "One Lives, One Dies in River Rafting Mishaps", *HCN*, May 2, 1994, p. 1.

40. Indian Lake Town Board, (1994). "Town Board Meeting", *ILTBM*, May 4, 1994, Indian Lake, NY, p. 352.

41. Craig, E. (1994). "Indian Lake Town Board Meeting", *HCN*, May 10, 1994, p. 6.

42. Indian Lake Town Board, (1994). "Town Board Meeting", *ILTBM*, May 9, 1994, Indian Lake, NY, p. 354.

43. Craig, E. (1994). "Indian Lake Town Board Meeting", *HCN*,, May 17, 1994, p. 6.

44. Craig, E. (1995). "Article on Indian Lake Town Board Meeting", *HCN*, December 19, 1994, p. 10.

45. Morse, R. (2002). "Detailed Accident Report: Hudson, New York", in *US Whitewater Accident Database*, www.americanwhitewater.org/safety/archive.

46. Glens Falls Post Star (1996). "Raft Fatality", *Glens Falls Post Star*, June 28, 1996, p. A1.

47. Sagamore Institute (no date). Flier describing the drift boat trips. No date or author but early 1990s date most likely, archived at DEC office in Northville, NY.

48. Indian Lake Town Board, (1984-6). "Town Budgets for 1984-1986", *ILTBM,* Indian Lake, NY.

49. Indian Lake Town Board, (1986). "Town Board Meeting", *ILTBM,* July 14, 1986, Indian Lake, NY, p. 244.

50. Indian Lake Town Board, (1986). "Town Board Meeting", *ILTBM,* July 29, 1986, Indian Lake, NY, p. 246.

51. Indian Lake Town Board, (1988). "Town Board Meeting", *ILTBM,* August 8, 1988, Indian Lake, NY, p. 34.

52. Indian Lake Town Board, (1988). "Town Board Meeting", *ILTBM,* December 23, 1988, Indian Lake, NY, p. 55.

53. Indian Lake Town Board (1980). "First Agreement Between the Town and Rafters Providing for Releases", *ILTBM*, February 2, 1980, p. 275.

54. Indian Lake Town Board (1981). "Board Discusses Approving Dam Releases for Rafting", *ILTBM*, February 2, 1981, p. 27.

55. Indian Lake Town Board (1981). "Wayne Hockmeyer Goes before the Board to Express Support for Town Involvement in Rafting at the Put-in and to Support charging outfitters a fee", *ILTBM*, March 2, 1981, p. 31.

56. Indian Lake Town Board (1982). "Discussion on Charging Outfitters a Fee", *ILTBM,* March 8, 1982, p. 70.

57. Hamilton County News, (1982). "Indian Lake Town Board Meeting", *HCN,* July 12, 1982, p. 16.

58. Hamilton County News, (1983). "Indian Lake Town Board Meeting", *HCN,* November 22, 1983, p. 2.

59. Indian Lake Town Board, (1989). "Town Board Meeting", *ILTBM,* May 8, 1989, Indian Lake, NY, p. 75.

60. Indian Lake Town Board, (1989). "Town Board Meeting", *ILTBM,* August 21, 1989, Indian Lake, NY, p. 85.

61. Indian Lake Town Board, (1989). "Town Board Meeting", *ILTBM,* September 18, 1989, Indian Lake, NY, p. 89.

62. Indian Lake Town Board, (1992). "Town Board Meeting", *ILTBM,* March 9, 1992, Indian Lake, NY, p. 241-2.

63. Indian Lake Town Board, (1992). "Town Board Meeting", *ILTBM,* April 13, 1992, Indian Lake, NY, p. 241-2, 255.

64. Ibid., p. 255.

65. Craig, E. (1992). "Rafting Negotiations Facing Rough Waters", *HCN*, April 21, 1992, p. 1, 16.

66. Ibid., p. 16.

67. Ibid., p. 16.

68. Ibid., p. 16.

69. Indian Lake Town Board, (1992). "Town Board Meeting", *ILTBM,* April 27, 1992, Indian Lake, NY, p. 261.

70. Craig, E. (1992). "Indian Lake Disenchanted with Rafting", *HCN*, August 18, 1992, p. 1.

71. Indian Lake Town Board, (1992). "Town Board Meeting", *ILTBM,* August 8, 1992, Indian Lake, NY, p. 13, 26.

72. Craig, E. (1992). "Indian Lake", p. 20.

73. Ibid., p. 20.

74. Ibid., p. 20.

75. Craig, E. (1992). "Chamber Presents Plan to Keep Rafting Afloat", *HCN*, September 22, 1992, p. 1.

76. Ibid., p. 8.

77. Indian Lake Town Board, (1992). "Town Board Meeting", *ILTBM,* September 14, 1992, Indian Lake, NY, p. 33.

78. Ibid., p. 33.

79. Ibid., p. 33.

80. Indian Lake Town Board, (1992). "Town Board Meeting", *ILTBM,* October 26, 1992, Indian Lake, NY, p. 63.

81. Indian Lake Town Board, (1992). "Town Board Meeting", *ILTBM,* November 30, 1992, Indian Lake, NY, p. 80.

82. Schmale, M. (2010). Personal interview on *Rafting on the Hudson River*, North River, NY.

83. Indian Lake Town Board, (1993). "Town Board Meeting", *ILTBM,* February 8, 1993, Indian Lake, NY, p. 97.

84. Indian Lake Town Board, (1993). "Town Board Meeting", *ILTBM,* March 8, 1993, Indian Lake, NY, p. 136.

85. Indian Lake Town Board, (1993). "Town Board Meeting", *ILTBM*, April 12, 1993, Indian Lake, NY, p. 160.

86. Indian Lake Town Board, (1995). "Town Board Meeting", *ILTBM*, October 9, 1995, Indian Lake, NY, p. 143.

87. Indian Lake Town Board, (1995). "Town Board Meeting", *ILTBM*, November 9, 1995, Indian Lake, NY, p. 157.

88. Earley, S. (1993). "Whitewater Rafting Guides Anticipate Strong Season", *Glens Falls Business Journal,* May 1993, p. 12.

89. Ibid., p. 12.

90. Glens Falls Post Star (1993). "Whitewater Events Set at Blue Mountain Lake", *Glens Falls Post Star,* May 3, 1993, p. B9.

91. Earley, S. (1993). "Whitewater', p. 12.

92. Town of Indian Lake (1983-96). *1983-96 Raft Attendance Records,* archived at DEC Office, Northville, NY.

93. Town of Indian Lake (1985). *1985 Raft Attendance Records,* archived at DEC Office, Northville, NY.

94. Earley, S. (1993). "Whitewater", p. 12.

95. Ibid., p. 12

96. Schmale, M (1996). Letter on "Economics of Rafting on the Hudson", *ILTBM*, January 18, 1996, p. 217.

97. Geandreau, R., ed. (1982). *A Proposal,* p. 3.

98. Town of Indian Lake (2009). 2009 *Raft Attendance Records,* archived at DEC Office, Northville, NY.

99. Geandreau, R., ed. (1982). *A Proposal*, p. 3-8.

100. Herwig, D. (1981). Warren County Tourism Rafting Brochure draft, September 14, 1981, Warrensburg, NY, p. 3.

101. Hamilton County News, (1989). "Hudson River Raft Company", *HCN,* March 21, 1989, p. 13.

102. DEC, (1995). *Blue Mountain*, p. 77.

103. Indian Lake Town Board, (1992). "Town Board Meeting", *ILTBM,* March 30, 1992, Indian Lake, NY, p. 251.

104. Grondahl, P. (1987). "A Rare Chance For Rafting on the Hudson This Summer", *Albany Times-Union*, August 12, 1987, p. C1.

105. Schmale, M. (2010). Personal interview.

106. Indian Lake Town Board (1987). "Local Outfitters ask to run the Gorge", *ILTBM*, August 13, 1987, p. 281.

107. Grondahl, P. (1987). "A Rare Chance", p. C1.

108. Schmale, M. (2010). Personal interview.

109. Hamilton County News, (1982). "Indian Lake Town Board Meeting", *HCN*, June 23, 1982, p. 21.

110. Indian Lake Town Board, (1983). "Town Board Meeting", *ILTBM,* June 13, 1983, Indian Lake, NY, p. 123.

111. Indian Lake Town Board, (1996). "Town Board Meeting", *ILTBM,* January 18, 1996, Indian Lake, NY, p. 217-18.

112. DEC, (1995). *Blue Mountain*, p. 77.

113. Indian Lake Town Board, (1996). "State of Hudson River Rafting", *ILTBM*, April 11, 1996, p. 260.

114. Ibid., p. 260.

115. Ibid., p. 260-1

116. Indian Lake Town Board (1996). "Consideration and Approval of Summer Rafting on the Hudson", *ILTBM*, May 13, 1996, p. 273.

117. Ibid., p. 274

118. Indian Lake Town Board (1996). "Town Recreation Plan", *ILTBM*, August 12, 1996, p. 5.

119. Indian Lake Town Board (1996). "Town Board Meeting", *ILTBM*, January 18, 1996, Indian Lake, NY, p. 218.

120. Indian Lake Town Board (1996). "Town Board Meeting", *ILTBM*, April 11, 1996, Indian Lake, NY, p. 260.

121. Indian Lake Town Board (1997). "Town Board Meeting", *ILTBM*, July 8, 1997, Indian Lake, NY, p. 168.

122. Indian Lake Town Board (1996). "Town Board Meeting", *ILTBM*, December 9, 1996, Indian Lake, NY, p. 66.

123. Indian Lake Town Board, (1996). "Marko Reports His Summer Numbers", *ILTBM*, September 9, 1996, p. 19.

124. Indian Lake Town Board (1996). "Town Board Meeting", *ILTBM*, December 9, 1996, Indian Lake, NY, p. 66.

125. Indian Lake Town Board (1997). "Town Board Meeting", *ILTBM*, February 10, 1997, Indian Lake, NY, p. 91.

126. Indian Lake Town Board (1997). "Town Board Meeting", *ILTBM,* May 12, 1997, Indian Lake, NY, p. 145.

127. Indian Lake Town Board (1997). "Town Board Meeting", *ILTBM,* June 23, 1997, Indian Lake, NY, p. 159.

128. Indian Lake Town Board (1997). "Town Board Meeting", *ILTBM,* November 10, 1997, Indian Lake, NY, p. 259.

129. Town of Indian Lake (2010). *Hudson River Raft Attendance Records,* archived at DEC office, Northville, NY.

130. Howard, P. (2000). *Town of Indian Lake Rafting Report,* archived at DEC office, Northville, NY, p. 1.

131. North Creek News Enterprise (2010). Front page photo of Governor Paterson rafting the Narrows, *North Creek News Enterprise,* August 28, 2010, p. 1.

132. USGS (2011). *Hudson River Gauge,* USGS Archives, April 28, 2011.

Bibliography

Aber, T. (1982). <u>Adirondack Folks</u>. Prospect Books: Prospect.

Aber, T. & King, S. (1965). <u>The History of Hamilton County</u>. Willard Press: Boonville.

Adams, A. (1996). <u>The Hudson River Guidebook.</u> Fordam University Press: NY.

Adams, A. (1996). <u>The Hudson Through the Years</u>. Fordam University Press: NY.

Addison, G. (2000). <u>Whitewater Rafting: The Essential Guide to Equipment and Techniques</u>. Stackpole Books: Mechanicsburg.

Adirondack Daily Enterprise, (1983). Article on *Rafting the Hudson*, <u>Adirondack Daily Enterprise,</u> May 20, 1983, p. 10, archived at DEC office in Northville, NY.

Adirondack Ecological Center, (no date). Copy of *Hudson River Log Driving System, Finch, Pryne 1929 Map*, Adirondack Ecological Center: Newcomb, NY.

Adirondack Ecological Center, (2012). <u>Adirondack Ecological Communities,</u> www.esf.edu/aec/adks/forestcomm.htm

Adirondack Life, (1982). *Raft Advertisements,* Adirondack Life, May/June, 1982, p. 36-7.

Adirondack Museum Staff, (2010). Lecture on mining and logging in the Adirondacks entitled *Working For the Man,* Fall 2010, North Creek, NY.

Adirondack Museum Archive, (2011). *Articles of Agreement for Driving Logs on the Hudson River and its Tributaries,* Adirondack Museum, Blue Mountain Lake, NY.

Adirondack Museum Archive, (2011). *Log Marks from Town of Queensbury,* Adirondack Museum, Blue Mountain Lake, NY.

Adirondack Museum Archive, (2012). *Maps of the Adirondack Region,* Adirondack Museum, Blue Mountain Lake, NY.

Adirondack Museum Photo Archives, (2013). www.adirondackhistory.org., Adirondack Museum, Blue Mountain Lake, NY.

Adirondack Museum web site, (2013). *Olive Gooley, 1859-1946.* www.adirondackhistory.org/new guides/olive.

Adirondack Park Agency, (2001). *Wild, Scenic, and Recreational Rivers.* www.apa.state.ny.us/documents/laws_regs/slmp PDF 2001.pdf.

Adirondack Park Agency, (2003). *State Land Classification Definitions.* www.apa.ny.gov/stateland/definitions.htm

Adirondack Park Agency, (2012). *Adirondack Park State Land Master Plan,* www.apa.ny.gov/Documents/Laws_Regulations/SLMP.

Adirondack River Outfitters, (1982). *Rafting Brochure,* Indian Lake Chamber of Commerce, Indian Lake, NY.

Allen, M. (1978). *Rafting Through Kennebec Gorge on the Silver Bullet,* Yankee, May 1978, archive.yankeemagazine.com/article.

Amos, W. (1972). The Infinite River: A Biologist's Vision of the World of Water. Ballantine Books: New York.

Angus, C. (2002). The Extraordinary Journey of Clarence Petty. Syracuse University Press: Syracuse.

Argus, The (1872). *The Water Question,* March 10, 1872, archived at Adirondack Museum, Blue Mountain Lake, NY.

Armstead, L. (1994). Whitewater Rafting In North America. The Globe Pequot Press: Old Seybrook.

Bacon, E. (1902). The Hudson River From Ocean to Source. G.P. Putnam & Sons: NY.

Baldigo, B., Mulvihill, C., Ernst, A., Boisvert, B. (2010). *Effects of Recreational Flow Releases on Natural Resources of the Indian and Hudson Rivers in the Central Adirondack Mountain, 2004-2006.* USGS Scientific Investigations Report, 2010-5223, p. 72.

Barkley, K. (2010). Personal interview on *Recollections of Running the Hudson River,* June, 2010, The Forks, Maine.

Barnett, L. (1974). The Ancient Adirondacks. Time Life Books: New York.

Bayse, J. (2011). E-mail on *Northern Frontier Camp Staff Use of the Hudson River Gorge,* dated April 1, 2011.

Bearor, B. (1988). *The Guides Column,* Barkeater 5:3, p. 39.

Bechdel, L. & Ray, S. (1985). River Rescue. Appalachian Mountain Club: Boston.

Beetle, D. (1984). <u>Up Old Forge Way</u>. Utica Observer Dispatch: Utica.

Belknap, B. & Evans, L. (2000). <u>Grand Canyon River Guide</u>. Westwater Books: Evergreen.

Bennet, J. (1996). <u>The Complete Whitewater Rafter</u>, Ragged Mountain Press: Camden, ME.

Benton, L. (2009). E-mail on *Hudson River Stories,* dated March 12, 2009.

Binger, D. (1967). *The Log,* <u>American Whitewater Journal</u>, Autumn 1967, p. 17.

Bird, B. (1952). <u>Calked Shoes: Life in Adirondack Lumber Camps</u>. Prospect Books: Prospect.

Blanchard, A. (2013). Personal interview on *Ernie Blanchard's role in Rafting Releases*, Indian Lake, April, 2013.

Board of the Hudson River Regulating District, (1923). *Official Plan of the Hudson River Regulating District,* NYS Archives, www.archives.nysed.gov.

Bond, H. (1995). <u>Boats and Boating in the Adirondacks</u>. Syracuse University Press: Syracuse.

Boyle, R. (1969). <u>The Hudson River: A Natural and Unnatural History</u>. W.W. Norton: New York.

Bradley, D. (1965). *Conservation Comment.* <u>American Whitewater Journal</u>, Autumn 1965, p. 26-7.

Brebner, J. (1955). <u>The Explorers of North America: 1492 – 1806</u>, Doubleday & Co.: Garden City.

Briggs, J. (1982). *Whitewater – Indian Lake Gold,* Hamilton County News, 35:29, May 12, 1982, p. 14.

Briggs, J. (1982). *Whitewater Fever,* Hamilton County News, 35:30, May 19, 1982, p. 9.

Briggs, J. (1982). *Rafting the Upper Hudson,* Clearwater Navigator, July 1982.

Briggs, J. (1985). *Economic Impact of Whitewater,* Hamilton County News, 38:16, February 6, 1985, p. 9.

Briggs, J. (1985). *Whitewater Guide Training to be Offered,* Hamilton County News, 38:16, February 6, 1985, p. 5.

Briggs, J. (1986). *Indian Lake Welcomes Whitewater Rafters,* Hamilton County News, April 16, 1986.

Brown, E., ed. (1969). *Conservation Highlights,* Adirondac, 33:3, May – June, 1969.

Brown, E. (1985). The Forest Preserve of New York State: A Handbook for Conservationists.

Brown, P. (1999). The Longstreet Highroad Guide to the New York Adirondacks. Longstreet: Atlanta.

Bruce, W. (1907). The Hudson: Three Centuries of History, Romance, and Invention. Bryant Union Company: NY.

Buck, R. (1972). *The Hudson Continued.* Adirondack Life 3:2, p. 24-7.

Buckell, B. (1999). Boldly into the Wilderness: Travelers in Upstate New York 1010- 1646. Buckle Press: Queensbury.

Burns, M. (2009). Personal interview with Milda Burns, daughter of Jack Donohue on *River Driving on the Hudson River,* North River, NY.

Burns, M. (2013). Personal interview with Milda Burns, daughter of Jack Donohue on *River Driving on the Hudson River,* North River, NY.

Burns, P. (2011). Personal conversation on the *Origins of the Virgin Falls Story,* Indian Lake, NY, August 2011.

Butler, T. (1997). *Confessions of a River Rat,* North Creek News Enterprise supplement Yesterday's River, May 1997.

Butler, T. (2009). Personal interview on *Memories of Running the Hudson,* North Creek, NY, June 27, 2009.

Calahan, T. (2009). Personal interview on *Commercial Rafting on the Hudson,* Blue Mountain Lake, NY, October 14, 2009.

Canan, K. (2010). Personal conversation on *Effects of Commercial Rafting on the Hudson River for Town of Indian Lake Court,* Indian Lake, NY, July 2010.

Canham, H. (1981). *Forest Recreation: New York State Forest Resources Assessment Report #10,* DEC: Albany, NY.

Carlson, D. (1986). *Official Map of River Names: Hudson River Gorge,* no publisher given.

Carlson, D. (2008). *A Whitewater Tale,* Winter Guide to the Gore Mountain & Lake George Area. Interface Communications, Weavertown, NY.

Carlson, R. (2010). Personal interview on *Early Days of Rafting on the Hudson River,* North Creek, NY.

Carlson, R. (2013). Personal interview on *Early Days of Rafting on the Hudson River,* North Creek, NY.

Carman, B. (1979). *Doing It,* Adirondack Life, May–June 1979, p. 36-7, 59-60.

Carmer, C. (1974). The Hudson. Holt, Rinehart, and Winston: New York.

Carr, S. (1986). *Q and A,* New York Times, May 11, 1986, p. XX4.

Carrey, J. & Conley, C. (1978). River of No Return. Backeddy Books: Cambridge.

Carson, R. (1973). Peaks and People of the Adirondacks. Adirondack Mountain Club: Glens Falls.

Carpenter, C. (1979). *Rescue in the Hudson River Gorge.* Adirondack Life, 10:2, p. 12-15, 44-7.

Cipperly, R. (1983). *DEC Raft Questionnaire,* September 29, 1983, archived at DEC Northville office, Northville, NY.

Cipperly, R. (1983). *DEC Raft Questionnaire Results,* September, 1983, archived at DEC Northville office, Northville, NY.

Cipperly, R. (1984). *Minutes of DEC/Town of Indian Lake Meeting with Rafting Companies,* October, 24, 1984, archived at DEC Northville office, Northville, NY.

Cipperly, R. (1984). *Minutes of DEC - Town of Indian Lake Rafting Meeting,* November 9, 1984, archived at DEC Northville office, Northville, NY.

Cipperly, R. (1985). Hand written note on green legal pad to Dick Cipperly from an unknown person on *Past Activity in the Hudson River Gorge,* archived at DEC office in Northville, NY.

Cipperly, R. (1987). Letter dated March 17, 1987, on *Contracts between the DEC and the Town,* archived at DEC office in Northville, NY.

Cipperly, R. (2011). Personal interview on *Early Days of Commercial Rafting on the Hudson River,* Warrensburg, NY.

Clarity, J. (1967). *Kennedy Falls Out of Kayak Shooting Hudson Rapids,* New York Times, May 7, 1967, p. 1, 70.

Clarke, G. (2011). Personal interview on the *Early Days of Commercial Rafting on the Hudson River,* Beachburg, Ontario.

Cobb, T. (1990). *A Profile of Outdoor Recreation Opportunities in the Adirondack Park* in Adirondack Park in the 21st Century, v.1. New York State: Albany.

Cobb, T. (1990). *An Overview of National Park, National Forest, and Other Protected Area Management Systems with Selected Institutional Case Examples,* Adirondack Park in the 21st Century, v.1. New York State: Albany.

Cole, Dane (2011). Personal interview on *Early Commercial raft trips on the Hudson River,* Indian Lake, NY.

Cole, Doug. (2010). Personal interview on *Rafting on the Hudson River,* Weavertown, NY.

Colvin, V. (1994). *The Discovery of Lake Tear,* The Adirondack Reader. Adirondack Mountain Club: Lake George.

Colvin, V. (1872). *The Water Question,* The Argus. Adirondack Museum Archives, Blue Mountain Lake, NY.

Colvin, V. (1874). Topographical Survey of the Adirondack Wilderness of New York, Weed, Parsons and Company: Albany.

Connelly, J. & Porterfield, J. (1987). <u>Appalachian Whitewater: Volume II, The Northern Mountains</u>. Menasha Ridge Press: Birmingham.

Connely, J., Grove, E., Porterfield, J., & Walbridge, C. (1999). <u>Appalachian Whitewater: Northeastern States</u>. Menasha Ridge Press: Birmingham.

Cooney, D. (1971). *Hydrological Characteristics of the Upper Hudson.* <u>American Whitewater Journal</u>, Summer 1971, p. 61-3.

Craig, E. (1990). *Whitewater World: Emphasis is on Safety,* <u>Hamilton County News</u>, December 12, 1990, p. 10.

Craig, E. (1991). Article on *Indian Lake Town Board meeting,* <u>Hamilton County News</u>, May 21, 1991, p. 8.

Craig, E. (1992). *Rafting Negotiations Facing Rough Waters,* <u>Hamilton County News</u>, April 21, 1992, p. 1, 16.

Craig, E. (1992). *Indian Lake Disenchanted with Rafting,* <u>Hamilton County News</u>, August 18, 1992, p. 1.

Craig, E. (1992). *Chamber Presents Plan to Keep Rafting Afloat,* <u>Hamilton County News</u>, September 22, 1992, p. 1, 8.

Craig, E. (1993). *Dwindling Pike Population is Blamed on Short Rations,* <u>Hamilton County News</u>, April 13, 1993, p. 7.

Craig, E. (1994). *One Lives, One Dies in River Rafting Mishaps,* <u>Hamilton County News</u>, May 2, 1994, p. 1.

Craig, E. (1994). Article on *Indian Lake Town Board meeting,* <u>Hamilton County News</u>, May 10, 1994, p. 6.

Craig, E. (1994). Article on *Indian Lake Town Board meeting,* <u>Hamilton County News</u>, May 17, 1994, p. 6.

Craig, E. (1995). Article on *Indian Lake Town Board meeting*, <u>Hamilton County News</u>, December 19, 1994, p. 10.

Crooker, B. (1983). *First Steps to Whitewater Canoeing*, <u>Adirondac</u>, March, 1983, p. 9-11.

Cromie, W. (2011). CD on the *History of Adirondack Wildwaters Rafting*.

Cunningham, P. (2012). Personal conversation on the *First Inflatable Raft Trips in the Hudson River Gorge*, September, 2012, Blue Mountain Lake.

Cummins, P. (2009). Personal conversation on *Tubing on the Hudson*, Indian Lake, NY, June, 24, 2009.

Davis, G. & Huber, J. (1970). *Care, Custody, and Control Guidelines for the Adirondack Park Forest Preserve: Wild, Scenic, and Recreational Rivers* in <u>Temporary Study Commission on the Future of the Adirondacks, Technical Report 1, vol. B, Private and Public Land,</u> Albany: NY.

Dawson, C. (2009). *Recreation and Tourism in the Adirondacks* in <u>The Great Experiment in Conservation: Voices From the Adirondacks,</u> Porter, W., Erickson, J., and Whaley, R., ed., Syracuse University Press: Syracuse.

DEC, (1970). *Water Resources, Technical Report 3: Forests, Minerals, Water, and Air* in <u>Temporary Study Commission on the Future of the Adirondacks, Technical Report 1, vol. B, Private and Public Land,</u> DEC: Albany.

DEC, (1971). *Hudson River Gorge Primitive Area Unit Management Plan Draft*, Albany, NY, archived at DEC office in Northville, NY.

DEC, (1982). Letter dated March 12, 1982, *DEC was considering expanding the scope of the Unit Management Plan*, archived at DEC office in Northville, NY.

DEC, (1982). Letter dated April 21, 1982 on *Progress of the Hudson River Gorge Unit Management Plan,* archived at DEC office in Northville, NY.

DEC, (1982). Memo dated June 10, 1982 on *Guide Licensing Committee,* archived at DEC office in Northville, NY.

DEC, (1985). *SEQR Negative Declaration for the Operation of the Indian River Waterway Access,* dated February 15, 1985, archived at DEC office in Northville, NY.

DEC, (1995). *Blue Mountain Wild Forest Unit Management Plan,* Department of Environmental Conservation: Albany.

Denis, M. (1984). *Fishing, Rafting, & Hunting–Still Good in the Adirondacks,* <u>Barkeater</u>, no further reference available.

Department of Interior, (1966). *Focus on the Hudson: Evaluation of Proposals and Alternatives,* booklet archived in Adirondack Museum, Blue Mountain Lake, NY.

Department of State, New York State (2012). New York State Constitution, Article XIV, Conservation, Forest Preserve to be forever kept wild.
www.dos.ny.gov/info/constitution.htm.

Duel, A. (1979). *Faltbooting Mit Silulium,* <u>American Whitewater Journal</u>, July–September, 1979, p. 10-15.

Diamond, H., ed. (1962). <u>Wilderness and Recreation: A Report on Resources, Values, and Problems</u>. Sierra Club Books: San Francisco.

Dickerman, P. (1991). <u>Adventure Travel North America</u>. Adventure Guides Inc.: New York.

DiNunzio, M. (1984). <u>Adirondack Wildguide: A Natural History of the Adirondack Park</u>. Brodock Press: Utica.

Division of Water Resources, DEC, (1970). <u>Temporary Study Commission on the Future of the Adirondacks, Technical Reports 1, v. B, Private and Public Land</u>. New York State: Albany.

Donaldson, A. (2002). <u>A History of the Adirondacks, Vol. I</u>. Purple Mountain Press: Fleischmanns.

Donohue, R. (2009). Personal interview on *River Driving on the Hudson River,* Newcomb, NY August, 2009.

Donohue, H. & Conroy, D. (1994). *The Hamlet of North River* in <u>Rivers, Rails, and Ski Trails: The History of the Town of Johnsburg,</u> Johnsburg Historical Society, ed. Sawyers Press: North Creek.

Dunwell, F. (2008). <u>The Hudson: America's River</u>. Columbia University Press: NY.

Earley, S. (1993). *Whitewater Rafting Guides Anticipate Strong Season,* <u>Glens Falls Business Journal</u>, May, 1993, p. 1, 12.

Ebert, T. (2009). E-mail on *Personal Recollections of Rafting on the Hudson River,* March 4, 2009.

Evans, L. & Belknap, B. (1975). <u>Flaming Gorge Dinosaur National Monument: Dinosaur River Guide.</u> Westwater Books: Boulder City.

Fabin, J. (1984). *Hudson River Access Issues,* letter to Dick Cipperly dated November 2, 1984, archived at DEC office in Northville, NY.

Fabin, J. (2010). Personal interview on *Early Days of Rafting on the Hudson River,* Indian Lake, NY.

Failing, W. (1992). Letter dated January 20, 1992 to Dick Cipperly with S*pecific Suggestions for the Improvement of the Put-in,* archived at DEC office in Northville, NY.

Failing, W. (2009). Personal interview on *Early Days of Rafting on the Hudson River,* Indian Lake, NY, April 2009.

Fanning, J. (1881). *Report on Water Supply for New York and Other Cities of the Hudson Valley,* archived at Adirondack Museum, Blue Mountain Lake, NY.

Fanning, J. (1884). *Report No. 2 on a Water Supply for New York and Other Cities of the Hudson Valley,* archived at Adirondack Museum, Blue Mountain Lake, NY.

Farnum, C. (1992). Excerpt from Chronicles of the Hudson, Roland Van Zandt, Black Dome Press: Hensonville.

Fenton, R. (1990). Personal notes from a conversation with Dick Nason, Finch, Pryne historian, archived at DEC office in Northville, NY.

Fenton, R. (1991). Personal notes from an interview with Dick Purdue, Indian Lake Town Supervisor, archived at DEC office in Northville, NY.

Fenton, R. (1992). *Draft of Hudson River Gorge Unit Management Plan* dated February 1992, archived at DEC office in Northville, NY.

Fenton, R. (1993). Personal notes on *Lake Abanakee fishing,* archived at DEC office in Northville, NY.

Fenton, R. (1994). Personal notes on *Sagamore dory trips*, archived at DEC office in Northville, NY.

Fenton, R. (1994). Personal notes on *Checking Conditions at Blue Ledges*, archived at DEC office in Northville, NY.

Fenton, R. (1996). Personal notes from Rich Preall on *Lake Abanakee Fishing*, archived at DEC office in Northville, NY.

Fenton, R. (2010). Email letter dated December 28, 2010 on *Hudson River Gorge Unit Management Plan.*

Fenton, R. (2011). Email dated on *Hudson River Gorge Unit Management Plan.*

Fosburgh, H. (1955). The Sound of Whitewater. Charles Scribbner: NY.

Fosburgh, P. (1947). *Big Boom*, New York Conservationist. 1:5, p. 16-17.

Fox, W. (1976). History of the Lumber Industry in the State of New York. Harbor Hill Books: Harrison.

Finch, Pruyn, (no date). *The History of the Finch, Pruyn Farm,* Undated article on Finch, Pruyn logging operations in Newcomb, NY.

Gaines, E. (2003). *The Re-signification of Risk in Whitewater: Ritual Initiation and the Mythology pf River Culture* in Case Studies in Sport Communication. Greenwood Publishing: Westport, CT.

Garand, D. (2009). Personal interview on *Early Rafting in the Hudson River Gorge,* Newcomb, NY, August 2009.

Gargan, E. (1985). *In the Adirondacks, River Rafters Get Adventure and Challenge,* New York Times, April 16, 1985, p. B1.

Garren, J. (1987). Idaho River Tours. Garren Publishing: Portland.

Gabler, R. (1981). New England Whitewater River Guide. Appalachian Mountain Club: Boston.

Geandreau, R. (1981). Letter on *Organizing Outfitters,* business letter to Hudson River Outfitters dated March 12, 1981.

Geandreau, R, ed. (1982). *A Proposal Affecting the Future of Our Township,* unpublished paper dated January, 1982, prepared by the Indian Lake Chamber of Commerce.

Geandreau, R. (1982). Letter from Wayne Hockmeyer to DEC's Mark Brown on *Hudson River Professional Outfitters Association position on Guide Licensing Proposals,* May 16, 1982.

Geandreau, R. (1982). Letter to Wayne Hockmeyer dated May 24, 1982 on *Hudson River Gorge Unit Management Plan advisory committees.*

Gilborn, A. (1982). *Down the Wild River,* Adirondack Life, 13:3, p. 30-7.

Glens Falls Post Star, (1979). *Weather Forecast,* Glens Falls Post Star, April 5, 1979, p. 10.

Glens Falls Post Star, (1979). *Weather Forecast,* Glens Falls Post Star, April 6, 1979, p. 10.

Glens Falls Post Star, (1979). *Weather Forecast,* Glens Falls Post Star, April 7, 1979, p. 1, 8, 10.

Glens Falls Post Star, (1979). *Weather Forecast,* Glens Falls Post Star, April 9, 1979, p. 10.

Glens Falls Post Star, (1979). *Weather Forecast,* Glens Falls Post Star, April 14, 1979, p. 1, 6.

Glens Falls Post Star, (1982). *Weather Forecast,* <u>Glens Falls Post Star,</u> April 16, 1982, p. 10.

Glens Falls Post Star, (1982). *Weather Forecast,* <u>Glens Falls Post Star,</u> April 17, 1982, p. 1, 9.

Glens Falls Post Star, (1982). *Raft Capsizes; 2 People Missing,* <u>Glens Falls Post Star</u>, April 19, 1982, p. 1.

Glens Falls Post Star, (1982). *Flood Warning Issued,* <u>Glens Falls Post Star,</u> April 19, 1982, p. 9.

Glens Falls Post Star, (1982). *Missing Rafters Found,* <u>Glens Falls Post Star,</u> April 20, 1982, p. 13.

Glens Falls Post Star, (1993). *Whitewater Events Set at Blue Mountain Lake,* <u>Glens Falls Post Star</u>, May 3, 1993, p. B9.

Glens Falls Post Star, (1996). Article on Raft Fatality, <u>Glens Falls Post Star,</u> June 28, 1996, p. A1.

Goodspeed, S. (1997). From *Mountain Views* in <u>Yesterday's River,</u> North Creek News-Enterprise, Sawyer Press: North Creek.

Graham, F. (1984). <u>The Adirondack Park: A Political History</u>. Syracuse University Press: Syracuse.

Grinnel, L. (1956). <u>Canoeable Waterways of New York State</u>. Pageant Press: NY.

Grondahl, P. (1987). *A Rare Chance For Rafting on the Hudson This Summer,* <u>Albany Times-Union,</u> August 12, 1987, p. C1.

Gruspe, A. (2009). *A History of Whitewater Rafting in West Virginia,* <u>West Virginia Historical Society Quarterly</u>, www.wvculture.org/history/wvhs124.html.

Haley, A. (2010). Personal interview on *Early Days of Northern Outdoors Rafting on the Hudson River,* October 2010, Schohegan, ME.

Hall, R. (1967). *The Unsullied Hudson – It Sings, It Skips, It Dances.* New York Times, July 16, 1967, p. 296.

Hamilton County News, (1975). *Hudson River Whitewater Derby supplement,* Hamilton County News, May 1, 1975, p. 8.

Hamilton County News, (1978). *Hudson River Whitewater Derby supplement,* Hamilton County News, May 1978, p. 8.

Hamilton County News, (1979). Hamilton County News, March 28, 1979, p. 1.

Hamilton County News, (1979). *Huge Snowstorm Hits County,* Hamilton County News, April 11, 1979, p. 1.

Hamilton County News, (1979). *Indian Lake Chamber of Commerce ads for Hudson River Whitewater Derby,* Hamilton County News Supplement dated May 2, 1979, p. 5.

Hamilton County News, (1980). *Rafting Down Indian River Ok'd by Indian Lake Board,* Hamilton County News, 32:2, February 13, 1980, p. 12.

Hamilton County News, (1980). *Indian Lake,* Hamilton County News, 31:6, March 12, 1980, p. 2.

Hamilton County News, (1980). *Rafting Down the Rivers: Indian Lake to North River,* Hamilton County News, 34:9, May 7, 1980, p. 1.

Hamilton County News, (1981). *Indian Lake,* Hamilton County News, February 11, 1981, p. 8.

Hamilton County News, (1981). *Indian Lake,* Hamilton County News, March 11, 1981, p. 7.

Hamilton County News, (1982). Ads for Hudson River Raft Company, American Hotel raft packages, night entertainment, <u>Hudson River Derby Suppliment</u> April 23, 1982, p. 3-4.

Hamilton County News (1982). *Indian Lake,* <u>Hamilton County News</u>, June 23, 1982, p. 21.

Hamilton County News, (1982). Article on *Indian Lake Town Board*, <u>Hamilton County News,</u> July 12, 1982, p. 16.

Hamilton County News, (1983). Article on *Indian Lake Town Board*, <u>Hamilton County News</u>, November 22, 1983, p. 2.

Hamilton County News, (1984). *Rafting To Start,* <u>Hamilton County News</u>, April 4, 1984, p. 1.

Hamilton County News, (1984). *Lost Couple Found on River,* <u>Hamilton County News</u>, June 6, 1984, p. 2.

Hamilton County News, (1984). <u>Hamilton County News</u>, June 13, 1984, p. 8.

Hamilton County News, (1984). *Students Learn Rafting,* <u>Hamilton County News</u> June 20, 1984, p. 18.

Hamilton County News, (1985). *Whitewater Guide School Changed,* <u>Hamilton County News</u>, January 20, 1985, p.

Hamilton County News, (1985). *Dates Set For Whitewater Raft Training,* <u>Hamilton County News,</u> March 13, 1985, p. 6.

Hamilton County News, (1986). *Snow Times in the Adirondacks* supplement to <u>Hamilton County News</u>, February, 1986, p. 4-5, 8.

Hamilton County News (1986). *Guides to be Issued Contingent Licenses,* <u>Hamilton County News</u>, March 26, 1986, p. 5.

Hamilton County News (1988). *Hudson River Rafting Company Celebrates 10th Birthday,* Hamilton County News, April 20, 1988, p. 9.

Hamilton County News, (1989). Article on *Hudson River Raft Company,* Hamilton County News, March 21, 1989, p. 13.

Hamilton County News (1991). Article has info on *Meeting of Lake Abanakee Owners objecting to releases,* Hamilton County News, September 24, 1991, p. 11.

Harper, J. (2008). *Woman Guides Live Their Dreams,* Adirondack Explorer, March/April 2008.

Harrigan, R. (1968). *Robert Francis Kennedy,* American Whitewater Journal, 13:1, Spring 1968.

Harris, E. (1989). Mississippi Solo: A River Quest. Harper & Row: New York.

Hatch, D. (2008). *Don Hatch River Expeditions.* donhatchrivertrips.com/hatch-legacy.php.

Hathaway, S. (1982). Letter to Terry Healey dated April 21, 1982 on the *Status of the Hudson River Gorge Unit Management Plan,* archived at DEC office in Northville, NY.

Hathaway, S. (1982). Letter to Norm VanValkenburg dated June, 10, 1982 on *Hudson River Gorge Unit Management Plan,* archived at DEC office in Northville, NY.

Hawksley, O. (1967). *River Protective Legislation: Now or Never.* American Whitewater Journal, Summer 1967, p. 8-10.

Hawksley, O. (1968). *Conservation Comment.* American Whitewater Journal, Summer 1968, p. 23.

Headley, J. (1982). <u>The Adirondack or Life In the Woods</u>. Harbor Hill Books: Harrison.

Healy, B. (1999). <u>The High Peaks of Essex: The Adirondack Mountains of Orson Schofield Phelps.</u> Purple Mountain Press: Fleischmanns.

Hendee, J., Stankey, J., Lucas, R. (1978). <u>Wilderness Management</u>. United States Forest Service: Washington.

Hennigan, R. (2007). *To be or Not To Be Dammed in New York State.* <u>Clearwaters</u>, Summer 2007, p. 22.

Herwig, D. (1981). *Warren County Tourism Rafting Brochure,* Warrensburg, NY.

Hill, M. (2009). *Rapid Transit.* <u>Adirondack Life,</u> 40:3, p.28 – 33, 76-7.

Hixon, E. (2010). Canoeist, phone interview on *Canoe Experiences on the Hudson River Gorge,* Indian Lake, NY, January 16, 2010.

Hixon, E. (2010). Personal interview on *Recreational boating in the Hudson River Gorge*, Saranac Lake, NY.

Hochschild, H. (1993). <u>Lumberjcaks and Rivermen in the Central Adirondacks 1850-1950</u>. Adirondack Museum: Blue Mountain Lake.

Hockmeyer, S. (2010). Personal interview on *Early Days of Northern Outdoors Rafting on the Hudson River,* June, 2010, The Forks, ME.

Hockmeyer, S. (2010). *A Few More Details on Black Sunday,* email dated June 27, 2010.

Hockmeyer, S. (2011). E-mail on *River Access Issues,* dated .

Hockmeyer, W. (1982). Letter to DEC's Mark Brown on *Hudson River Professional Outfitters Association position on Guide Licensing Proposals,* May 16, 1982.

Hockmeyer, W. (1982). *Letter of thanks* to Indian Lake Town Board dated May 20, 1982.

Hockmeyer, W. (1984). Letter to Dick Cipperly on *Access to the Hudson River for Rafting,* October 15, 1984.

Hockmeyer, W. (2009). *First Few Years on the Hudson,* email dated September 28, 2009.

Hockmeyer, W. (2009). Phone interview on *Early Days of Northern Outdoors Rafting on the Hudson River,* Indian Lake, NY.

Hockmeyer, W. (2010). *More on Black Sunday and 1ˢᵗ Day on the Hudson,* email dated July 2, 2010.

Hockmeyer, W. (2011). *E-mail response to Black Sunday Draft,* dated.

Hockmeyer, W. (2011). Email on *Over Use on the Hudson River,* dated January 28, 2011.

Hoffman, C. (1970). Wild Scenes In the Forest and Plain, Vol 1. Literature House: Upper Saddle River, NJ.

Houston, M. (1985). *Rapid Transit,* Utica Observer–Dispatch, April 20, 1985, p. 9, 11.

Howard, P. (2000). *Raft Attendance Report,* Town of Indian Lake, archived at DEC office, Northville, NY.

Hudowalski, G., ed. (1940). *Canoeing in the Adirondacks.* Cloudsplitter June 1940.

Hudson River Professional Outfitters (1981). *Articles and Bylaws of Hudson River Professional Outfitters,* Spring 1981.

Hull, R., ed. (1967). *Editorial,* in <u>Warrensburg – Lake George News,</u> May 11, 1967.

Hutchins, B. (2010). Personal interview on *Early Days of Rafting on the Hudson River,* Indian Lake, NY, July, 2010.

Hyde, F. (1985). *Resources for the Taking* in <u>A Century Wild</u>, Neal Burdick, ed. The Chauncy Press: Saranac Lake, NY.

Indian Lake Chamber of Commerce, (1982). *Whitewater Raft Tours* in Indian Lake Community Directory.

Indian Lake Town Board, (1979). *Bob Geandreau goes before the Board,* Indian Lake Town Board Minutes, May 7, 1979.

Indian Lake Town Board, (1979). *Bob Geandreau asks board to Approve Raft trips,* Indian Lake Town Board Minutes, September 4, 1979.

Indian Lake Town Board, (1980). *First Agreement Between the Town and Rafters Providing for Releases,* Indian Lake Town Board Minutes, February 2, 1980, p. 275.

Indian Lake Town Board, (1981). *Board Discusses Approving Dam Releases for Rafting,* Indian Lake Town Board Minutes, February 2, 1981, p. 27.

Indian Lake Town Board, (1981). *Wayne Hockmeyer Goes before the Board,* Indian Lake Town Board Minutes, March 2, 1981, p. 31.

Indian Lake Town Board, (1982). *Discussion on Charging Outfitters a Fee,* Indian Lake Town Board Minutes, March 8, 1982, p. 70.

Indian Lake Town Board, (1982). *Resolution to Include Rafting in the Hudson River Gorge UMP*, Indian Lake Town Board Minutes, dated April 12, 1982, p. 72.

Indian Lake Town Board, (1983). *Appointment of Barry Hutchins as Raft Attendant*, Indian Lake Town Board Minutes, March, 24, 1983, p. 111.

Indian Lake Town Board, (1983). *Resolution to Limit River Access for Eastern River Expeditions*, Indian Lake Town Board Minutes, April 4, 1983, p. 112.

Indian Lake Town Board, (1983). *Minutes of Town Board Meeting*, June 13, 1983, Indian Lake, NY, p. 123.

Indian Lake Town Board, (1983). *Resolution to Approve Raft Contracts*, Indian Lake Town Board Minutes, December 12, 1983, p. 138.

Indian Lake Town Board, (1984). *Effects of Rafting on Lake Abanakee*, Indian Lake Town Board Minutes, June 11, 1984, p. 158.

Indain Lake Town Board (1984). *Methods For Charging Rafters*, Indian Lake Town Board Minutes, September 10, 1984, p. 169.

Indian Lake Town Board Minutes, (1985). March 11, 1985, p. 197.

Indian Indian Lake Town Board, (1986). *Town Budgets for 1984-1986*, Indian Lake Town Board Minutes, Indian Lake, NY.

Indian Indian Lake Town Board, (1986). *Minutes of Town Board Meeting*, July 14, 1986, Indian Lake, NY, p. 244.

Indian Indian Lake Town Board, (1986). *Minutes of Town Board Meeting*, July 29, 1986, Indian Lake, NY, p. 246.

Indian Lake Town Board, (1987). *Local people express concern over the effects of releases,* Indian Lake Town Board Minutes, May 11, 1987, p. 276.

Indian Lake Town Board, (1987). Local Outfitters ask to run the Gorge, Indian Lake Town Board Minutes, August 13, 1987, p. 281.

Indian Indian Lake Town Board, (1988). *Minutes of Town Board Meeting,* August 8, 1988, Indian Lake, NY, p. 246

Indian Indian Lake Town Board, (1988). *Minutes of Town Board Meeting,* December 23, 1988, Indian Lake, NY, p. 55.

Indian Indian Lake Town Board, (1989). *Minutes of Town Board Meeting,* May 8, 1989, Indian Lake, NY, p. 75.

Indian Indian Lake Town Board, (1989). *Minutes of Town Board Meeting,* August 21, 1989, Indian Lake, NY, p. 85.

Indian Indian Lake Town Board, (1989). *Minutes of Town Board Meeting,* September 18, 1989, Indian Lake, NY, p. 89.

Indian Lake Town Board, (1990). *Minutes of Town Board Meeting,* December 1990, Indian Lake, NY.

Indian Lake Town Board, (1991). *Minutes of Town Board Meeting,* October 14, 1991, Indian Lake, NY.

Indian Lake Town Board, (1991). *Minutes of Town Board Meeting,* November 29, 1991, Indian Lake, NY.

Indian Lake Town Board, (1992). *Minutes of Town Board Meeting,* February 27, 1992, Indian Lake, NY.

Indian Lake Town Board, (1992). *Minutes of Town Board Meeting,* March 9, 1992, Indian Lake, NY, p. 241-2.

Indian Lake Town Board, (1992). *Minutes of Town Board Meeting,* March 30, 1992, Indian Lake, NY.

Indian Lake Town Board, (1992). *Minutes of Town Board Meeting,* April 13, 1992, Indian Lake, NY, p. 241-2, p. 255.

Indian Lake Town Board, (1992). *Minutes of Town Board Meeting,* April 27, 1992, Indian Lake, NY, p. 261.

Indian Lake Town Board, (1992). *Minutes of Town Board Meeting,* May 5, 1992, Indian Lake, NY.

Indian Lake Town Board, (1992). *Minutes of Town Board Meeting,* July 27, 1992, Indian Lake, NY.

Indian Lake Town Board, (1992). *Minutes of Town Board Meeting,* August 8, 1992, Indian Lake, NY, p.13, 26.

Indian Lake Town Board, (1992). *Minutes of Town Board Meeting,* September 14, 1992, Indian Lake, NY, p. 33.

Indian Lake Town Board, (1992). *Minutes of Town Board Meeting,* October 26, 1992, Indian Lake, NY, p. 63.

Indian Lake Town Board, (1992). *Minutes of Town Board Meeting,* November 30, 1992, Indian Lake, NY, p. 80.

Indian Lake Town Board, (1992). *Minutes of Town Board Meeting,* December 28, 1992, Indian Lake, NY.

Indian Lake Town Board, (1993). *Minutes of Town Board Meeting,* February 8, 1993, Indian Lake, NY, p. 97.

Indian Lake Town Board, (1993). *Minutes of Town Board Meeting,* March 8, 1993, Indian Lake, NY.

Indian Lake Town Board, (1993). *Minutes of Town Board Meeting,* April 12, 1993, Indian Lake, NY, p. 160.

Indian Lake Town Board, (1993). *Minutes of Town Board Meeting,* August 9, 1993, Indian Lake, NY.

Indian Lake Town Board, (1994). *Minutes of Town Board Meeting,* April 8, 1994, Indian Lake, NY.

Indian Lake Town Board, (1994). *Minutes of Town Board Meeting,* May 4, 1994, Indian Lake, NY.

Indian Lake Town Board, (1994). *Minutes of Town Board Meeting,* May 9, 1994, Indian Lake, NY.

Indian Lake Town Board, (1995). *Minutes of Town Board Meeting,* February 13, 1995, Indian Lake, NY.

Indian Lake Town Board, (1995). *Minutes of Town Board Meeting,* October 9, 1995, Indian Lake, NY, p.143.

Indian Lake Town Board, (1995). *Minutes of Town Board Meeting,* November 9, 1995, Indian Lake, NY.

Indian Lake Town Board, (1996). *Minutes of Town Board Meeting,* January 18, 1996, Indian Lake, NY, p. 217-18.

Indian Lake Town Board, (1996). *State of Hudson River Rafting,* Indian Lake Town Board Minutes, April 11, 1996, p. 260-1.

Indian Lake Town Board, (1996). *Minutes of Town Board Meeting,* April 11, 1996, Indian Lake, NY, p. 260-1.

Indian Lake Town Board, (1996). *Consideration and Approval of Summer Rafting on the Hudson,* Indian Lake Town Board Minutes, May 13, 1996, p. 273-4.

Indian Lake Town Board, (1996). *Town Recreation Plan,* Indian Lake Town Board Minutes, August 12, 1996, p. 5.

Indian Lake Town Board, (1996). *Minutes of Town Board Meeting,* August 29, 1996, Indian Lake, NY.

Indian Lake Town Board, (1996). *Marko reports his summer numbers,* Indian Lake Town Board Minutes, September 9, 1996, p. 19.

Indian Lake Town Board, (1996). *Minutes of Town Board Meeting,* December 9, 1996, Indian Lake, NY, p. 66.

Indian Lake Town Board, (1997). *Minutes of Town Board Meeting,* 1997, Indian Lake, NY.

Indian Lake Town Board, (1997). *Minutes of Town Board Meeting,* February 10, 1997, Indian Lake, NY, p. 91.

Indian Lake Town Board, (1997). *Minutes of Town Board Meeting,* May 12, 1997, Indian Lake, NY, p. 145.

Indian Lake Town Board, (1997). *Minutes of Town Board Meeting,* June 23, 1997, Indian Lake, NY, p. 159.

Indian Lake Town Board, (1997). *Minutes of Town Board Meeting,* November 10, 1997, Indian Lake, NY, p. 259.

Ingersoll, E. (1905). Guide To the Hudson River, 13th ed. Rand McNally: Chicago.

Isachsen, Y. (1992). *Still Rising After All These Years,* Natural History, May 1992, p. 31-3.

Jamieson, P. (1986). Adirondack Pilgrimage. Adirondack Mountain Club: Glens Falls.

Jamieson, P. (1994). The Adirondack Reader. Adirondack Mountain Club: Lake George.

Jenkinson, M. (1973). Wild Rivers of North America. E.P. Dutton & Co.: NY.

Jennings, V. (1988). *Drawdowns May Effect Fish,* Hamilton County News, May 25, 1988, p. 9.

Jensen, C. (1970). Outdoor Recreation In America. Burgess Publishing: Minneapolis.

Johnson, D. (1984). Business letter dated November 2, 1984 on *Hudson River Rafting Legal Issues,* archived at DEC office in Northville, NY.

Kapelewski, T. (1994). Letter to Mike Wilson dated April 14, 1994 on *Wilson's concerns for the Hudson River Gorge Unit Management Plan*, archived at DEC office in Northville, NY.

Karlin, R. (2004). *A Message Carried on the Current,* Albany Times – Union, July 7, 2004, p. B1.

Kaufman, J. (1994). *The Upper Hudson* in The Adirondack Reader, Paul Jamieson. Adirondack Mountain Club: Lake George.

Keller, J. (1980). Adirondack Wilderness: A Story of Man and Nature. Syracuse University Press: Syracuse.

Ketchledge, E. (1996). Forests and Trees of the Adirondack High Peaks Region. Adirondack Mountain Club: Lake George.

Kohl, M. (2011). *Personal conversation on river names.* June 2011, North River, NY.

Komroff, M. (1969). The Hudson: From Lake Tear of the Clouds to New York Harbor, McGraw-Hill: NY.

Kovach, B. (1970). *Rural Upstaters Denounce City's Call for More Dams to Expand the Water Supply*. New York Times, February 1970, p. 23.

Kowalski, J. (2010). Phone interview on *Early Years on the Hudson*. Indian Lake, NY, May, 2010.

Kowalski, J. (2011). Email letter dated February 2, 2011 on *Early Commercial Rafting on the Hudson*.

Knapp, C. (1987). *Summer Times,* Hamilton County News Suppliment, May 20, 1987, p. 4.

Krakel II, D. (1987). Downriver: A Yellowstone Journey. Sierra Club Books: San Francisco.

Kudish, M. (1996). Railroads of the Adirondacks: A History. Purple Mountain Press: Fleishmanns.

Kuhne, C. (1995). Whitewater Rafting: An Introductory Guide. Lyons & Buford: NY.

LaForest, J. & LaForest, A. (2004). *Along the Cedar River*. Self-published book archived at Town of Indian Lake Library: Indian Lake, NY.

LeBlanc, A. (2010). Personal recollections on *Rafting on the Hudson River,* Indian Lake, NY, June, 2010.

LeBrun, F. (2003). *Effect of Rafting,* Albany Times-Union, July 10, 2003.

Lessels, B. (1998). Classic Northeastern Whitewater Guide, 3rd ed. Appalachian Mountain Club Boston.

Lewis, T. (2000). The Hudson: A History. Yale University Press: New Haven.

Leydet, F. (1968). *Time and the River Flowing: Grand Canyon*. Sierra Club–Ballantine Books: New York.

Lorrie, P. (1995). River of Mountains: A Canoe Journey Down the Hudson. Syracuse University Press: Syracuse.

Lossing, B. (1972). The Hudson From Wilderness to the Sea. New Hampshire Publishing Company: Somersworth.

Luciano, D. (1984). Legal letter dated April 11, 1984 on *Access to the Hudson River*, archived at DEC office in Northville NY.

Mallette, D. (1982). Letter on *Usage of the Put-in Area*, February 23, 1982, archived at DEC office in Northville NY.

Manchester, L. (2010). Tales From the Deserted Village. www.cefles.org/version 1.03.

Marshall, G. (1973). *Preface* in Peaks and People of the Adirondacks, Adirondack Mountain Club: Glens Falls.

Masten, A. (1968). The Story of Adirondac. Syracuse University Press: Syracuse.

Masters, B. & Smith, C. (1970). *Whitewater Wilderness: Adventure in the Upper Hudson*. Adirondack Life, 1:2, p. 24-7, 44.

McCall & McCall, (1977). Outdoor Recreation: Forest, Park and Wilderness, Benziger, Bruce, & Glencoe: Beverly Hills.

McKenney, K. (2010). Phone conversation on *Northern Frontier Camp in the Hudson River Gorge*, Indian Lake, NY.

McKenney, R. (2011). Personal interview on *Northern Frontier Camp in the Hudson River Gorge*, Indian Lake, NY.

McKinstry, L. (1984). *Town Day Raft Tour Set,* Hamilton County News, April 4, 1984, p. 3.

McKinstry, L (1984). *Raft Accident Occurs in Indian Lake,* Hamilton County News, May 9, 1984.

McKinstry, L. (1993). *Whitewater Claims a Life,* Hamilton County News, May 4, 1993, p. 1.

McLelland, J. & Selleck, B. (2009). *Geology of the Adirondacks* in The Great Experiment in Conservation: Voices From the Adirondacks, Porter, W., Erickson, J., and Whaley, R., ed., Syracuse University Press: Syracuse.

McMartin, B. (1990). *Discover the Northwestern Adirondacks.* Backcountry Publications: Woodstock.

McMartin, B. (1992). Discover the Central Adirondacks. Backcountry Publications: Woodstock.

McMartin, B. (1993). Discover the South Central Adirondacks. Backcountry Publications: Woodstock.

McMartin, B. (1994). The Great Forests of the Adirondacks. North Country Books: Utica.

McMartin, B. (1996). Discover the Adirondack High Peaks. Lake View Press: Canada Lake.

Merrill, R. (2007). *Log Marks on the Hudson.* Nicholas Burns: Utica.

Metivier, D. (1967). *Winners Listed In Canoe Races,* in Warrensburg – Lake George News, May 11, 1967

Miller, B. (1984). *The Adirondacks: Central Mountains,* series of combined maps based on USGS maps, Plinth, Quoin, & Cornice: Keene Valley, NY.

Miller, B. (1985). *The Adirondacks: High Peaks Region,* series of combined maps based on USGS maps, Plinth, Quoin, & Cornice: Keene Valley, NY.

Miller, I. (1985). *History of Hudson River Gorge,* handwritten notes from Greg George, Blue Mountain Lake, NY.

Mills, B. (1955). *Tupper to Tahawus,* <u>Adirondac,</u> 44:7, May-June 1955.

Minerva Historical Society (1967). <u>Minerva 1817-1967: A History of a Town in Essex County,</u> p. 128.

Mitchell, J. (1994). *The Watering Place,* <u>Adirondack Life</u>: 25:6, p. 59.

Molton, D. (2011). *Personal Conversation on the History of Rafting on the Hudson River,* May 2011, Indian Lake, NY.

Monroe, T. (1982). Letter to the Editor on *Response to Alice Gilborn Rafting Article,* <u>Adirondack Life,</u> May 19, 1982.

Monthoney, J. (2010). Phone conversation on *John Monthoney's Rafting on the Hudson,* Indian Lake, NY, March, 5, 2010.

Monthoney, K. (2010). Personal interview on *Early Days of Rafting on the Hudson River,* North Creek, NY, May, 2010.

Monthoney, K. (2010). *John Monthoney's Early Role in Rafting on the Hudson River,* hand written note sheet dated September 17, 2010.

Moore, L. (2010). Personal interview on *Early Days of Rafting in Indian Lake,* Indian Lake, NY, April 2010.

Morrison, C. (1982). DEC memo dated July 9, 1982 on *Lake Abanakee Releases for Canoers in 1976,* archived at DEC office in Northville, NY.

Morse, R. (2002). *Detailed Accident Report: Hudson, New York,* in US Whitewater Accident Database, www.americanwhitewater.org/safety/archive.

Myers, T. (2003). *Grand Canyon River Trip Safety,* Grand Canyon River Outfitters Association, www.gcroa.org/Pages/safety.

Nash, R. (1982). Wilderness and the American Mind, 3rd ed. Yale University Press: New Haven.

Nason, M. (1967). *Kennedys, Secretary Udall Turn Spotlite on 10th Anniversary of Whitewater Derby,* Glens Falls Post Star, May 8, 1967.

Nason, R. (2009). Lecture on *Log Drives on the Hudson,* Glens Falls, NY, October, 29, 2009.

Neuman, L. (2009). Personal interview on *Recollections of Rafting on the Hudson,* April 12, 2009, North Creek, NY.

New York State Archives, (2013).Map of *Ground Plan of Beds and Veins of Magnetic Oxide of Iron,* Digital Collection, NYS Archives, NYSA B1405-96 310, www.iarchives.nysed.gov.

NYS Environmental Conservation Law, (1982). *Wild, Scenic, and Recreational Rivers System,* Title 27, Article 15. New York State Environmental Conservation Law: Albany.

New York State Water Supply Commission, (1907). *New York's Water Supply and Its Conservation, Distribution, and Uses,* archived at Adirondack Museum, Blue Mountain Lake, NY.

New York Times, (1969). *Protect Adirondack Park.* New York Times, February 24, 1969, p. 36.

New York Times (1969). *Adirondack Town Fears Extinction in Dam Plan,* New York Times, July 13, 1969, p. 64.

New York Times, (1971). *Other Proposals for Park*. New York Times, January 3, 1971, p. 60.

New York Times, (1971). *Danger in the Adirondacks*. New York Times, March 5, 1971, p. 34.

New York Times, (1975). *Flow Gently*. New York Times, June 5, 1975, p.36.

New York Times, (1986). *Question and Answer: Northeast Rafting*, New York Times, May 11, 1986, p. XX4.

New York Times, (1987). *Question and Answer: Raft Trips*, New York Times, April 19, 1987, p. XX4.

Northern Outdoors Staff (2000). *Pioneer Rafting Days on Maine's Kennebec River*, Northern Outdoors web site, www.northernoutdoors.com/blog/whitewater-rafting.

North Creek News Enterprise (2010). *Front page photo of Governor Paterson rafting the Narrows*, North Creek News Enterprise, August 28, 2010, p. 1.

NYS Environmental Conservation Law, (1982). *Wild, Scenic, and Recreational Rivers System*, Title 27, Article 15. New York State Environmental Conservation Law: Albany.

Olbert, D. (2009). *Early Newcomb Rafters on the Hudson*, email dated August 11, 2009.

Oliver, F. (1969). *The President's Page*. Adirondac, July–August 1969, p. 67.

Payne, P. (2012). Phone conversation on the *New York State Wild, Scenic, and Recreational Rivers Act of 1972*.

Perls, J. (1999). <u>Paths Along the Hudson: A guide to Walking and Biking</u>, Rutgers University Press: New Brunswick.

Perrin, J. (1984). *Hudson River Access Issues,* letter to Dick Cipperly dated October 29, 1984, archived at DEC office in Northville, NY.

Phillips, M. (1965). *Hudson Proposed As a Key Source City's Water.* <u>New York Times</u>, August 12, 1965.

Pocono Whitewater World, (1982). *Whitewater Rafting Brochure,* Jim Thorpe, PA.

Porter, W. (2009). *Forestry in the Adirondacks*, in <u>The Great Experiment in Conservation: Voices From the Adirondacks</u>, Porter, W., Erickson, J., and Whaley, R., ed., Syracuse University Press: Syracuse.

Porter, W. & Whaley, R. (2009). *Public and Private land-use Regulation of the Adirondacks* in <u>The Great Experiment in Conservation: Voices From the Adirondacks</u>, Porter, W., Erickson, J., and Whaley, R., ed., Syracuse University Press: Syracuse.

Powell, J. (1961). <u>The Exploration of the Colorado River and its Canyons</u>, Dover Publishing: NY.

Powley, K. (1984). *Hudson River Access Issue,* letter to Dick Cipperly dated October 29, 1984, archived at DEC office in Northville, NY.

Prichard, B. (1967). *Wilderness Canoe Trip on the Hudson River Near It's Source.* <u>Cloudsplitter</u>, 18:3, p. 2, archived at Town of Long Lake Library, Long Lake, NY.

Prime, W. (1967). *The Kennedy Hudson Hegira.* <u>American Whitewater Journal</u>, Autumn 1967, p. 15-18.

Proskine, A. (1984). <u>Adirondack Canoe Waters: South and West Flow</u>. Adirondack Mountain Club: Lake George.

Purdue, R. (2010). Personal interview on *Town of Indian Lake Involvement with Rafting on the Hudson River,* Indian Lake, NY, July, 2010.

Quist, R. (2008). *History of Utah River Running,* www.utah.com/raft/history.htm.

Rafferty, R. (2009). *Early Remembrances on the Hudson,* email dated March 10, 2009.

Randolph, J. (1961). *Wood, Field, and Stream.* <u>New York Times</u>, May 2, 1961.

Reinicker, R. (1985). Letter to John English of the DEC on the <u>Hudson River Gorge Unit Management Plan</u> dated January 14, 1985, archived at DEC office in Northville, NY.

Rist, L. (1970). *Compiles Record of White Water Men Who Lost Lives in Bygone Adirondack River Drives During Peak Years of Logging,* <u>Tupper Lake Free Press</u>, September 24, 1970.

Rist, L. (1969). Letter to Indian Lake town historian Katherine Early on *Fatalities on Hudson River Log Drives,* dated April 28, 1969.
Rose, H. (2009). *Personal conversation on Early Days of Rafting,* North River, NY, August 2009.

Rosenthal, J. (1996). Letter of the Lake Abanakee Civic Association dated November 1, 1996, highlights the *Concerns of the Association with Regards to Lake Abanakee Water,* archived at DEC office in Northville, NY.

Sagamore Institute, (1990). Flier describing the *drift boat trips.* No date or author but early 1990's date most likely, archived at DEC office in Northville, NY.

Satterlee, S. (1979). *High on Whitewater,* Hamilton County News supplement, May 2, 1979, p. 6.

Satterlee, S. (1979). *River Rafting Facts,* Hamilton County News supplement, May 2, 1979, p. 7.

Savarie, B. (1997). *River Drives,* North Creek News Enterprise supplement, Yesterday's River, May 1997.

Schaefer, P. (1989). Defending the Wilderness: The Adirondack Writings of Paul Schaefer. Syracuse University Press: Syracuse.

Schaefer, P. (1989). *The Forest Preserve and the Recreation Needs of the People of New York State* in Defending the Wilderness: The Adirondack Writings of Paul Schaefer, Syracuse University Press: Syracuse.

Schanberg, S. (1967). *New Reservoirs Urged For State.* New York Times, December 20, 1967, p. 57.

Schenectady Chapter, Adirondack Mountain Club, (1968). *Why Gooley Dam,* Adirondac, September-October, p. 85-7.

Schmale, M. (1996). *Letter on Economics of Rafting on the Hudson,* Indian Lake Town Board Minutes, January 18, 1996, p. 217-18.

Schmale, M. (2009). Personal interview on *Early rafting on the Hudson,* North River, NY, May 28, 2009.

Schmale, M. (2010). Personal interview on *Rafting on the Hudson River,* North River, NY.

Schmale, M, Greene, D, Cunningham, P, Thomas, & Heidrich, (1994). *Recreation and Sports* in Rivers, Rails, and Ski Trails: The History of the Town of Johnsburg, Johnsburg Historical Society, ed. Sawyers Press: North Creek.

Schurman, J. (2010). Phone interview on *Early Days of Rafting on the Hudson River,* Indian Lake, NY, March, 2010.

Seaman, F. (1970). *Refinding Hudson Spring,* Adirondac, 34:5, September–October 1970.

Severo, R. (1975). *Natural Wonders of Adirondacks Inventoried.* New York Times, July 11, 1975, p. 31-2.

Shaunghnessy, J. (1997). Delaware & Hudson. Syracuse University Press: Syracuse.

Shaw, G & R. (no date).*Tahawus–Newcomb and Long Lake.* Reference in Saranac Free Library, Saranac Lake, NY.

Silk, S. (1987). *Riding the Wild Whitewater Rafting Down Hudson a Great Thrill of Spring,* Albany Times–Union, May 23, 1987, p. B3.

Silk, S. (1987). *Finding Outfitters for a Trip in Gorge,* Albany Times-Union, May 23, 1987, p. B3.

Smith, C. (1976). The Adirondacks. Viking Press: New York.

Smith, H. (1885). The History of Essex County. D. Mason & Company: Syracuse.

Smith, M. (1985). *Big Water: The Hudson Gorge,* Adirondack Life, 16:2, p. 21-6.

Spring, T. (2011). Phone interview on *Early Days of Commercial Rafting in Indian Lake,* Indian Lake, NY, March, 2011.

Soucie, A. (2008). Echos of the Forest: Canada's Lumbering Story From past to Present. Bak Pak Productions: Ottawa.

Staab, G. (2009). Conversation on the *Early Years of Rafting on the Hudson River,* North River, NY. August, 2009.

Staab, G. & Carlson, R. (2010). Personal interview on *Rafting on the Hudson River,* North River, NY, August 2010.

Staab, G. (2011). Personal interview on the *Early Years of Commercial Rafting on the Hudson River,* North River, NY, September, 2011.

Staveley, G. (2009a). *A Brief History of Grand Canyon River Running.* Gcroa/pages/history.htm.

Staveley, G. (2009b). *The Caynoneers Story.* Canyoneers.com/pages/canyoneers.htm#principals.

Street, A. (1993). The Indian Pass: Source of the Hudson. Purple Mountain Press: Fleishmanns.

Stoddard, S. (1983). The Adirondacks Illustrated. Excelsior Printing: North Adams.

Sulavick, S. (2007). Adirondacks: Of Indian and Mountains. Purple Mountain Press: Fleischmanns.

Suchecki, M. (1988). *Rafting Helps North Country Bridge Economic Seasons,* Albany Times–Union, April 3, 1988, p. E1.

Swedberg, J. (2009). *A Few Remembrances,* email dated March 15, 2009.

Swedberg, J. (2011). Personal interview on *Rafting on the Hudson River,* Indian Lake, NY, March, 2011.

Sylvester, N. (1973). Historical Sketches of Northern New York and the Adirondack Wilderness. Harbor Hill Books: Harrison.

Temporary Study Commission on the Future of the Adirondacks, (1970). *Forest, Minerals, Water and Air, Technical Report 3*, Albany: New York.

Terrie, P. (1973). *Introduction* in <u>Peaks and People of the Adirondacks</u>, Carson. R., Adirondack Mountain Club: Glens Falls.

Terrie, P. (1997). <u>Contested Terrain: A History of Nature and People in the Adirondacks</u>. Syracuse University Press: Syracuse.

Terrie, P. (2009). *Cultural History of the Adirondack Park* in <u>The Great Experiment in Conservation: Voices From the Adirondacks</u>, Porter, W., Erickson, J., and Whaley, R., ed., Syracuse University Press: Syracuse.

Thomas, B. (2009). Raft guide, personal interview on *Early Years at Whitewater Challengers,* North River, NY, May 23, 2009.

Thompson, H. (1967). <u>New York State Folktales, Legends, and Ballads</u>, Dover Publications: NY.

Tillich, P. (1957). *Dynamics of Faith,* Harper Colophon Books, New York.

Tom, D. (1982). *Raft Capsizes; 2 People Missing,* <u>Glens Falls Post Star</u>, April 19, 1982, p. 1.

Town of Indian Lake (1983). *1983 Raft Attendance Records,* archived at DEC Office, Northville, NY.

Town of Indian Lake (1985). *1985 Raft Attendance Records,* archived at DEC Office, Northville, NY.

Town of Indian Lake (1986). *1986 Raft Attendance Records,* archived at DEC Office, Northville, NY.

Town of Indian Lake (1987). *1987 Raft Attendance Records,* archived at DEC Office, Northville, NY.

Town of Indian Lake (2009). 2009 *Raft Attendance Records,* archived at DEC Office, Northville, NY.

Town of Indian Lake (2010). *Hudson River Raft Attendance Records,* archived at DEC office, Northville, NY.

Trautwein, B. (1971). *The Rip Trip,* Cloudsplitter, Summer, 1971, archived at Town of Long Lake Library, Long Lake, NY.

Trudell, D. (1980). *Hudson River Trip Report* in Bow & Stern, June 1980, at www.vtpaddlers.net/talk/bowstern/archive.

Twain, M. (1986). The Adventures of Huckleberry Finn. Penguin Books: New York.

Udall, S. & Olsen, K. (1989). *Too Many Dammed Rivers.* New York Times, November 25, 1989, p. 23.

Unicorn, (1982). *Rafting Brochure,* Indian Lake Chamber of Commerce, Indian Lake, NY.

USGS, (2010). United States Geological Service river gage archives for Hudson River at North Creek for April 7, 1979, www.waterdata. usgs.gov.

USGS, (2010). United States Geological Service river gage archives for Hudson River at North Creek for April 14, 1979, www.waterdata. usgs.gov.

USGS, (2010). United States Geological Service river gage archives for Hudson River at North Creek for April 18, 1982, www.waterdata. usgs.gov.

USGS, (2012). United States Geological Service river gage archives for Hudson River at North Creek for April 28, 2011, www.waterdata. usgs.gov.

USGS, (2013). Topographical map archives, 1898 Newcomb, NY, quadrangle, www.usgs.gov.

Van Zandt, R. (1992). Chronicles of the Hudson. Black Dome Press: Hensonville.

Vandrei, C. (2009). *Explorateur: Samuel Champlain, Intrepid Explorer,* The Conservationist, 64:1, p. 10-13.

Virgil, G. (2009). Personal interview on *Impact of Rafting in Indian Lake,* Indian Lake, NY, June 15, 2009.

Virgil, G. (2010). Personal interview on *Rafting on the Hudson River,* Indian Lake, NY, February 2010.

Vorhees, J. (2010). Personal interview on *Early Days of Rafting on the Hudson River,* Indian Lake, NY, June, 2010.

Wallace, E.R. (1894). Descriptive Guide to the Adirondacks, Watson Gill: Syracuse.

Wallace, W. (1982). *Outdoors: Rafting Emerges in the East,* New York Times, May 17, 1982, p. C9.

Wallace, W. (1988). *An Undercurrent of Safety Questions,* New York Times, March 21, 1988, p. C8.

Wallack, J. (1996). What the River Says: Whitewater Journeys Along the Inner Frontier. Blue Heron Publishing: Hillsboro, OR.

Warrensburg News, (1903). *Preparing For River Drives,* no further citation given.

Warrensburg News, (1904). *Lumbering Operations*, no further citation given.

Weber, S. (2001). <u>Mt. Marcy: The High Point of New York</u>. Purple Mountain Press: Fleischmanns.

Wellner, A. (1997). *Americans at Play: Demographics of Outdoor Recreation and Travel*. New Strategist Publishing: Ithaca.

Wells, G. (1968). <u>Handbook of Wilderness Travel</u>. Colorado Outdoor Sports: Denver.

Welsh, P. (1995). <u>Jacks, Jobbers, and Kings: Logging the Adirondacks 1850-1950</u>. North Country Books: Utica.

Wessels, W. (1961). <u>Adirondack Profiles</u>. Adirondack Resorts Press: Lake George.

Wheat, D. (1983). <u>Floater's Guide to Colorado</u>. Falcon Press: Billings.

White, W. (1983). <u>Adirondack Country</u>. Alfred A. Knoff: New York.

Whitewater Challengers (2012). www.whitewaterchallengers.com/lehigh/lehigh-guides.

Whitewater World, (1982). *Rafting Brochure,* Indian Lake Chamber of Commerce, Indian Lake, NY.

Whiting, M. (1984). *Hudson River Access Issues,* letter to Dick Cipperly dated October 29, 1984, archived at DEC office in Northville, NY.

Wilderness Raft Expeditions, (1982). *Rafting Brochure,* Indian Lake Chamber of Commerce, Indian Lake, NY.

Wilderness Tours (2011). www.wildernesstours.com/the-river/history.

Wildwater Rafting (2012). www.wildwaterrafting.com/mediacobackground.

Wilke, L. (2010). Personal interview on *Early Raft Trips on the Hudson,* North River, NY, February, 19, 2010.

Wilson, L. (1986). The Northwoods Club 1886–1986, Leila Wilson: NY, archived at DEC office Northville, NY.

Wolff, B. (2010). Personal conversation on *Early Days of Whitewater Challengers on the Hudson River,* North River, NY.

Woodard, B. (1982). *Level of Use Record for Hudson River,* attendance report archived at DEC Office in Northville, NY.

Woodard, B. (1984). *Hudson Gorge Level of Use and Impact Report Summary,* archived at DEC office in Northville, NY.

Zwick, D. (1969). *Fast Water Canoeing.* Adirondac, March–April 1969, p. 29-32.

Made in the USA
Columbia, SC
09 June 2017